THEORY-BASED TREATMENT PLANNING FOR MARRIAGE AND FAMILY THERAPISTS

Integrating Theory and Practice

THEORY-BASED TREATMENT PLANNING FOR MARRIAGE AND FAMILY THERAPISTS

Integrating Theory and Practice

DIANE R. GEHART, PH.D.
California State University, Fresno
AMY R. TUTTLE, M.S.

BROOKS/COLE
CENGAGE Learning™

Australia • Brazil • Japan • Korea • Mexico • Singapore • Spain • United Kingdom • United States

Theory-Based Treatment Planning for Marriage and Family Therapists: Integrating Theory and Practice
Diane R. Gehart, Ph.D., Amy R. Tuttle, M.S.

Sponsoring Editor: Julie Martinez
Marketing Manager: Caroline Concilla
Marketing Assistant: Mary Ho
Assistant Editor: Shelly Gesicki
Editorial Assistants: Amy Lam, Mike Taylor
Project Editor: Kim Svetich-Will
Production: Shepherd, Inc.
Manuscript Editor: Jeanne Patterson
Permissions Editor: Sue Ewing
Cover Design: Andrew Ogus
Cover Art: Jose Ortega/Stockart.com
Print Buyer: Vena Dyer
Compositor: Shepherd, Inc.

Library of Congress Control Number: 2002110922

ISBN-13: 978-0-534-53616-9
ISBN-10: 0-534-53616-6

Brooks/Cole
20 Davis Drive
Belmont, CA 94002-3098
USA

Cengage Learning is a leading provider of customized learning solutions with office locations around the globe, including Singapore, the United Kingdom, Australia, Mexico, Brazil, and Japan. Locate your local office at:
www.cengage.com/global.

Cengage Learning products are represented in Canada by Nelson Education, Ltd.

To learn more about Brooks/Cole, visit
www.cengage.com/brookscole.

Purchase any of our products at your local college store or at our preferred online store **www.cengagebrain.com.**

Printed in the United States of America
14 15 16 17 18 19 18 17 16 15

We dedicate this book to our parents,
Anna and Guenther Gehart and Shirley Ito Endersbe,
who have tirelessly supported, inspired, and loved us,
and
to our clients and colleagues who have taught us that anything is possible
when we create space for each other and
embrace our humanity.

CONTENTS

PREFACE

This is book I (DG) never anticipated writing. Having trained in a collaborative, social-constructionist approach that views therapeutic dialogue as fluid and changing, the idea of constructing a single plan early in treatment has never seemed particularly practical. My unenthusiastic attitude toward treatment planning has been further reinforced in practice, where I have found that therapy rarely goes according to plan, especially when I think I have it "all figured out." The problem I first address with a client often does not remain the focus of treatment because life circumstances change, new areas of concern emerge, and new people enter the conversation. However, as an educator and a practitioner in California, my perspective and attitude regarding treatment planning have changed. To be licensed in California, each intern must pass an intense oral examination that requires a detailed theory-based treatment plan. In addition, third-party reimbursement, whether state or private, always requires an extensive treatment plan. As an educator, I need to teach this skill to my students to ensure their success.

The challenge for me has been to develop treatment plans that are consistent with my epistemological position as a marriage and family therapist while addressing the requirements of third-party payers and state regulatory bodies. When medically based third-party payers started demanding detailed treatment plans from therapists, they adopted a symptom-based medical model without consideration of the significant differences between medical and psychotherapeutic treatment approaches. As third-party payers began requiring measurable behavioral goals, therapists were required to conceptualize the case from a behavioral perspective, regardless of how they were trained. Due to the new agenda managed care placed on therapists, a mushrooming occurred in commercial treatment-planning guides that describe this symptom-based model; therapists needed instruction in this model because it did not reflect how most therapists, especially family therapists, conceptualize and conduct their work. Therefore, my search was to find a treatment-planning model that reflected and facilitated how I actually conduct my work; so I returned to the theory and literature that guide my practice to find direction for developing meaningful treatment plans. This book is designed to help you do the same.

The purpose of this book is to fill the ever-widening gap between formal training in theory and actual practice in managed-care-dominated workplaces through the development of theory-based treatment plans. A well-designed treatment plan is difficult to craft since it must reflect a mastery of theory as well as an understanding of a specific client's or family's needs. The treatment plan is the place where theory and practice meet. Balancing the two—theory and practice—has always been and will continue to be one of the greatest challenges facing new and seasoned practitioners. It is precisely in this tension that we grow as clinicians and theoreticians. This book provides methods and guidelines to help clinicians integrate theory and practice in their treatment planning. Rather than a cookbook approach to treatment planning, this book provides tools to help each clinician develop treatment plans that are consistent with his or her theoretical approach and that are meaningful to the client whose problems they are intended to address.

Treatment plans generally are expected to provide an outline of goals and interventions that address a client's concerns based on professional and theoretical knowledge. Theory provides a foundation to help clinicians address client concerns in an effective and consistent manner. We have included a comprehensive yet condensed review of 11 commonly used family therapy theories to aid in treatment planning. These overviews provide the essential information for conceptualizing treatment from these approaches. Of course, each theory can be practiced in a variety of styles, and individual practitioners commonly adapt and modify interventions to address the needs of each client. These adaptations may be included in treatment plans as well. We intend for the overviews of each theory to be a starting point for thinking about treatment planning rather than a restrictive list.

We have also included sample treatment plans for each theory, including plans for individual, couple, and family cases. Although some of the theories reviewed were originally intended only for couple or family treatment, in today's practice environment, most theories are applied more broadly. These treatment plans are examples of how theory can be applied to a client's concern and should not be considered templates to simply copy and replicate. A well-designed treatment plan is unique. It should reflect the needs and wishes of the client as well as the style of the therapist. We strongly recommend that therapists collaborate with clients to create treatment plans that are meaningful and appropriate for them. We have found that such openness greatly facilitates the therapy process and strengthens the client-therapist relationship. We hope you find the book an invitation to creatively design treatment plans that are beneficial to clients, meaningful to you, and appreciated by third parties.

ACKNOWLEDGMENTS

Finally, we would like to acknowledge that the chapters that follow represent what we have learned from our students and clients in our mutual attempts to better meet life's challenges. The ideas in this book were developed in response to their questions, concerns, life experiences, successes, and failures. We hope to honor their voices and share the wisdom that we have gained by sharing in their struggles. We would also like to thank the incredible editors and staff at Brooks/Cole, especially Julie Martinez and Shelly Gesicki, creative director Vernon Boes, our project editor, Kim Svetich-Will, and the staff at Shepherd, Inc., for their generous assistance and enthusiastic support. They have been a joy to partner with and have done the unseen and often unappreciated work that has made this book a reality. We would also like to acknowledge the contributions of our reviewers, who graciously provided feedback and guidance in the development of this text: Donald R. Bardill, Florida State University; Peter Emerson, Southern Louisiana University; Susan Lane, LMFT; Margaret Pinder, Amberton University; Art Sanchez, California State University, Chico; and Thomas Scofield, University of Nebraska, Kearney.

Diane R. Gehart
Amy R. Tuttle

TREATMENT PLANNING

CHAPTER 1

Treatment planning is an increasingly critical and required skill for family therapists in every practice context: hospitals, private practice, nonprofits, government, and agency settings. Any new hire in the field, from a novice intern to a seasoned practitioner, is generally expected to start developing treatment plans immediately upon commencing clinical work. However, treatment planning is rarely addressed in university curricula, textbooks, or professional literature. Reviewing the entirety of professional family therapy literature and educational textbooks is not likely to yield a single example of a treatment plan (at least, we are still searching). So why are therapists expected to have this skill, and where are they expected to learn it? Strangely, most therapists have learned this skill from the sources *outside* the field who have the greatest stake in treatment planning: third-party payers and managed-care organizations. As these organizations increasingly require treatment plans for reimbursement, they have needed to create guidelines to efficiently manage their paperwork. These guidelines have been the most explicit source on how to construct treatment plans. However, as any family therapist will quickly notice, these treatment plan guidelines reveal a symptom-based, medical-model foundation, which is consistent with the overall culture and focus of third-party payers yet vastly different from family therapy theory and methods. Most family therapists find themselves speaking one language with third-party payers and another with colleagues. In this book, we hope to provide a means to reduce this gap between payers and therapists, theory and practice.

WHAT IS A TREATMENT PLAN?

As the name implies, a *treatment plan* articulates how the therapist intends to address the concerns a client brings to therapy; or, more systemically stated, it is a plan for how to elicit change in the system to address the presenting problem. Treatment plans can have many forms, from formal to informal. However, with the influence of third-party payers, most therapists today expect treatment plans to include a list of clinical goals and related interventions. Goals usually address the concerns identified by clients and/or the issues identified by the therapist's assessment, including any diagnosis. In family therapy, the goals often address relational issues related to the presenting problem.

Treatment plans are simply that: plans. Plans often need to be modified because of outside factors, unanticipated events, or unrealistic expectations. So, the therapist must remember that these are simply tools—tools that ideally are useful to the clinician and client as well as to reimbursing parties. This book provides one method for making treatment plans more useful to clinicians who work from systemic or postmodern therapy perspectives. However, different therapists will find that they have different needs for treatment plans in various contexts and situations and they should adjust the proposed treatment plan strategy accordingly.

WHY USE TREATMENT PLANS?

Different professionals in the family therapy field have varying perspectives and uses for treatment plans. Therefore, as with all written documents, the author, the audience, and the needs of each must always be kept in mind.

Licensed Clinicians

"I use treatment plans because 'it pays.'"

Many licensed and seasoned clinicians use treatment plans simply because they are required for third-party reimbursement. Of course, some also find them helpful in planning treatment; but, for many experienced clinicians, the explicitly detailed plans required for reimbursement may not always seem necessary for competent treatment. Experienced clinicians may find that treatment planning occurs spontaneously as they work and think through a case. The motivation to put it down on paper is often external.

However, some therapists believe that structured, written plans are better than informal plans and, therefore, should be created with or without external motivation. Clark (1991) maintains that a comprehensive, structured treatment plan based on theoretically hypothesized case conceptualization will reduce treatment failure. Furthermore, Clark asserts that the treatment plan may assist in overcoming disruptive patterns in treatment and increase the opportunity to achieve beneficial outcomes. By organizing theory-specific goals and interventions, the potential for treatment confusion, failure, and dysfunctional patterns may be reduced. Further research on the actual impact of treatment planning on the therapy process may provide experienced clinicians with additional incentives for treatment planning.

Interns and Trainees

"Treatment plans help me figure out where I am going."

Interns and trainees are often required to develop treatment plans in training situations but may also find many other sources of motivation to create treatment plans. Early in training, treatment planning provides an excellent springboard for discussion with supervisors and peers about how to engage and intervene with clients. New interns often feel a strong need for structure, especially after the initial period of joining and assessing the client's situation, and treatment plans can be an efficient means of helping trainees conceptualize their case and determining how to proceed next. Treatment plans can also be an opportunity to explore and deepen understanding of an intern's chosen theory by providing a structured format for applying theory to an actual case over a sustained period of time. Treatment plans encourage the intern or trainee to keep the broader treatment picture in mind, and they facilitate integration of theory and practice.

Supervisors and Trainers

"I have interns develop plans to help them focus and think through what they are doing."

Supervisors and trainers have two good reasons to encourage treatment planning with their interns. First, as already mentioned, treatment planning provides an efficient means of checking in and providing supervision to supervisees on their cases. Structuring case consultation around treatment planning provides opportunities to address theoretical and practical training needs, as well as assessing how the therapist is connecting to clients.

Second, treatment planning can also serve a more legal function of documenting adequate oversight of supervisees' cases. Increasingly, supervisors are expected to closely monitor the cases seen by supervisees. Such oversight can be a daunting task for supervisors who work with multiple supervisees, especially in group settings. Reviewing treatment plans for each case seen by supervisees is an efficient means of documenting that the supervisor is monitoring all supervisee cases.

Managed-Care-Utilization Review Specialists

"Treatment plans are the only evidence I have that our money is doing what it is supposed to."

Managed care is the increasingly dominant form of mental health care delivery in our society, which has resulted in a focus on accountability and cost containment. Managed-care organizations are perhaps the most adamant about treatment planning. Treatment plans are one form of "evidence" that therapists can easily produce to document that they are doing what these companies are paying them to do. Of course, the ability to create a plan in no way guarantees that the clinician can carry out the plan effectively, but the outcomes in this field are otherwise difficult to document and so therapists tend to rely (perhaps thankfully) on treatment plans.

Lawyers

"Treatment plans protect my client, the therapist."

Treatment plans also serve the legal and ethical purpose of helping to document competent services. Current ethics guidelines require therapists to maintain adequate records of their treatment. Guideline 3.6 of the ethics code of the American Association for Marriage and Family Therapy states, "Marriage and family therapists maintain accurate and adequate clinical and financial records" (AAMFT, 2001). Similarly, some states have made this a legal obligation as well. For example, Section 4982 of the *California Business and Professions Code* states, "Unprofessional conduct shall include, but not be limited to, the failure to keep records consistent with sound clinical judgment, the standards of the profession, and the nature of the services being rendered" (Leslie, 2001, p. 33).

Although not specifically named in ethical or legal guidelines at the moment, there is an increasing expectation that some form of treatment planning be documented as part of "adequate records." Richard Leslie, maintains that records serve to assist in the treatment process and that "good record keeping will enable you to plan the continued treatment of your client and will enable you to document your treatment plan or approach and the patient's response to that treatment" (Leslie, 2001, p. 34). As treatment plans become increasingly "standard" in the profession, the ethical and legal mandate to maintain these becomes clearer.

TYPES OF TREATMENT PLANS

Although many styles of treatment plans can be created, two basic approaches to written treatment plans are identified here: symptom-based and theory-based treatment plans.

Symptom-Based Treatment Plans

Symptom-based treatment plans derive from the medical model and are generally the plans promoted by third-party payers. Therapists using this treatment plan model identify the client symptoms and then outline measurable goals and corresponding interventions. In this model, symptoms are limited to those defined in psychiatry, such as depressed mood, aggressive conduct, or poor appetite. Jongsma and Peterson have developed a successful series of symptom-based treatment planners, including such titles as *The Complete Adult Psychotherapy Treatment Planner* (Jongsma & Peterson, 1999), *The Child Psychotherapy Treatment Planner* (Jongsma, Peterson, & McInnis, 2000), and *The Family Therapy Treatment Planner* (Jongsma & Datillio, 2000).

The symptom-based approach requires "behaviorally stated, measurable objectives [that] clearly focus the treatment endeavor" (Jongsma & Peterson, 1999, p. 2). The limitation of this model is just that: that the focus is the symptom. *Outside of behavioral models, no marriage and family therapy theory is symptom focused.* In fact, systemic family therapy theories were designed to expand the therapists' thinking beyond the basic level of individual symptoms, which are viewed as "functional" in the larger relational context. Similarly, solution-focused therapists do not view symptom descriptions as necessarily useful to identifying solutions to problem issues. Therefore, a symptom-based treatment plan model can be an unwelcome distraction from the family therapist's theory rather than a supportive tool. More critically, if newer therapists are not mindful, they will find that managed care will choose their theory for them because these treatment plans embody a specific epistemology that is most directly expressed in behavioral therapy.

Furthermore, by limiting the focus to symptoms, the symptom-focused approach fails to incorporate the majority of professional knowledge in the field and, instead, limits the therapist to behavioral and medical models of case conceptualization. When adhered to, this treatment plan model limits the tools therapists have at their discretion because of the limited possibility for problem construction. For example, when focusing on reducing the frequency of a child's tantrums, a therapist may entirely miss the larger family, school, peer, and social processes that support the tantrums. As many postmodern therapists have noted, as the descriptions of problems are limited, so too are the possibilities (Anderson, 1997). Therefore, the symptom-based model quickly becomes a model that limits case conceptualization and treatment possibilities, thereby limiting the potential to be helpful to the greatest number of clients.

Theory-Based Treatment Plans

Theory-based treatment planning is anchored in the therapist's therapeutic model, which becomes the source for goal definition and treatment options. Family therapy models generally encourage a broad view of the problem situation, including family and social influences on the presenting problem. This treatment plan model inspires a careful and rich case conceptualization beyond basic behavioral problems and may include psychological, relational, cultural, and social factors. In most family therapy approaches, case conceptualization requires not just an abstract theoretical description but also the client's perception of the situation. Therefore, the two critical elements become (a) the therapist's theory and (b) the client's perspective.

THEORY-BASED TREATMENT PLANS: INTEGRATING THEORY AND PRACTICE

In the context of theory and treatment planning, *integration* is referred to as the direct application of the therapist's theoretical perspective in the therapy process (Carlson, Sperry, & Lewis, 1997). A theory-based treatment plan is a concrete tool that can be used to facilitate this integration. When developing a theory-based treatment plan, therapists are encouraged to identify how theoretical goals and interventions can be integrated into the interview, goal setting, treatment planning, and intervention processes for each client. Integrating theory in the treatment-planning process maximizes the therapist's understanding of a client's situation and provides well-informed and practical intervention options. The process also ensures a comprehensive assessment of issues based on theory and provides treatment options that are specifically and theoretically related to the identified problem. By using theory-based treatment plans to integrate theory and practice, therapists are more likely to provide *consistent* and *coherent* treatment from the initial to final stages of therapy than if only symptoms are attended to.

TREATMENT PLAN COMPONENTS

Treatment plans have increasingly become defined by two primary components: goals and interventions. Therefore, we have designed theory-based treatment plans to include these two primary elements; however, these are not required components, and therapists are encouraged to be creative in applying their theory and adapting to their working environments.

Goals

The establishment of a theory-based treatment plan includes theory-specific (a) goals and (b) interventions, which help guide treatment. The *goals,* sometimes referred to as *objectives,* should simultaneously address (a) the client's problem issues and (b) the therapist's theoretical perspective. Because they address these two issues, goals are the critical bridge between theory and practice. When therapists are working with managed-care companies, their goals must usually be behavioral, measurable, and specific. That is not necessarily the case in theory-based treatment planning. Certain therapy models, such as solution-focused and cognitive-behavioral models, recommend highly specific goals. Other models, such as intergenerational and experiential models, have more growth-oriented goals, which may not be as easily quantified. Therefore, therapists should determine the necessary specificity of goals based on their theory and practice context.

Goals for Whom?

In symptom-based treatment planning, the goals are generally for the client. However, when a broader theoretical view of treatment is taken, the goals should address *the entire therapeutic process.* Therefore, in theory-based treatment planning, the goals can also be relevant for the therapist. For example, in most theories, achieving a working therapeutic relationship is critical for successful therapy and therefore can be included in the treatment plan as an initial goal for treatment. In this way, theory-based treatment plans include treatment-specific goals that would not be included in a symptom-focused plan, which is more consistent with the systemic and postmodern premises that underlie most family approaches.

Interventions

Interventions identify what the therapist will do to accomplish specific goals. For each goal, the therapist should specify what actions will be taken by the therapist and/or client to achieve the goal. In many marriage and family therapy approaches, the interventions focus on the system and familial relationships; they may also include referrals, psychoeducation, homework, and other out-of-session tasks.

TREATMENT PLAN STRUCTURE

The general, theory-based treatment plan we propose is based on the therapist's theory and is structured to include early-, middle-, and late-phase goals and interventions (see Figure 1.1).

Early-Phase Goals

Early-phase goals generally address (a) the development of the therapeutic relationship, (b) problem assessment, (c) goal setting, and (d) early referrals. Virtually all schools of therapy emphasize the importance of creating a solid working relationship with clients in this early phase. Research consistently attests to the importance of the therapeutic relationship, which some maintain is more critical than theory-informed interventions (Miller, Duncan, & Hubble, 1997). During this initial relationship-building phase, the therapist should attend to cultural and diversity issues. This stage also involves assessment, which can include theory-based assessment, crisis assessment, and more traditional psychiatric models of assessment. Joint goal setting with clients is also common in family therapy approaches in the early phases of treatment, as are referrals to community resources based on the assessment and agreed-upon goals.

Middle-Phase Goals

The middle phase of therapy is generally considered the "working phase" of therapy in which presenting and/or assessed problems are more specifically addressed. The goals in this phase are generally client specific. This is often the phase in which the therapist relies most heavily on theory, applying theory-specific goals, techniques, and interventions.

Late-Phase Goals

Late-phase goals generally include (a) addressing long-term issues, (b) solidifying gains, (c) strategies for handling future issues, and (d) referrals. Often, a specific theory will have a predetermined long-term goal, such as differentiation in intergenerational therapy. In addition, many clients state long-term

FIGURE 1.1 | TREATMENT PLAN OUTLINE

Early-Phase Goals: In most approaches, early phase goals address (a) development of the therapeutic relationship, (b) problem assessment, (c) goal setting, and (d) early referrals.

Goal 1. Theory-based goal that addresses client need
a. Intervention to address specific client problem
b. Intervention to address specific client problem

Goal 2. Theory-based goal that addresses client need
a. Intervention to address specific client problem
b. Intervention to address specific client problem

Middle-Phase Goals: The middle phase is the "working" phase of therapy in which the majority of change-oriented goals and interventions take place. Both the presenting problems and theory-based concepts on health and change (i.e., theoretical formulations about family structure, communication stances, etc.) should inform the goals.

Goal 1. Theory-based goal that addresses client need
a. Intervention to address specific client problem
b. Intervention to address specific client problem

Goal 2. Theory-based goal that addresses client need
a. Intervention to address specific client problem
b. Intervention to address specific client problem

Late Phase Goals: Late-phase goals generally include (a) addressing long-term issues, (b) solidifying gains, (c) strategies for handling future issues, and (d) referrals.

Goal 1. Theory-based goal that addresses client need
a. Intervention to address specific client problem
b. Intervention to address specific client problem

Goal 2. Theory-based goal that addresses client need
a. Intervention to address specific client problem
b. Intervention to address specific client problem

goals at the beginning of treatment: "After we address our child's behavior issues, we also want to address how the family communicates in general." In addition to these long- or longer-term goals, most therapists also address maintenance of gains, strategies for handling future problems, and community referrals during this phase.

COLLABORATIVELY CONSTRUCTING A PLAN

There are many ways to go about constructing a plan, but we suggest always starting by first talking with clients about their intentions for treatment. Research indicates that clients who collaborate in treatment planning report higher satisfaction with the outcome of treatment (Chinman, Allende, Weingarten, Steiner, Tworkowski, & Davidson, 1999). In addition, many therapy models such as collaborative, solution-focused, and narrative therapy also support the idea of jointly working with clients to determine goals and how best to proceed. The early-phase goal of establishing goals with clients essentially begins this process. Clients can be directly asked: "What are your hopes or goals for our meeting together?" Therapists can then continue to inquire about the specifics of clients' goals. In addition, it can also be helpful to directly ask, "Do you already have ideas about how best to achieve these goals?" Often clients do, but sometimes they do not. In either case, therapists can then share some of the possibilities they are considering. We have found that offering multiple options rather than one generally encourages more active involvement on the part of clients in terms of providing feedback about what they are willing and not willing to try. Therapists may also choose to jointly write up the discussed plan with clients. A collaborative and open discussion about the plans for treatment can strengthen the client-therapist relationship and increase the motivation and involvement of all involved.

ISSUES TO CONSIDER WHEN CREATING A TREATMENT PLAN

When developing a treatment plan, there are many issues to consider besides the client's presenting problem and the therapist's theoretical model. Additional client and contextual issues are important to consider when designing a useful treatment plan.

Whom to See

In devising a theory-based treatment plan, therapists must consider several factors that influence whom to see in therapy. Given that the goal is to help clients achieve success in a way that makes sense to them, treatment must be individualized to the client/family system. The determination of whom to see should be considered within the context of the individual-couple-family social system, as well as within the therapist's theoretical perspective. As a result, therapy can involve the individual, the couple, the family, and/or other social configurations. Treatment plans can also specify more than one client configuration. For example, it is common in systemic approaches such as structural and intergenerational approaches to sometimes meet with parents separate from the children or with an individual separate from the couple. When individual treatment is warranted, most family therapy approaches encourage therapists to assess the client's relational context, including marital, family, and sociocultural factors, and to consider these factors when defining the problem and developing a treatment plan.

How the therapist and client jointly define the problem essentially determines who needs to be in therapy. In addition to theory-specific questions, therapists may want to consider the following questions when determining who needs to be in session:

- Who makes the first call and attends the first session?
- Who wants to be there? Who does not?
- Who does each person think should be there?
- What does each person say the problem is? Whom do they identify as involved with the problem?
- Who is able to attend?
- What does the therapist's theory say about who needs to be in treatment?
- What is the therapist's assessment of the situation?

Exploring these questions with a client generally provides some clear directions about who needs to come to the sessions. Most marriage and family therapy theories, including systemic and postmodern theories, prefer to work with all significant family members and involved persons. Theories such as collaborative and narrative theories would also not hesitate to periodically bring in friends, extended family members, "unofficial" family members, or other significant people in a person's life. However, in some cases, family members may refuse or be unable to attend, in which case the therapist and client will need to determine whether individual treatment is a workable alternative. Therefore, we encourage therapists to be creative and flexible in determining who needs to be in session.

Client's Perspective

The client's perspective for treatment, as well as his or her definition of the presenting problem, is one of the most important issues to consider when constructing a treatment plan. Most family therapy approaches pay careful attention to the specific terms and labels the client uses to define the problem. This language can either be used to construct meaningful interventions, as in strategic, experiential, or Milan therapies, or to join with clients in constructing new meanings, as in the narrative and collaborative therapies. In most every situation, starting with the client's perspective is critical to establishing an effective therapeutic relationship. Therapists can explore the client's perspective by inquiring about:

- How each person involved describes the problem, including extended family members, friends, legal systems, school personnel, involved medical specialists, and so on

- How and why each involved person believes the problem developed
- What each person believes to be the best way to address the problem situation
- How each person sees the role of the therapist and therapy process in addressing the situation

Client's Motivation

Treatment planning should also take into account the client's level of motivation. Motivation is a central issue in how clients perceive therapy and the problem issue. de Shazer (1988) classified clients into three types based on level of motivation: visitor, complainant, and customer. "'Visitors' must have somebody to visit with, 'complainants' somebody to complain to, and 'customers' somebody from which to buy" (p. 87). The *visitor* enters therapy without an identified complaint or problem issue, often at the request or demand of another, and therefore may have little personal motivation to change. Therapists must take extra care when developing treatment plans with visitors so that the plans acknowledge the perceptions and agenda of the person in the room rather than only attending to the concerns of the person who sent them; otherwise treatment is not likely to be successful. The *complainant* identifies a complaint and/or problem issue and is looking for solutions. The *customer* is similar to the complainant in that each identifies a complaint; however, the customer will more readily use behavioral tasks, while the complainant will utilize observational or thinking tasks. The client's motivation behind entering counseling, whether characteristic of the visitor, the complainant, or the customer, contributes to the client's attitude in counseling and the establishment of a therapeutic relationship. Client motivation and expectations should be addressed in the early stages of therapy to ensure that the therapist is able to meet the client at that client's motivational level.

Mandated Treatment

Increasingly, clients are required to seek treatment by child-protection service agencies, legal systems, employers, or other outside parties. Voluntary clients are typically open to new possibilities for change. Clients mandated to treatment may be more cautious or may not want help at all. As a result, therapists may need to spend extra time early in therapy to develop a solid therapeutic relationship. Furthermore, the therapist should address the client's level of commitment in the early phase of therapy and adjust the pacing of treatment and goals accordingly.

Contacting the person or agency that mandated treatment is often helpful when developing a treatment plan to ensure that the concerns of the referring party are addressed, which often is critical in meeting the client's ultimate goal (e.g., obtaining custody of an abused child, fulfilling probation requirements, etc.). Issues to consider when treating people mandated to treatment include:

- What is the client's perspective on what his or her problem "really" is?
- What, if any, are the referring party's stated goals for treatment?

- If the goals are different, what are the client's options? Is the client willing to work toward the "mandated goals" in any form? Are there alternative or related goals that address the concerns of both the client and the referring party? If not, what are the consequences? Is the client aware of the consequences?

Therapists must not assume that mandated clients are going to simply "go along" with the mandated goals and, instead, should explore the client's attitudes and willingness to work toward these goals. In most cases, clients mandated to treatment are cooperative and successful if the therapist carefully and respectfully develops a treatment plan with input from all parties and avoids simply imposing a treatment plan on the client.

Diversity Considerations

When constructing a theory-based treatment plan, therapists should keep in mind diversity issues and individual differences present in society's heterogeneous population. Diversity should be considered with *all* clients when developing a treatment plan. Diversity may include an individual's culture, ethnicity, gender, age, sexual identity/orientation, economic status, political affiliation, religion, disability, and family structure. Individual differences significantly influence the therapeutic process. Diversity affects (a) assessment, (b) goals, and (c) intervention choices. For example, when working with clients in a first-generation East Asian family, the therapist may need to adjust how emotional expression is assessed, the appropriateness of goals related to emotional expression, and how emotionally focused interventions are implemented. Therapists who follow "standard" diagnostic procedures and theoretically informed assessment procedures without attending to diversity issues are likely to develop treatment plans that will not work for their clients.

When developing a treatment plan, therapists should consider how diversity issues will affect the therapy process.

- Will the differences between the therapist and the client affect the time it takes to establish a therapeutic relationship and/or to make the client feel comfortable with the therapeutic process?
- Are the cultural, age, gender, and other differences between the therapist and the client likely to affect communication and mutual understanding? How can this be addressed?
- How might the diversity issues affect how the therapist defines or diagnoses the problem? Are the identified problems "normal" or "expected" given the client's background?
- Do certain theories, goals, or interventions seem appropriate to the therapist that are not consistent with the client's beliefs, values, or way of being? Is the therapist willing to adjust?
- Is the therapist willing to openly discuss with the client differences in values or beliefs that may be affecting the therapy process?
- Is the therapist willing and able to respect and work with the client's values and beliefs? If not, does the therapist need to refer out or seek consultation?

Diversity and Theory

When working with families, therapists must be mindful of how they choose and/or adapt their theory to address diversity issues such as gender, culture, ethnicity, and socioeconomic status. Unfortunately, no simple guidelines exist for matching theory to diversity because each person and each family make sense of dominant social issues differently. For example, research indicates that therapists generally approach male and female clients based on the assumption that women prefer a more emotionally focused approach. However, only half of the female clients in a recent study indicated that they found an emotionally focused approach helpful; the other half reported that they preferred a more pragmatic, problem-focused approach (Gehart & Lyle, 2001). The same was reported by men in the study. Therefore, therapists must carefully assess each person's perspective to collaboratively construct a treatment approach and plan that will be useful to the client, which often involves modifying the therapist's theoretical approach to account for the client's unique experience of diversity issues. Therapists should also be careful to not let stereotypes determine their approach to diversity but instead work with the client to determine how best to adapt their approach.

Diagnostic and Medical Issues

In the majority of contexts in which treatment plans are required, a mental health diagnosis is also required. When this diagnosis and/or other medical problems are assessed, the treatment plan should address these issues in some way. A medical or psychiatric assessment may be helpful or even ethically required in these cases, and the therapist should develop a working relationship with the medical professionals and develop treatment plans in conjunction with the medical services.

Generally, diagnostic issues and reduction of related symptoms are addressed in the middle and late phases of therapy. These are often easily incorporated into theory-based goals, such as clarifying enmeshed boundaries to increase the sense of agency and hopefulness with someone diagnosed with depression. The better the therapist understands the chosen theory, the easier it is to identify the links to diagnostic concerns. Additionally, referrals for medication and other medical evaluations should be considered in treatment planning, particularly in the early phase of treatment.

Safety and Crisis Issues

Safety and crisis issues must be carefully assessed before creating a treatment plan. These issues include threats of harm to self or others, prior or current child and elder abuse, partner violence and abuse, emotional abuse, eating disorders, and self-harm without suicidal intent (i.e., cutting, self-mutilation). Unfortunately, many of these issues are difficult to assess because clients are often ashamed or afraid of the consequences of discussing such issues. Many therapists ask clients to complete information forms that inquire into these areas. However, therapists should not rely entirely on forms to assess potential crisis because many people are not willing to put such information down in writing, especially at the time of the first session. Therefore, therapists should also directly ask clients about safety issues whenever they suspect a problem.

Once a therapist determines that a safety issue exists, the therapist must take some form of action to respond to the threat. Most states have specific laws about how to handle suspected child and elder abuse/neglect, as well as laws that address threats of harm to self; others; and, in some states, property. In addition to following these laws, it is generally helpful to develop *safety plans* with clients currently or recently in any type of safety or crisis situation. Safety plans should identify specific actions or steps a client will take the next time his or her safety is threatened. For example, safety plans with women who are in physically abusive relationships may identify where they plan to go, what they need to take, and/or whom they might call the next time they become fearful of being hurt or are hurt. Similarly, clients who have urges to harm themselves, either with or without suicidal intent, often benefit from creating plans about whom to call, where to go, and other specific actions to take to prevent hurting themselves. These plans can be added to treatment plans.

Alcohol and Substance Abuse

Another important issue to assess when planning treatment is alcohol and substance abuse. Like other crisis issues, substance abuse can be difficult to detect, so therapists must be attentive to this issue. When asking about substance use, therapists should inquire about (a) what types of substances are being used; (b) how much; (c) how often; (d) the effects of the use on relationships, work, finances, and health; (e) the larger sociocultural context; and (f) the client's and the family's perspectives on whether or not the substance use is a problem. The distinction between abuse and heavy social use is sometimes difficult to assess, especially when larger family, social, and cultural issues are taken into consideration.

How substance abuse affects the treatment plan depends on the therapist's theoretical approach and practice context. Many therapists will not see a client who is actively using and abusing substances under any circumstances and will require the person to seek specialized substance abuse treatment elsewhere. However, therapists who work from a systemic family therapy approach may feel comfortable working with certain individuals and families in which there is a substance use or abuse issue; these theoretical approaches have a long tradition of working with substance use as part of the family dynamics. Postmodern therapists also have well-developed models for treating substance use (Berg & Miller, 1994; Miller, 1994; Winslade & Smith, 1997). Therefore, therapists must carefully determine whether the substance abuse case is within their scope of competence and develop treatment plans that include prudent adjunctive referrals, such as detoxification programs, support groups, and/or inpatient treatment.

Time Constraints

Therapists receiving reimbursement by insurance companies, managed-care organizations, or other third-party payers may experience time constraints on the therapeutic process. Third-party payers increasingly cover fewer sessions with the expectation that therapists maximize their effectiveness and focus only on "medically necessary" treatment (Chinman et al., 1999; Domino, Salkever, Zarin, & Pincus, 1998; Johnson, 1997; Peake, Meyers, & Duenke, 1997). To comply with the time constraints, treatment plans may need to be altered to address the most severe or critical problem issues. Additional referrals and alternative services may also need to be considered.

The time constraints encouraged by insurance and managed-care companies encourage a brief therapeutic approach to treatment. Fortunately, many marriage and family therapy approaches are considered "brief" therapies. For example, the solution-focused approach is often referred to as "brief" therapy. Other marriage and family therapy theories, such as the Milan systemic approach and the Mental Research Institute (MRI) approach, structure therapy into a limited number of sessions. Many marriage and family therapy theories fit comfortably with a brief, time-restricted approach to treatment.

Community Resources and Referrals

When developing a treatment plan, therapists should consider available resources for the individual, couple, or family system. Community resources and alternative adjunct services can directly assist in creating the desired outcome or may be used to address problems less central to the clinical issues, such as housing or legal services. These resources may include group and support counseling, shelter and housing information, school services, community legal services, medical services, religious community resources, and other social services. Community resources generally enhance treatment and provide clients with additional outside support. In the therapeutic process, community resources and referrals are important to identify and utilize during the early- and late-phase goals. Therapists should familiarize themselves with community resources and services and periodically reassess the status of available community resources.

CHOOSING A THEORY

Many new therapists agonize over choosing their theory, while some find it easy to choose. In either case, we believe it is helpful to remember that the theory is essentially a *tool* for the therapist rather than the *answer* for the client. Theory gives therapists a vocabulary to discuss what they do, provides ideas about how to make sense of what clients bring to therapy, and gives direction about how to address these concerns. Any theory can be helpful, just as any theory—improperly practiced—can be harmful. Therefore, we recommend that therapists choose a theory that preserves their "humanity" and reminds them to honor the dignity of the people with whom they work. Although the ideas about how to assess and intervene are helpful at times, we believe therapy is most essentially a way of *being* with others; our theories provide guidance in how to do this in ways that are helpful. So, we encourage all therapists to seek training in their preferred approach. Having a solid theoretical foundation to conceptualize one's work can greatly reduce one's sense of being overwhelmed and "burned out."

THEORY INTEGRATION

Some therapists may choose to integrate more than one theory in their therapeutic approach and treatment plans. Several models exist for integrating theories (see Nichols & Schwartz, 2001). However, we strongly recommend that practitioners attend to epistemological issues when considering integration. Bateson (1977) maintained that "You cannot claim to have no epistemology. Those who so claim have nothing but a bad epistemology" (p. 147). One's epistemology provides the "lens" through which one interprets the theories one integrates. For example, a "therapeutic letter" will be viewed and utilized quite differently depending on one's epistemology. A modernist therapist would view a therapeutic letter as a vehicle for expressing emotion to reduce distress and symptoms, whereas a systemic therapist might view the letter as a form of positive or negative feedback, and a postmodernist would view the letter as a means of creating space for alternative descriptions and voices. Therefore, the same intervention has very different uses depending on one's epistemological assumptions. We find that many therapists are not as effective as they could be because they are not clear about their epistemological stance as they try to integrate concepts and methods from therapies based on vastly different epistemologies. Therefore, we encourage therapists wanting to develop integrated treatment plans to carefully consider the epistemological underpinnings of their approach to therapy and use the sample treatment plans closest to their epistemological position as a basis for adapting various techniques and methods.

THEORY-BASED TREATMENT PLANS IN TRAINING

Theory-based treatment planning is an especially beneficial training tool for students, trainees, and interns. The theory-based treatment plans provide one of the few methods that directly facilitate the integration of theoretical knowledge and practice, which is one of the most difficult tasks in early training. Theory-based treatment planning can be used in both course curriculum and supervision to encourage theoretical case conceptualization and applications. Theory-based treatment plans can be integrated into existing family therapy coursework and supervision in a variety of ways:

- Theory-based treatment plans can be used in introductory theory courses with vignettes for the various theories covered in the course. They can be included as class exercises, parts of exams, or take-home assignments. For example, the vignettes can be used as a foundation for role plays that enact selected stages of treatment plans in the text or treatment plans developed by students/instructors.

- Theory-based treatment plans can be incorporated into basic skills classes as part of the foundational knowledge required for basic practice and used to address issues in role plays, videos, or other assignments.
- Theory-based treatment plans can easily be adopted as the "treatment plan format of choice" in training centers and agencies that do not have a third party requiring a specific treatment plan format.
- Theory-based treatment plans are an excellent choice for inclusion in qualifying or comprehensive exams to allow students to demonstrate their ability to integrate theory and practice.
- Theory-based treatment plans can be discussed in both individual and group supervision to simultaneously address theoretical and specific client issues. These plans are an excellent tool for encouraging all members in the supervision process to stay connected with theory and practice.

The Dialectic of Reading and Practice

To facilitate the learning of theory-based treatment planning, we have found it very helpful to encourage students and interns to continue reading while practicing. Most academic programs are structured with the majority of theory courses in the early phase of training and practice courses occurring later. This separation often makes it difficult to understand how theory works in practice. Although many pre- and post-degree interns intend to continue studying their chosen theory, practical experiences are often so demanding that the literature is often neglected. However, this is a critical time for new therapists to be reading and exploring theory. There is a dialectic process whereby continually moving between theoretical readings and practice begins to make each more understandable. Instructors and supervisors can encourage this dialectic process by including theoretical readings as part of clinical training.

THEORY-BASED TREATMENT PLANS IN A MANAGED-CARE ENVIRONMENT

Theory-based treatment planning is highly relevant to those therapists working in managed-care environments and in situations that require symptom-based treatment plans. Most symptom-based plans require three components: (a) specific symptoms, (b) measurable goals, and (c) interventions. Obviously, the specification of a symptom is the most significant difference between the two treatment planning models. However, what symptoms a therapist notices are always a product of that therapist's epistemology, which underlies specific theories. For example, an experiential therapist is more likely to notice and document emotional symptoms (i.e., depressed mood), whereas a behavioral or strategic therapist is apt to notice behavioral symptoms (i.e., anxiety). Therefore, even the "objective, medical" symptoms the therapist notes are a reflection of that therapist's epistemology and theory. This subtle distinction is the first place that the role theory plays in a symptom-based treatment plan can be noticed.

The specified goals and interventions in a symptom-based treatment plan can usually be directly converted from theory-based plans, particularly the middle- and late-phase goals. The theory-based treatment plan goals may need to be more directly related to the assessed symptoms and stated in more behavioral or measurable terms. The basic "formula" for converting theory-based treatment goals to symptom-based goals is as follows:

Theory-based goal + "to reduce" + specific symptoms (+ "to be evidenced by" + measurable goal)

Alternatively, the goal may be stated in positive terms:

Theory-based goal + "to increase" + preferred behaviors (+ "to be evidenced by" + measurable goal)

For example, if the original theory-based goal addressed "interrupting destructive family games/interactions," the symptom-based goal may be to "interrupt destructive family games to reduce frequency of child's tantrums" or to "increase frequency of child's cooperative behaviors." If measurable goals are required, this can also be stated as "interrupt destructive family games to reduce frequency of child's tantrums, which will be evidenced by no more than one episode over a one-month period." Therapists who understand their theory well can easily extrapolate symptom-based goals to fit the requirements of their local third-party payers, thus being allowed to work from their chosen approach rather than having to adopt the case-conceptualization method implicit in symptom-based plans.

WHY USE THEORY-BASED TREATMENT PLANS?

Alternative to Symptom-Based Treatment Planning

Theory-based treatment plans provide an alternative to symptom-based approaches to treatment. Theory-based treatment planning encourages therapists to draw from the field's rich theoretical traditions for case conceptualization and treatment rather than limiting themselves to a medical or behavioral model, which is presupposed in symptom-based treatment planning. Especially when working with couples and families, therapists are likely to find theory-based treatment planning superior in addressing the complex relational dynamics that typically cannot be fully captured by symptomatic or behavioral descriptions.

Greater Clinical Relevance

Many therapists, especially traditionally trained marriage and family therapists, will find that theory-based treatment plans are more clinically relevant and fit better with their approach to therapy than symptom-based models. Theory-based plans address the complex issues of systemic assessment and family functioning by allowing therapists to address broader issues beyond the presenting symptom. For therapists trained in postmodern approaches, theory-based treatment plans allow for problem descriptions that are not predetermined by medical language and that can include the client's constructions more directly.

Training Tool

Theory-based treatment plans are efficient and effective training tools for supervisors and instructors who want to teach students and interns how to integrate theory and practice. Interns can use this treatment planning approach to explore the specific implications of theory with each family with which they work. In addition, it encourages interns to do a comprehensive assessment of clients and consider the long-term considerations for treatment. Similarly, in the classroom, theory-based treatment plans are an excellent tool for allowing students to examine the practical implications of the theories they study.

HOW TO USE THIS BOOK

Each of the following chapters covers theory-based treatment planning for a specific theory. The theories covered in this book include structural, strategic, MRI, Milan systemic, Satir's communication, symbolic-experiential, intergenerational, cognitive-behavioral, solution-focused, narrative, and collaborative approaches. Each chapter is structured as follows:

- *Theoretical overview:* Overview of key theoretical concepts, which is not intended to be an exclusive or restricted list but is representative of common practices
- *General treatment plan:* A general treatment plan that outlines possible goals and interventions without reference to a specific case
- *Case vignettes:* Individual, couple, and family case vignettes with space to "practice" developing theory-based treatment plans
- *Sample treatment plans:* For each theory, sample treatment plans that address the three case vignettes

Readers may choose to use some or all of these sections. Therapists wanting to apply theory-based treatment planning in a clinical setting may find it helpful to review the theoretical concepts, the general treatment plan, and the sample treatment plans to develop a treatment plan method for their practice.

Trainees, interns, students, and those studying for licensure may find it helpful to "test" themselves by first reviewing the key concepts and general plan and then trying to create treatment plans for each of the vignettes. Afterward, readers can compare the plans they developed to the samples. We anticipate that each reader's plan will differ from the samples, because many ways exist to conceptualize and treat a case even within a single approach. Therefore, the samples should not be interpreted as the "correct" treatment plans but as "possible" treatment plans.

Goals for Therapeutic Process

Additionally, we want to remind readers that the goals in these treatment plans—particularly, early-phase goals—are different than goals proposed in symptom-based plans because the goals are for the *therapeutic process* rather than for just the client. Both systemic and postmodern theories view the therapist as part of the therapeutic or language system rather than as an external change agent. Therefore, it is theoretically consistent for the goals to apply to the process rather than to one part of the therapy system. Such goals are particularly helpful to those learning how to do therapy, because they capture all phases of the therapy process rather than just the final goals for clients, as is expected in symptom-based planning. Goals for the proposed plans can be changed to a more traditional focus by deleting process goals (e.g., joining with the system, etc.) if a clinician finds it more useful in a specific work setting.

References

American Association of Marriage and Family Therapists. (2001). *AAMFT ethical guidelines*. [Online]. Available: www.aamft.org

Anderson, H. (1997). *Conversations, language, and possibilities: A postmodern approach to therapy.* New York: Basic Books.

Bateson, G. (1977). The thing of it is. In M. Katz, W. Marsh, & G. Thompson (Eds.), *Explorations of planetary culture at the Lindisfarne conferences: Earth's answer.* New York: Harper & Row.

Berg, I., & Miller, S. (1994). *Working with the problem drinker: A solution-focused approach.* New York: Norton.

Carlson, J., Sperry, L., & Lewis, J. A. (1997). *Family therapy: Ensuring treatment efficacy.* Pacific Grove, CA: Brooks/Cole.

Chinman, M. J., Allende, M., Weingarten, R., Steiner, J., Tworkowski, S., & Davidson, L. (1999). On the road to collaborative treatment planning: Consumer and provider perspectives. *Journal of Behavioral Health Services & Research, 26*(2), 211–218.

Clark, D. A. (1991). Case conceptualization and treatment failure: A commentary. *Journal of Cognitive Psychology: An International Quarterly, 13*, 331–336.

de Shazer, S. (1988). *Clues: Investigating solutions in brief therapy.* New York: Norton.

Domino, M. E., Salkever, D. S., Zarin, D. A., & Pincus, H. A. (1998). The impact of managed care on psychiatry. *Administration and Policy in Mental Health, 26*(2), 149–157.

Gehart, D., & Lyle, R. (2001). Client experiences of gender in therapeutic relationships: An interpretive ethnography. *Family Process, 40*, 443–458.

Johnson, S. L. (1997). *Therapist's guide to clinical intervention: The 1-2-3's of treatment planning.* San Diego, CA: Academic Press.

Jongsma, A. E., & Datillio, F. M.(2000). *The family therapy treatment planner.* New York: Wiley.

Jongsma, A. E., & Peterson, L. M. (1999). *The complete adult psychotherapy treatment planner.* New York: Wiley.

Jongsma, A. E., Peterson, L. M., & McInnis, W. P. (2000). *The child psychotherapy treatment planner* (2nd ed.). New York: Wiley.

Leslie, R. (2001, July). Treating children, confidentiality and other legal issues. In *Should I keep clinical records?* AAMFT-CA Division Conference, San Diego, CA.

Miller, S. D. (1994). Some questions (not answers) for brief treatment of people with drug and alcohol problems. In M. F. Hoyt (Ed.), *Constructive therapies 1* (pp. 92–110). New York: Guilford Press.

Miller, S. D., Duncan, B. L., & Hubble, M. (1997). *Escape from Babel: Toward a Unifying language for psychotherapy practice.* New York: Norton.

Nichols, M. P. & Schwartz, R. C. (2001). *Family therapy: Concepts and methods* (5th ed). Boston: Allyn & Bacon.

Peake, T. H., Meyers, T. L., & Duenke, S. D. (1997). Options for brief psychotherapy: Cognitive and psychodynamic variations. *Journal of Mental Health, 6,* 217–235.

Winslade, J., & Smith, L. (1997). Countering alcoholic narratives. In G. Monk, J. Winslade, K. Crocket, & D. Epston (Eds.), *Narrative therapy in practice: The archaeology of hope* (pp. 158–192). San Francisco, CA: Jossey-Bass.

"Structural family therapy provides a template for mapping out the relational aspects of family communication and interactional patterns, while highlighting and acknowledging internal, covert rules" (Minuchin, 1974; Minuchin & Fishman, 1981).

2 CHAPTER STRUCTURAL FAMILY THERAPY

KEY THEORISTS

Harry Aponte
Charles Fishman
Salvador Minuchin
Braulio Montalvo

HISTORICAL OVERVIEW

Salvador Minuchin, born and raised in Argentina, is the child psychiatrist who developed the theoretical foundations for structural theory. Early in his career, he trained under Nathan Ackerman at the Jewish Board of Guardians in New York and also worked with child survivors of the Holocaust in Israel. After returning from Israel, Minuchin worked with children from poverty-stricken areas in New York and further refined his ideas about the importance of the social and familial contexts. During this time, he worked and collaborated with Jay Haley. In 1965, Minuchin became the director of the Philadelphia Child Guidance Clinic, where he further developed the approach that is now referred to as "structural." In 1974, Minuchin published *Families and Family Therapy,* generally regarded as the first book on the structural approach.

KEY CONCEPTS

View of Families

Structural family therapists view the family as a system structured according to set patterns and rules that govern family interactions. The family is composed of multiple subsystems that function within the whole (or *holon,* Minuchin & Fishman, 1981). The therapist should "look at the family as more than an aggregate of differentiated subsystems" and must consider it as "an organism in itself" (p. 13). With this systemic perspective, the therapist works with the family by educating and assisting family members to become aware of structure, boundaries, patterns, rules, and detrimental familial processes.

Structure

"Family structure is manifested in a variety of transactions that obey the same system rules and which are therefore dynamically equivalent" (Minuchin & Fishman, 1981, p. 123). The systemic structure of a family is associated with the establishment of rules for family interactions. Structure is defined by the system and compiled into a set of covert rules that govern family interactions. The covert rules and interactional patterns are usually not explicitly stated or consciously recognized (Minuchin, 1974). These rules and patterns are established through communication on overt and covert levels.

The interactional rules address the management of closeness and distance, referred to as the *relationship rules.* Minuchin (1974) noted that nonverbal cues, such as the pitch of the voice, frequent hesitations, and when an individual speaks, are indicative of the internal structure and interactional patterns of the family. Other interactional patterns include issues associated with "closeness, hierarchies, areas of specialization and expertise, and patterns of cooperation" (Minuchin & Fishman, 1981, p. 23). Overall, interactional patterns and rules are defined by the family and contribute to the structure of the system.

"Family members relate according to certain arrangements, which govern their transactions" (Minuchin, 1974, p. 89). Internal rules and norms work together to influence structure. More specifically, cultural differences and cultural norms, associated with gender and marital expectations, influence interactional and transactional patterns. For example, "if both spouses come from patriarchal families, . . . they may simply take it for granted that the woman will do the dishes" (Minuchin & Fishman, 1981, p. 16). As a result, cultural issues influence the internal structure of the family system.

In addition to the influence of cultural norms and interactional patterns, family history and intergenerational rules are relevant factors in the formation of family structure. The uniqueness of an individual's family of origin and the associated intergenerational rules and patterns influence the structure of the new system. Minuchin (1974) maintained that individuals face the task of separating from their family of origin and transitioning into a newly defined structure. The processes of accommodation and negotiation are necessary components in determining the new family structure. When two individuals join to create a new family, they enter the union with remnants of rules and interactional patterns from their families of origin.

Subsystems

"Families are highly complex multi-individual systems, but they are themselves subsystems of larger units—the extended family, the block, the society as a whole" (Minuchin & Fishman, 1981, p. 16). Every individual is a subsystem, as are dyads and larger groupings formed by generation, gender, or task. Subsystems that are often targeted in evaluating a family include the parental, marital/spousal, and sibling subsystems.

Development of Subsystems Subsystems are formed in congruence with developmental stages and tasks (Minuchin, 1974; Minuchin & Fishman, 1981). The *individual* is a subsystem that maintains structure and rules based on past experience, family of origin, cultural influences, and other interrelated factors. In the initial stage of family development, an individual joins with another individual to form a *spousal subsystem.* "Learning, creativity, and growth" are elements that become apparent within the spousal subsystem (Minuchin, 1974, p. 56). According to Minuchin (1974), the spousal subsystem is established with the "purpose of forming a family" (p. 56).

With the birth of a new child, the spousal subsystem is transformed into a parental unit, referred to as the *parental subsystem.* The parental subsystem maintains responsibility for nurturing and caring for children (Minuchin, 1974). As the developmental stages of the family are experienced, additional subsystems are formed, such as the *sibling subsystem* (between two or more siblings). Furthermore, individuals from different generations within the family may bond, resulting in the emergence of *intergenerational subsystems.* Additionally, subsystems may form around gender, interests, hobbies, or other factors.

Problem Subsystems: Covert Coalitions Minuchin and Fishman (1981) note that the establishment of a family system and the formation of an increasing number of subsystems have the potential to become problematic. Conflict and other problematic issues arise when two members join and form a coalition against one or more family members. This process is referred to as a *covert coalition* (Minuchin & Fishman, 1981). In the covert coalition, the members establish a destructive coalition, which serves as a source of conflict.

Boundaries

Boundaries refer to invisible barriers that regulate the amount and type of contact one has with others. They are the "rules defining who participates, and how" (Minuchin, 1974, p. 53). Boundaries are directly associated with the interaction and communication within a subsystem. Development in a family system is dependent on the subsystem's boundaries and its "freedom from interference by other subsystems" to negotiate with others to develop appropriate skills and problem-solving techniques (Minuchin, 1974, p. 54). Further, it is actually subsystems (rather than the family itself) that tend to be enmeshed or disengaged. For example, the couple may be disengaged but the mother is enmeshed with her children (Minuchin, 1974, p. 55).

The clarity of a subsystem's boundaries is apparent by the level of communication, interaction, and involvement in relationships. Boundaries can be described as *diffuse, rigid,* or *clear.* Family subsystems fall into "a continuum whose poles are the two extremes of diffuse boundaries and overly rigid boundaries" (Minuchin, 1974, p. 54). Subsystems with rigid boundaries have difficulty or lack in communication and maintain overly structured, restrictive interactional patterns. Rigid boundaries have the potential to lead to *disengagement.* On the other end of the spectrum, subsystems characterized by intense levels of communication and overinvolvement have diffuse boundaries (Minuchin, 1974). For example, diffuse boundaries are apparent when the behavior of one member in the system immediately affects the entire system. Diffuse boundaries have the potential to result in *enmeshment.*

In the middle of the spectrum, between highly rigid and diffuse boundaries, exists a normal range of communication and interactional patterns. These are referred to as *clear boundaries* (Minuchin, 1974). Clear boundaries define "normal" relationships and appropriate family functioning. Clear boundaries are well defined and allow the members of the system to function with levels of independence and interdependence.

Boundaries are used to describe levels of communication, independence, and interdependence within a family system. The system's boundaries are developed and maintained by each individual's cultural norms, family-of-origin influences, experiences, and worldview. Assessment of a system's boundaries requires the sensitive consideration of cultural influences.

Boundaries are referred to when assessing and describing interactional and communication patterns within a subsystem. "The adequacy of these boundaries is one of the most important aspects to the viability of the family structure" (Minuchin & Fishman, 1981, p. 17). Most important, boundaries serve to protect differentiation and autonomy of the family and its subsystems by managing proximity and hierarchy (Minuchin, 1974).

Focus of Treatment

A therapist arranges information and facts provided by the family to develop a *focus of treatment* (Minuchin & Fishman, 1981). However, while the problem presented by the family is never ignored, the therapist must be aware of other relevant data and systemic processes that may be affecting the situation. The therapist must use clinical judgment in considering the focus of treatment, which may not be directly related to the presenting symptom. For example, if a family presents with child behavior as the problem, a structural therapist will also assess the marital subsystem to determine whether poor boundaries and hierarchy in this system are affecting the parent-child system. Therefore, the interrelated nature of the system requires exploration of all subsystem relations regardless of the presenting problem.

GOALS OF THERAPY

The ultimate goal in the structural approach is to obtain assurance that the structural process will provide benefits for the entire family (Minuchin, 1974). More specifically, the goal is to alter the dysfunctional structure to promote problem solving and "to facilitate the growth of the system to resolve symptoms and encourage growth in individuals, while also preserving the mutual support of the family" (Nichols & Schwartz, 2001, p. 247). In this process, family structure is transformed and subsystems are restructured and reorganized to eliminate the presenting complaint, resulting in a well-defined and structured system.

The process of restructuring the family system is not attained by a single intervention but involves a constant effort toward achieving the therapeutic goal or "target," a healthy, well-defined, structured system. Thus, the goal can be identified as a healthy functioning family that possesses specific characteristics that are concurrent with structural family therapy, including the establishment and maintenance of:

- Generational hierarchy
- A parental coalition
- A spousal subsystem
- Clear boundaries between all individuals and subsystems

The transformation or restructuring of the family system leads to a change in interactional patterns and ways individuals "relate" to one another. As the therapist assists the family in restructuring the system, the presenting problem and symptoms are concomitantly resolved.

STRUCTURE OF THERAPY

The structural approach involves a structured, therapeutic intervention process that provides key elements and assessment procedures that aid in facilitating transformation and restructuring the family system (Minuchin, 1974). The structure of therapy is divided into three phases: (a) joining and accommodating, (b) mapping family structure, and (c) intervening.

Joining and Accommodating

Joining and accommodating are the processes in which the therapist enters the family system in a hierarchical stance as the "leader" (Minuchin, 1974). The key component in the process deals with the therapist's ability to adapt, accommodate, and join the system's rules, patterns, and worldview.

FIGURE 2.1 | FAMILY MAPS

Balanced Parental Hierarchy	Hierarchical Father	Parental Conflict	Coalition Between M and C
M F	F	M——I I——F	F
------------	M		————
C	------------		M C
	C		

F = father
M = mother
C = child

Mapping Family Structure

The structure of the family system is assessed and determined through the construction and conceptualization of a *family map* (Minuchin, 1974; Minuchin & Fishman, 1981). The family map is a static entity that identifies each family member's position in the family while highlighting interaction patterns, conflicts, and coalitions (Figure 2.1).

In the process of mapping the systemic structure, the therapist devises an initial hypothesis, compiles diagnostic information, and begins initial goal-setting procedures (Minuchin, 1974; Minuchin & Fishman, 1981). The hypothesis of family interactional patterns is observed and represented within the family map. Diagnosing "is the working hypothesis that the therapist evolves from his [her] experiences and observations upon joining the family" (Minuchin, 1974, p. 129). Through the process of identifying and delineating components within the system and the family map, goals are established and explored. Furthermore, the process of assessing and constructing the family map overlaps with the intervention techniques.

Intervening

After joining and observing the system's dynamics and structure, the therapist *intervenes* with techniques that strengthen and clarify structure and boundaries. Interventions, such as enactments, boundary making, unbalancing, and challenging assumptions, are applied while focusing on restructuring the family system to address the problem.

ASSESSMENT

Assessment requires that the entire family be addressed and included to appropriately determine structure and boundaries. The assessment of the system's structure most critically includes (a) boundaries, (b) complementarity, (c) hierarchy, and (d) conflict management.

Boundaries

When assessing a family, the therapist identifies the boundaries and relational rules between members. The therapist assesses the quality of boundaries (clear, diffuse, or rigid) in each subsystem with the awareness that diffuse boundaries in one subsystem often are counterbalanced with rigid boundaries in another.

Complementarity

A relationship between two family members has the potential to develop reciprocal or complementary aspects (Minuchin & Fishman, 1981). The dichotomous perception of individuals within the system may result in effective teamwork; however, when exaggerated, it leads to problems, such as pursuer-distancer, active-passive, and dominant-submissive reciprocal characteristics within the relationship.

Hierarchy

Hierarchy is determined and maintained by the system's rules, boundaries, and interactional patterns (Minuchin, 1974; Minuchin & Fishman, 1981). Hierarchy refers to the arrangement and structural delineation of power within the system. Functioning families with appropriate boundaries and subsystems have a well-established hierarchy between the parental and children subsystems, as well as between older and younger siblings. The parental hierarchy should be appropriate for the developmental needs of the children.

Conflict Management

Conflict management refers to the system's ability to resolve conflict and negotiate solutions. The manner in which a system deals with conflict management and resolution "identifies family members who operate as detourers of conflict and family members who function as switchboards" (Minuchin & Fishman, 1981, p. 69). In disengaged families, members avoid contact to avoid conflict. In enmeshed families, there exists a tendency to develop *cross-generational coalitions* to manage conflict.

TECHNIQUES

Joining

"Joining a family is more an attitude than a technique" (Minuchin & Fishman, 1981, p. 31). It involves the therapist entering the family system; *tracking* interaction and communication; and adapting and accommodating to their style, rules, and patterns (Minuchin, 1974; Minuchin & Fishman, 1981). Joining involves *mimesis*, which includes using, matching, and acknowledging the system's metaphors and themes. In the joining process, the therapist displays empathy and confirms and acknowledges feelings to assist in decreasing anxiety while remaining sensitive to hierarchy, culture, language, and rules. The process of joining a family system contributes to establishing empathy and understanding while creating a sense of "working together."

Joining is synonymous to forming a partnership and involves the establishment of common therapeutic goals (Minuchin & Fishman, 1981). While the therapist is viewed as a leader in therapy, to be effective the therapist needs to ensure successful joining with the family system. To do so, therapists must examine their comfort with various levels of involvement and then establish an appropriate position from which to join.

In conjunction with joining, the structural therapist accommodates to the family system. *Accommodation* refers to the therapist's "adjustments" and alterations necessary to join the system (Minuchin, 1974). This process involves adaptation to the system's rules, interaction style, communication patterns, and organization. Furthermore, while the therapist is accommodating to the family system, the family is also accommodating to the therapist and the therapeutic process.

The technique of joining involves the accommodation of the system's interactional patterns, organization, cultural influences, and style (Minuchin, 1974). For example, the system's cultural values determine the initial communication process and which member is addressed first. The therapist must be mindful of the system's initial, covert, communication patterns to ensure a beneficial experience. Overall, the process of joining reflects the family therapist's ability to successfully meet the family where it is in the present moment.

Planning

Planning is a technique similar to that of an initial hypothesis. The therapist theorizes about the family structure while remaining curious about its structural reality. The initial hypothesis is tested in joining with the family and observing the structure and is then altered or discarded (Minuchin & Fishman, 1981). Additionally, the composition of the family serves as a basis for the initial hypothesis.

Family Mapping

Family maps are constructed through observations and interactions with the family during the process of joining and accommodating. Minuchin (1974) identified six areas to assess for when observing interaction:

1. Family structure and transactional patterns
2. Flexibility and the ability to restructure
3. Resonance ("sensitivity to the individual members' actions")
4. Family life context (support and stress)
5. Family life developmental stage
6. Ways the problem issue is maintained through family interactions (p. 130)

Therapists observe families to determine how the family's boundaries, hierarchy, and other structural features are related to the presenting problem. When assessing the family, the therapist should also consider the ways the family interacts with and responds to the therapist.

Enactments

"Enactment is the technique by which the therapist asks the family to dance in his [her] presence" (Minuchin & Fishman, 1981, p. 79). In enactments, the therapist observes each client in the here and now while interacting, responding, and behaving in a natural manner. An enactment allows the therapist to assess and identify structure. Three components are associated with enactments that are essential to the therapeutic process. First, the therapist recognizes sequences by observing the "spontaneous transactions of the family and decides which dysfunctional areas to highlight" (Minuchin & Fishman, 1981, p. 81). Then, the therapist directs the enactment (also known as "eliciting transactions") by directly asking the family to reenact a specific problem conversation or event. In the final phase, the therapist directly intervenes and redirects the interactions. This process involves presenting new options for change through alternatives and possibilities. If the enactment is not successful or experiences a break in the process, the therapist initiates a discussion of what went wrong or encourages the participants to continue.

Enactments provide direct involvement; responses; presentation of alternatives in the therapeutic session; and assessment of concrete, observable communication patterns while allowing for the familial reality to be challenged and restructured. In addition, the process of highlighting interaction provides the therapist with information about interactions within the family while providing the family with hope for change.

Spontaneous Behavioral Sequences

Spontaneous behavioral sequences are similar to enactments, except the behaviors (e.g., heated arguments, yelling, sulking) are spontaneous rather than directed by the therapist. In these situations, the therapist must stay focused on the relational process and direct the family's attention to the process by highlighting the interactional dynamics and behavioral sequences and redirecting the process toward a more beneficial interaction. Successfully intervening in these spontaneous situations requires that the therapist integrate training at a personal level (Minuchin & Fishman, 1981).

Challenging Family Assumptions

Families enter the therapy because "reality, as they have constructed it, is unworkable" (Minuchin & Fishman, 1981, p. 71). Therefore, the family therapist can intervene by challenging the family reality, constructs, and assumptions by reframing and highlighting possibilities.

Challenging family assumptions is a technique that involves discovering the family's "narrowed perception of reality" and challenging their reality by educating the family on appropriate family structure (Minuchin & Fishman, 1981, p. 207). The therapist may apply psychoeducation techniques to teach families about family structure. Furthermore, the technique can be applied genuinely or paradoxically (Minuchin & Fishman, 1981). For example, the therapist can either directly confront a father on his inability to consistently set limits or paradoxically exaggerate the lack of hierarchy by referring to how the father needs to ask permission from the son to be a father.

Challenging the Symptom, Structure, and Reality

While all theoretical foundations involve altering/changing the family system, the structural approach involves three identifiable strategies involving challenging and changing the organization of the family. They are (a) challenging the symptom, (b) challenging the family structure, and (c) challenging the family reality (Minuchin & Fishman, 1981). The changes and alterations that result in challenging the structure assist in reorganization and restructuring. Challenging can take the form of direct confrontation with verbal statements or indirect confrontation, such as unbalancing or rearranging chairs.

Reframing

Families enter a therapeutic situation with "their framing of the problem and their framed solution" (Minuchin & Fishman, 1981, p. 76). While the therapist considers the family's framing of the problem and solution, the framing is modified and reframed in relational terms to establish a more effective framing and a more constructive perspective. Enacting, focusing, and intensity are used in the process of reframing by allowing the family to experience the transactions (framed and/or reframed), display new meaning, and challenge unproductive familial frames.

Affective Intensity

Families are unique entities that respond to messages in a distinct manner. Therefore, therapists must gauge the family system and alter their degree of intensity (their responses, messages, and other communicative reflexes) to the particular needs of the family system. The techniques involved in the presentation of intensity are "repetition of message, repetition of message in isomorphic transactions, changing the time in which people are involved in a transaction, changing the distance between people involved in a transaction, and resisting the pull of a family transactional pattern" (Minuchin & Fishman, 1981, p. 118). For example, vivid and intense messages associated with a covert coalition can be commented on by saying, "When did you divorce your husband and marry your son?" In gauging intensity, the therapist must apply this technique in such a way that the family "hear[s] the therapist's message" (p. 141), ensuring that the message is neither too strong nor too soft.

Shaping Competence

Shaping competence is associated with highlighting the positive, strengths, and progress. It is applied to alter the direction of interaction rather than to criticize. The family is shown what they are doing right and/or are guided in that direction.

Boundary Making

"Boundary-making techniques regulate the permeability of boundaries separating holons" (Minuchin & Fishman, 1981, p. 147) and involve establishing and/or strengthening the structural boundaries in a system or a subsystem. In this process, the therapist restructures and strengthens individual and subsystem boundaries by intervening in the system. This is done by physically or verbally intervening, altering spatial proximity between members, focusing on specific individuals or subsystems, and/or recognizing and highlighting inappropriate boundaries (Minuchin, 1974; Minuchin & Fishman, 1981). For example, the therapist may actively strengthen boundaries by asking people to speak for themselves, rearranging chairs to affect boundaries, blocking interruptions, establishing individual or subsystem sessions, and/or highlighting how people's behaviors influence those around them.

Unbalancing

Unbalancing refers to altering the "hierarchical relationship of the members of a subsystem" (Minuchin & Fishman, 1981, p. 161). Minuchin (1974) referred to the unbalancing process as broadening the focus. Broadening the focus unbalances the system by focusing on another individual within the system or recognizing that the identified patient may be experiencing dysfunction due to dysfunction within the family.

Unbalancing involves temporarily taking sides to change family interaction (Minuchin & Fishman, 1981). Minuchin and Fishman identify several unbalancing techniques: alternating affiliation, ignoring family members, and forming a coalition against family members.

In the process of unbalancing and aligning with an individual in a lower hierarchical position in the family, the individual may be empowered by the affiliation, thus altering the system's rules and patterns and creating a possibility for resolution and restructuring (Minuchin & Fishman, 1981). For example, when one child is the identified patient (IP), the therapist might focus on problems with another child in the system. This process causes an unbalancing effect, resulting in a shift in the focus, thus inviting restructuring to occur. Furthermore, "by expanding the problem beyond the family focus, the therapist raises hope that a different way of looking at the problem will bring a solution" (Minuchin, 1974, p. 212).

STRUCTURAL TREATMENT PLANS

General Structural Treatment Plan

The following general treatment plan identifies possible goals and interventions for each stage of therapy that could be used in treating individuals, couples, and families. Not all goals and techniques are applicable to all clients.

Early-Phase Goals

1. Join with and accommodate to family rules, patterns, and structure.

Possible Interventions

a. Confirm family members' feelings and reflect a sense of empathy.
b. Track and maintain family interactional style while matching and acknowledging hierarchy and rules.

2. Assess/map family structure and boundaries and determine goals.

Possible Interventions

a. Inquire about each individual's perspective of the problem, family structure, and interaction.
b. Map family structure by observing enactments that reflect a discussion about the problem issue.
c. Identify structural patterns by observing spontaneous behavioral sequences.

Middle-Phase Goals

1. Reestablish the parental subsystem; adjust generational hierarchy; strengthen parental coalition.

Possible Interventions

a. Initiate enactments to provide couple/family with the opportunity to discuss issues in more productive manner.
b. Present affective intensity statements to assist in highlighting parent/child hierarchical power imbalance.
c. Unbalance the system by taking the least dominant family member's side to assist in increasing his/her position in family.
d. Initiate separate parental subsystem sessions.
e. When appropriate, apply boundary-making techniques by directing parental subsystem to sit in close proximity.
f. Use affective intensity or enactments to highlight and sever covert coalitions.

2. Strengthen spousal subsystem to increase intimacy and reduce enmeshment or increase contact.

Possible Interventions

a. Initiate separate couple sessions with the goal of focusing on the relationship/marriage.
b. Introduce enactments to help couple improve communication, strengthen boundaries, and/or reduce disengagement.
c. Use affective intensity to highlight imbalances in relationship, unrealistic assumptions, and/or emotional blocks.
d. Unbalance the system with couples who have unequal distributions of power.
e. Reframe problem behaviors to highlight reciprocal interactions.
f. Challenge the couple's assumptions about their relational boundaries.

3. Develop clear boundaries between all subsystems.

Possible Interventions

a. Reframe boundaries in relational terms to introduce a more helpful perspective.
b. Initiate enactments to help family be more respectful of each family member's boundaries.
c. Challenge family assumptions associated with relational boundaries.
d. Unbalance the system by taking sides with family scapegoat when appropriate.
e. Initiate boundary-making techniques, such as having clients arrange chairs to challenge current hierarchy, coalitions, and boundaries.
f. Challenge assumptions by presenting psychoeducational information.

Late-Phase Goals

1. Address and identify remaining individual, couple, and family problem issues, such as relationship with family of origin or outside systems.

Possible Interventions

a. Extend new behaviors and learning to other relationships by shaping competence.
b. Use affective intensity to highlight unresolved parent/child boundary imbalances.
c. Employ enactments to address remaining relational concerns.

2. Establish and solidify newly established family norms and structure.

Possible Interventions

a. Shape competence by focusing on what was learned and accomplished.
b. Reframe the structural alterations to assist in introducing each member's role.
c. Discuss previous family assumptions to highlight progress and structural alterations.

Vignette: Individual

Nancy was referred to counseling to address relationship issues. She has two young children and recently left an abusive relationship. Nancy was married for 9 years and states that the last 5 years included verbal and emotional abuse. She reports depressive symptoms, trouble in dealing with the separation, low self-esteem, and difficulty parenting her children.

Practice Structural Treatment Plan for Individual

Early-Phase Goals

1.
    a.
    b.

2.
    a.
    b.

Middle-Phase Goals

1.
    a.
    b.

2.
    a.
    b.

Late-Phase Goals

1.
    a.
    b.

2.
    a.
    b.

Vignette: Couple

The marital couple, Kimiko, a Japanese native, and John, a Caucasian American, initiated couple's counseling due to reported unresolved issues and feelings surrounding their inability to effectively communicate. John is employed full-time, and Kimiko cares for their two children and tends to household duties. The couple reports that they are expecting their third child in 5 months. Kimiko reported that the pregnancy has diminished her future for a career outside the home and states that she is resentful of John. John states that Kimiko is overly concerned about this and other marital issues, while she reports that she is unhappy and unsatisfied in the relationship.

Practice Structural Treatment Plan for Couple

Early-Phase Goals

1.
   a.
   b.

2.
   a.
   b.

Middle-Phase Goals

1.
   a.
   b.

2.
   a.
   b.

Late-Phase Goals

1.
   a.
   b.

2.
   a.
   b.

Vignette: Family

Tom and Fran are court mandated to counseling for child neglect. The parents lost custody of their three children because of the poor living conditions. The parents have regained custody of two children, Arthur, age 9, and Jennifer, age 4, and are still fighting for custody of their ill 2-year-old son, Collin. The parents complain that Arthur and Jennifer are constantly verbally and physically fighting, and Fran complains that Tom does not assist with parenting or household chores.

Practice Structural Treatment Plan for Family

Early-Phase Goals

1.
   a.
   b.

2.
   a.
   b.

Middle-Phase Goals

1.
   a.
   b.

2.
   a.
   b.

Late Phase Goals

1.
   a.
   b.

2.
   a.
   b.

Vignette: Individual

Nancy was referred to counseling to address relationship issues. She has two young children and recently left an abusive relationship. Nancy was married for 9 years and states that the last 5 years included verbal and emotional abuse. She reports depressive symptoms, trouble in dealing with the separation, low self-esteem, and difficulty parenting her children.

Structural Treatment Plan for Individual

Early-Phase Goals

1. Join with and accommodate to Nancy.
   a. Display a sense of empathy while acknowledging her feelings about her spouse, the abuse, and the separation.
   b. Track, maintain, and match Nancy's interactional style.

2. Assess Nancy's family structure, including subsystems, boundaries, and hierarchy.
   a. Map Nancy's family and relational structure by engaging in dialogue about the relationship and abusive acts.
   b. Inquire about Nancy's perspective of family structure and interaction; inquire about Nancy's perspective about the roles and rules in the family.

Middle-Phase Goals

1. Strengthen Nancy's boundaries in relation to her past husband and children to encourage better adjustment to separation, reduce depression, and improve self-esteem.
   a. Challenge assumptions about her role as wife that prevented her from asserting and/or protecting self in the relationship.
   b. Shape competency by highlighting how she was able to take care of herself and her children in various ways; identify her strengths and resources.
   c. Apply boundary-making techniques, such as identifying the influence and control Nancy's spouse has had on her; ensure that Nancy does not assume undue responsibility for the abuse.
   d. Reframe the abusive situation and the separation of the parental subsystem to reflect an alternative, constructive perspective that reflects her strength in being able to leave the abusive situation.
   e. Use affective intensity to highlight to reduce self-blame and guilt.
   f. Initiate enactments to help Nancy identify specific ways to enact "clear" boundaries.

2. Strengthen and increase parental hierarchy between Nancy and her children.
   a. Use enactments to guide Nancy in new ways to parent effectively.
   b. Use affective intensity to challenge Nancy to take a more active role with children.
   c. Initiate boundary-making techniques, such as having Nancy arrange chairs to represent current hierarchy and rearranging the chairs to represent her status as the parent.

3. Strengthen Nancy's role in the parental subsystem.
   a. Apply affective intensity statements to highlight inappropriate subsystem arrangement.
   b. Present enactments involving Nancy discussing her role in the parental subsystem and the abusive situation and reflect her new role as the primary parent.
   c. Challenge Nancy's assumptions about being the primary parental figure and provider for her children.

Late-Phase Goals

1. Assist Nancy in clearly defining and enacting her new role as single mother.
   a. Introduce family sessions to address and challenge assumptions and to provide Nancy with the opportunity to create an audience for new role and structural patterns.
   b. Present affective intensity statements to assist in maintaining and highlighting structural alterations.
   c. Offer individual sessions to address any remaining depressive symptoms.
   d. Challenge Nancy's assumptions by presenting psychoeducational information about domestic violence and the cycle of violence.

2. Highlight progress, gains, and the newly established structure.
   a. Shape Nancy's competence by highlighting what she has done right and continue guiding in a more helpful direction.
   b. Discuss previous family assumptions to assist in reflecting what was learned and what was done right.
   c. Reframe to assist in recognizing their new roles and structure.

Vignette: Couple

The marital couple, Kimiko, a Japanese native, and John, a Caucasian American, initiated couple's counseling due to reported unresolved issues and feelings surrounding their inability to effectively communicate. John is employed full-time, and Kimiko cares for their two children and tends to household duties. The couple reports that they are expecting their third child in 5 months. Kimiko reported that the pregnancy has diminished her future for a career outside the home and states that she is resentful of John. John states that Kimiko is overly concerned about this and other marital issues, while she reports that she is unhappy and unsatisfied in the relationship.

Structural Treatment Plan for Couple

Early Phase Goals

1. Join with and accommodate to couple's rules, patterns, and structure.
   a. Display a sense of empathy by acknowledging each member's feelings, thoughts, and perspectives.
   b. Track and match the couple's interactional style and patterns, attending to cultural issues and differences.

2. Assess the couple's structure and boundaries and the cultural expectations on structure and boundaries.
   a. Initiate enactments that highlight a discussion about the marital relationship and ineffective communication patterns, addressing roles of Japanese and American culture.
   b. Observe spontaneous behavioral sequences to identify structure and differing structural expectations.

Middle-Phase Goals

1. Work with couple to clarify and define relational "rules" for the marital subsystem, clarifying boundaries and hierarchical arrangements and attending to cultural issues.
   a. Initiate enactments around the discussion of couple issues to identify power imbalance between Kimiko and John.
   b. Unbalance the system by taking wife's side to raise her position in the family, while remaining sensitive to her cultural beliefs and individual expectations about hierarchy.
   c. Apply boundary-making techniques, such as asking Kimiko to speak for herself, rearranging chairs, and having couple sit together.
   d. Intervene with spontaneous behavioral sequences to clarify boundaries as problem behavioral sequences arise in session.
   e. Shape competence by highlighting areas of strength in the relationship and utilizing these to address concerns.
   f. Challenge couple assumptions about what a man and woman "must" do in a relationship while remaining sensitive to cultural and family traditions.

2. Increase and strengthen boundaries between Kimiko and John to reflect clear, appropriate boundaries that increase their sense of intimacy.
    a. Initiate enactments to highlight and modify interactions to allow each to speak for self and not for the other.
    b. Reframe the rigid boundary between the couple to highlight their ability to remain individual.
    c. Challenge the couple's assumptions about their relational boundaries and patterns while remaining mindful of the cultural differences.

Late-Phase Goals

1. Improve functioning co-parents and develop parenting skills.
    a. Invite children into the session and allow the couple to enact a discussion or activity to highlight alterations in the structure.
    b. Apply affective intensity statements to continue balancing power.
    c. Challenge lingering couple and family assumptions and present psychoeducational techniques.

2. Highlight progress and the couple's accomplishment of appropriate relational structure, and solidify their gains.
    a. Shape competence by highlighting progress, what was learned, and what they are doing right.
    b. Discuss previous family assumptions and cultural expectations and articulate how these have been renegotiated during therapy.
    c. Highlight new roles and structure and appropriate complementarity in their roles.

Vignette: Family

Tom and Fran are court mandated to counseling for child neglect. The parents lost custody of their three children because of the poor living conditions. The parents have regained custody of two children, Arthur, age 9, and Jennifer, age 4, and are still fighting for custody of their ill 2-year-old son, Collin. The parents complain that Arthur and Jennifer are constantly verbally and physically fighting, and Fran complains that Tom does not assist with parenting or household chores.

Structural Treatment Plan for Family

Early-Phase Goals

1. Join with and accommodate to family rules, patterns, and structure.
   a. Acknowledge family members' feelings and reflect a sense of empathy.
   b. Track and maintain family interactional style while matching and acknowledging hierarchy and rules.

2. Assess family structure and boundaries.
   a. Map family structure by observing enactments that reflect children arguing and parents discussing a specific problem.
   b. Identify structural patterns by observing spontaneous behavioral sequences.

Middle-Phase Goals

1. Reestablish the parental subsystem while increasing generational hierarchy to address children's acting-out behavior.
   a. Initiate enactments to provide parental subsystem with the opportunity to identify new ways to interact with children.
   b. Initiate parental subsystem sessions to address parenting.
   c. Present affective intensity statements to assist in highlighting parent/child hierarchical power imbalances.
   d. Unbalance the system by taking Tom's side to assist in increasing his position in family.
   e. Apply boundary-making techniques by directing spousal subsystem to sit in close proximity when with children.
   f. Shape competence by encouraging Tom to take a more active parenting role in and out of session.

2. Increase and strengthen boundaries to reflect clear, normal boundaries by assisting mother to be less intensively involved with the children and by having Tom become more appropriately involved.
   a. Reframe children's problem behavior as serving the purpose of getting mother's mind off of the ill child.
   b. Use unbalancing to increase Tom's engagement with the children.
   c. Initiate enactments to help family find ways to be more respectful of each family member's boundaries.
   d. Challenge family assumptions associated with a man's ability to parent.

Late-Phase Goals

1. Work with couple to redefine and clarify marital relationship, attending to effect of neglect charges and ill child on marital relationship.
   a. Increase separate couple sessions to explore and challenge marriage and family assumptions.
   b. Apply affective intensity statements to highlight unresolved couple boundary imbalances.
   c. Use enactments to increase direct communication between couple.

2. Establish and solidify newly established family norms and structure.
   a. Shape competence by focusing on what was learned and accomplished.
   b. Reframe to assist in introducing each member's role.

References and Suggested Readings

Aponte, H. J. (1994). *Bread and spirit: Therapy with the new poor: Diversity of race, culture, and values.* New York: Norton.

Aponte, H. J. (1996). Political bias, moral values, and spirituality in the training of psychotherapists. *Bulletin of the Menninger Clinic, 60*(4), 488–502.

Aponte, H. J. (1999). The stresses of poverty and the comfort of spirituality. In F. Walsh (Ed.), *Spiritual resources in family therapy.* New York: Guilford Press.

Aponte, H. J., & DiCesare, E. J. (2000). Structural theory. In F. M. Dattilio & L. J. Bevilacqua (Eds.), *Comparative treatments for relationship dysfunction.* New York: Springer.

Aponte, H. J., & Winter, J. E. (2000). The person and practice of the therapist: Treatment and training. In M. Baldwin (Ed.), *The use of self in therapy* (2nd ed.) pp. 127–165. Binghamton, NY: Haworth Press.

Minuchin, S. (1974). *Families and family therapy.* Cambridge, MA: Harvard University Press.

Minuchin, S., & Fishman, H. C. (1981). *Family therapy techniques.* Cambridge, MA: Harvard University Press.

Minuchin, S., & Nichols, M. P. (1993). *Family healing: Tales of hope and renewal from family therapy.* New York: Free Press.

Minuchin, S., Montalvo, B., Buerney, B. G., Rosman, B., & Schumer, F. (1967). *Families of the slums.* New York: Basic Books.

Minuchin, S., Rosman, B., & Baker, L. (1978). *Psychosomatic families: Anorexia in context.* Cambridge, MA: Harvard University Press.

Nichols, M. P., & Schwartz, R. C. (2001). Family therapy: Concepts and Methods (5th ed.) New York: Allyn & Bacon

"The symptom is not a 'bit' of information but is an analogy that has as its referents multiple aspects of the person's situation" (Haley, 1987, p. 106).

3 CHAPTER STRATEGIC THERAPY

KEY THEORISTS

Jay Haley Cloe Madanes

HISTORICAL OVERVIEW

Jay Haley and Cloe Madanes were influential in developing the strategic approach. Jay Haley worked with Gregory Bateson, Milton Erickson, and Salvador Minuchin and was involved in the MRI group. He left MRI in 1961 to go to the Philadelphia Child Guidance Clinic, where he worked with Minuchin, Montalvo, and Madanes. In the early 1970s, Haley and Madanes founded a clinic in Washington, D.C.; and they have published several influential strategic therapy books (Haley, 1963, 1973, 1976, 1980, 1981, 1984, 1996; Madanes, 1981, 1984, 1990; Madanes & Haley, 1977).

KEY CONCEPTS

Symptoms Serve a Purpose

Haley (1976) believed that "treating an individual for symptoms is like assuming a stick has one end" (p. 155). In strategic therapy, symptoms are viewed within the context of the family system (Haley, 1973; Madanes, 1981). Strategic family therapists maintain that symptoms serve the purpose of maintaining the family homeostasis and that they reflect the interdynamics between two or more persons; therefore, the symptom is viewed as "adaptive to relationships" (Madanes, 1981, p. 20). The problem or symptom is the system's attempt at maintaining homeostasis by implementing a solution, although the solution is a maladaptive solution. For example, Haley (1976) wrote that, in a marriage, the symptom serves a purpose and "there will be consequences in the marriage when a symptom is cured" (p. 155).

Hierarchy

The concept of *hierarchy* refers to the natural organization and distribution of power within any organizational system (Haley, 1976; Madanes, 1981, 1984). Madanes (1981) defines hierarchy as the "repetitive sequences of who tells whom what to do" (p. 145).

"When an individual shows symptoms, the organization has a hierarchical arrangement that is confused" (Haley, 1976, p. 103), thus resulting in problems, conflict, and power struggles. Symptoms are clues to the confused hierarchical boundaries. When family organization includes coalitions across levels of hierarchy (e.g., generations) and/or when the coalition is not overtly observable, the family becomes stuck.

A common disruption within the family refers to inappropriate hierarchical positioning of children and parents. "A hierarchical incongruity is the simultaneous coexistence of two conflicting hierarchies within the framework of one hierarchical organization, where one hierarchy frames the other and where the same people are involved in both hierarchies" (Madanes, 1981, p. 124). In this instance, the child or children take a more dominant hierarchical position in the system than the parents or adults in the system. When the hierarchy is inconsistent between generations, the goal is to draw a clear distinction between generations and prevent consistent coalitions between generations and hierarchical positions.

Family Development

Family development refers to the transitional points throughout the family life cycle (Haley, 1973). The family life cycle stages include:

1. The courtship period
2. Marriage
3. Childbirth and young children
4. Middle marriage
5. Weaning parents from children
6. Retirement and old age

"Symptoms appear when there is a dislocation or interruption in the unfolding life cycle of a family" (Haley, 1973, p. 42). Problems occur at the transition points in the family system's development.

Communication and Control

Overt and covert patterns of communication are viewed as an attempt to control or influence others. Control or influence is viewed as the motivation in interpersonal interactions, particularly problematic interactions.

Love and Violence

Madanes (1990) proposed that all problems that are brought to therapy can be conceptualized as a struggle between love and violence. She maintained that family problems develop around four basic intentions:

1. To dominate and control
2. To be loved
3. To love and protect others
4. To repent and forgive

GOALS OF THERAPY

Focus

Therapy focuses on helping people move on to the next stage of family life by preventing unfortunate sequences of actions from repeating (Haley, 1973; Madanes, 1981). In particular, strategic therapists attempt to interrupt covert hierarchical structure and address power struggles within the family.

Goals

Haley (1976) maintained that the simplest goal is to interrupt the covert hierarchical structure and covert alliances. Parental hierarchy and cross-generational coalitions are identified and challenged. This goal focuses on altering "a sequence [or interactional style] by preventing coalitions across generational lines" (p. 108).

Another common strategic goal is to change the style of interaction in the social unit of which the client is a member. The process of altering the interactional style within a social network or situation allows the individual or family to grow and develop and proceed to the next stage of the family life cycle (Haley, 1973). Other specific goals for each client are agreed upon at the beginning of treatment in a therapeutic contract (Haley, 1976).

STRUCTURE OF THERAPY

Initial Interview

In strategic therapy, the initial session is highly structured and divided into four stages: the social stage, the problem stage, the interaction stage, and the goal-setting stage (Haley, 1976). The structured nature of the initial session involves the entire family and is essential for establishing a therapeutic framework. Furthermore, the initial session "provides maximum information and begins a change" in the family system (Haley, 1976, p. 44).

Social Stage During the initial moment in the therapy session, the therapist addresses and obtains a "social response" from each family member. In this process of social interaction, the therapist observes family interaction, mood, relationship dynamics, and organization of the family members. Furthermore, Haley (1976) maintained that the therapist should not disclose the initial hypothesis and observations to family members.

Problem Stage In the problem stage, the therapist leads the discussion and there is a "shift to the therapy stage where the situation is no longer defined as social but as purposeful" (Haley, 1976, p. 19). In this stage, the therapist gathers information about the problem situation. The therapist directs the conversation by posing probing questions about the problem situation and the perspectives of each family member. Haley (1976) stated that "the more general and ambiguous the inquiry of the therapist is, the more room there is for the family members to display their point of view" (p. 21).

Interaction Stage The interaction stage involves a family discussion about the problem and provides the therapist with the opportunity to observe communication patterns, organization, and power hierarchies. In this process, the therapist's role shifts to the role of a facilitator and observer, and the conversational interaction between family members is encouraged. Furthermore, there is a shift from conversation to action and the therapist attempts to "bring the problem action into the room" (Haley, 1976, p. 38).

Goal-Setting Stage The initial session concludes by highlighting and clarifying the problem situation while addressing therapeutic goals and precisely defining the presenting problem. In this process, the therapist and the family define the problem in "operational" terms. The operational definition assists in the process of designing a contract to defining goals, which involve a means of measuring change.

The initial session often concludes by the therapist assigning a directive at the end of the first session (Haley, 1976). In subsequent sessions, the therapist inquires about the outcome of directives or homework assignments and uses this feedback to modify the hypothesis and inform in-session and out-of-session interventions.

ASSESSMENT

Strategic theory holds that traditional diagnosis and formal assessment create unsolvable problems by applying static, unchanging labels to fluid patterns of interaction. Therefore, strategic assessment focuses on understanding these subtle and evolving patterns of interaction.

Conceptualizing a Problem

When a therapist possesses the ability to think "clearly" about a problem and is able to understand a symptom, the therapist "can develop the right strategy to solve it" (Madanes, 1984, p. 188). Strategic therapists invoke several common metaphors to help conceptualize the problems that families bring to therapy.

Voluntary Versus Involuntary Typically, problems and symptoms are perceived as involuntary; however, all symptoms, except organic ones, are assumed to be "voluntary and under control of the patient" (Madanes, 1984, p. 141).

Helplessness Versus Power Problems can be viewed in relation to helplessness and power. In this view, those in power are dependent on the powerless to maintain their status (Madanes, 1984). To resolve the inadequate helplessness/power relation, strategic therapists highlight and redistribute power and the attendant responsibility. Madanes notes that the therapist's view of power and helplessness assists in the process of devising a strategy for change.

Metaphorical Meaning Versus Literal Meaning The symptom or problem may be viewed as a metaphor for problems at another level (Haley, 1973, 1976; Madanes, 1981, 1984). In these cases, the focus can be directed within the metaphorical or literal context, depending on what the therapist believes will be most helpful to the family.

Hierarchy Versus Equality The conceptualization of problems associated with hierarchy is similar to that of power and helplessness. The strategic therapist's decision to focus on hierarchy or equality is dependent on the therapist's perspective. However, many problems develop from disorganized hierarchy, especially between parents and children.

Personal Gain Versus Altruism The problem can be conceived by understanding the symptomatic person's motivation, whether hurting or helping others, and can lead to a strategy for change.

TECHNIQUES

Directives

In strategic therapy, *directives* are assignments to be performed inside and outside of the therapeutic session and are a key intervention. Directives can be defined as instructions, tasks, or a "message for the other person to do something" (Haley, 1976, p. 50). Furthermore, directives are not concerned with the past or with growth, but emphasize "communication in the present" (Madanes, 1981, p. 24). Examples of directives include instructions to take turns talking/listening for 10 minutes each night or, more paradoxically, to argue for 10 minutes at a set time each night.

There are two types of directives, genuine and paradoxical (Haley, 1976; Madanes, 1981). Directives serve several purposes: first, clients are encouraged to "behave differently"; second, treatment is intensified by involving the family between sessions and the therapeutic relationship is intensified; and, third, information about systemic structure and rules is gathered from the outcome of directives (Haley, 1976).

Metaphoric Task

Haley (1973, 1976) and Madanes (1981, 1984) highlight the use of *metaphor* in strategic therapy and refer to a metaphor as a statement or activity that represents or resembles something else. A *metaphoric task* is a directive in which the family engages in a conversation or an activity that is not about the problem, typically "an activity easier for the family members to deal with" (Haley, 1976, p. 67). The task indirectly facilitates change because of the symbolism and the content. For example, "in one case where a boy was reported to be afraid of dogs, the therapist learned that the boy had been adopted as an infant" (Haley, 1976, p. 65). The therapist introduced the idea of having the boy adopt a dog "who had a problem of being frightened" (Haley, 1976, p. 65). The therapist introduced the idea of the dog becoming ill, and the boy responded with the option to give the dog away. The therapist stated that once the boy adopted the dog he was responsible for caring for the dog, "no matter what" (Haley, 1976, p. 65). The concerns that the parents and child may have about the adopted boy were "discussed in metaphoric terms in relation to the proposed adoption of the puppy" (Haley, 1976, pp. 65–66).

Paradoxical Injunction

A *paradox* is "a directive or an extended message that is apparently inconsistent with itself or with the purpose of the therapy" (Madanes, 1984, p. 148). In applying a *paradoxical injunction,* the strategic therapist instructs clients to continue with "symptomatic" behavior in order to avoid a greater problem or for a reason consistent with the family's concerns. For example, a mother who chronically worries may be directed to spend 15 minutes worrying each morning. The underlying assumption is that conscious attempts to change habitual behavior rooted in relationships are often not successful. Prescribing the symptom changes the behavior from a spontaneous act to a conscious act. The four basic types of paradoxical injunctions are:

1. *Compliance-based (hoping for compliance):* For example, instruct "worrier" to worry for set period each day, which often reduces worry throughout day.
2. *Defiance-based (hoping for defiance):* For example, ineffective parents are instructed to ask permission from child before setting rules.
3. *Exposure-based (revealing covert alliances):* For example, father gives daughter a quarter each time she defies mother in situation where father and daughter have coalition against mother.
4. *Control-based (aims at gaining control of behavior):* For example, instruct couple to argue for 20 minutes each day to gain more awareness of how they start and stop an argument.

The intention behind the application of a paradoxical injunction is to "provoke a family to change by rebelling against the therapist" (Madanes, 1981, p. 7).

Ordeal Therapy

Ordeal therapy is a technique that assists in alleviating the symptom by making it more trouble to maintain the symptom than to give it up. In this process, an *ordeal,* usually a constructive or neutral activity, is presented to make it more difficult for the client to have a problem than to maintain it. Clients are typically instructed that they must engage in the ordeal activity before they are allowed to engage in the symptomatic activity. For example, a couple may agree that before engaging in an argument they will rearrange the living room furniture to resemble a court room and conduct the argument using this metaphor. Alternatively, a client may be instructed to give a present to a person with whom he/she has a poor relationship each time the symptom occurs.

Pretend Techniques

Developed by Madanes (1981, 1984), pretend techniques are less confrontational than many other strategic techniques. These techniques may involve asking symptom bearers to "pretend" to have the symptom (or enact the feared situation) and have the other family members respond in session; they may also involve pretending to have the symptoms at specified times between sessions, similar to paradoxical directives. Other members in the family can also be asked to pretend that they are experiencing particular symptoms. These techniques (a) allow the system to maintain homeostasis without the person genuinely suffering from the symptom, (b) often have a paradoxical effect of highlighting the control one actually has over the symptom, and (c) serve to disrupt problem patterns in the family.

Restraining and Going Slow

In restraining, the therapist attempts to "restrain the family from improving" or improving too fast by discouraging the possibility of change. This paradoxical technique suggests that the symptom may be helpful to the family (Haley, 1976; Madanes, 1981, 1984) with the hope that the family will rebel against the therapist and/or take a new position in relation to the problem. Similarly, families may be advised to "go slow" once changes have occurred, which normalizes possible setbacks in the future and simultaneously sends a paradoxical message about change.

Positioning

Positioning is a paradoxical technique in which the therapist addresses resistance by exaggerating it to hopelessness and "the illusion of no alternatives" (Madanes, 1984, p. 181). This paradoxical task highlights the therapist's hopelessness for resolution of the symptoms in an attempt to encourage the client family to "prove to the therapist that they are as good as other people" (Haley, 1976, p. 69). Positioning may involve the therapist taking the "one down" position.

STRATEGIC TREATMENT PLANS

The following general treatment plan identifies possible goals and interventions for each stage of therapy that could be used in treating individuals, couples, and families. Not all goals and techniques are applicable to all clients.

General Strategic Treatment Plan

Early-Phase Goals

1. Join system in the *social stage* of therapy.

Possible Interventions

a. Observe family interaction, mood, dynamics, and organization while discussing neutral or social topics.
b. Discuss problem issue and observe interaction and discussion while ensuring involvement of all members.
c. Inquire about the family's stage of development.

2. Gather information about the problem issue in the *problem stage.*

Possible Interventions

a. Direct questions and conversation about the problem.
b. Conceptualize problem and hypothesis in terms of voluntary/involuntary control, power, metaphor, hierarchy, and personal gain/altruism.
c. Encourage all members to attend; inquire about those who did not attend.
d. Discuss problem issue and observe interaction and discussion while ensuring involvement of all members in the *interaction stage.*

3. Establish goals with the client in the *goal-setting stage.*

Possible Intervention

a. Design a contract defining goals and utilize as a measure of the change.

Middle-Phase Goals

1. Interrupt covert hierarchical structure and covert alliances.

Possible Interventions

a. Apply directives that encourage the hierarchy to become disrupted.
b. Assign metaphoric task that highlights hierarchy imbalance, for example, parents ask for permission, child sits at head of table, and so on.
c. Present a paradoxical injunction to highlight the dysfunctional hierarchical structure.
d. Use pretend techniques to upset and highlight problem alliances.
e. Reframe problem dynamics in terms of love, control, helpfulness, and so on.

2. Alter unproductive interaction styles and patterns.

Possible Interventions

a. Use restraining techniques to paradoxically discourage changes in the system and prepare for setbacks.
b. Utilize positioning to exaggerate hopelessness.
c. Present an ordeal to assist in making the problem issue harder to maintain.
d. Present a paradoxical injunction, such as prescribing the symptom.
e. Reframe problem dynamics in terms of love, control, helpfulness, and so on.

Late-Phase Goals

1. Address any specific problem issues that still remain, particularly couple issues.

Possible Interventions

a. Inquire about specific problem issues.
b. Present directives, ordeals, and paradoxical injunctions to assist in relieving symptoms.

2. Highlight gains while focusing on the family's ability to transition through another stage of life.

Possible Interventions

a. Discuss problem issue and highlight the previous role the symptom played in the family.
b. Identify and discuss changes in the system and ways to avoid problems.
c. Advise family to "go slow" in making changes.

Vignette: Individual

Kurt is a recently divorced, Japanese American male with limited custody of his 4-year-old daughter. Kurt states that his wife Sarah "kicked him out" several months ago and reports that he did not identify any warning signs or precursors to the separation. Kurt states that he has been depressed, has few friends, is in a "dead-end" career, and is unsure how to rebuild his life. He states that he attempts to contact Sarah daily, but she hangs up on him. Kurt reports not wanting to initiate contact with his daughter, resulting from his statement that the quality of the relationship with his daughter has diminished.

Practice Strategic Treatment Plan for Individual

Early-Phase Goals

1.
   a.
   b.

2.
   a.
   b.

Middle-Phase Goals

1.
   a.
   b.

2.
   a.
   b.

Late-Phase Goals

1.
   a.
   b.

2.
   a.
   b.

Vignette: Couple

Joanne, age 33, and Richard, age 34, are a Hispanic couple that has been married for 7 years. They have been in and out of couples counseling to address interrelational conflict associated with lack of communication and infidelity. Joanne and Richard state that the previous counseling was helpful and diminished the level of conflict. However, since the birth of their daughter, Joanne reports feeling anxious and depressed. Richard and Joanne state that Richard's mother has been very active in the new child's life. They state that Richard's mother is at their house from 6 in the morning to 6 in the evening. While she's at Richard and Joanne's home, she reportedly cleans up after and "waits on" Richard. Joanne states that her mother-in-law's help was useful; however, Joanne felt overwhelmed by her presence and asked her to leave. This incident has resulted in a reemergence of conflict between Joanne and Richard, as well as a decrease in intimacy.

Practice Strategic Treatment Plan for Couple

Early-Phase Goals

1.
   a.
   b.

2.
   a.
   b.

Middle-Phase Goals

1.
   a.
   b.

2.
   a.
   b.

Late-Phase Goals

1.
   a.
   b.

2.
   a.
   b.

Vignette: Family

Malorie, a Causasian American single parent struggling with reported depressive symptoms, initiated counseling services. During a 20-year marriage to Doug, an African American male, she had three children; 17-year-old daughter Kristin, 15-year-old daughter Julia, and 12-year-old son Brad. Malorie reports that Kristin is highly disruptive at home and at school, and she suspects that she is using drugs and alcohol. Malorie states that Julia and Brad have become more withdrawn from the family by staying in their rooms and spending time with friends due to Kristin's adverse behavior.

Pratice Strategic Treatment Plan for Family

Early-Phase Goals

1.
    a.
    b.

2.
    a.
    b.

Middle-Phase Goals

1.
    a.
    b.

2.
    a.
    b.

Late-Phase Goals

1.
    a.
    b.

2.
    a.
    b.

Vignette: Individual

Kurt is a recently divorced, Japanese American male with limited custody of his 4-year-old daughter. Kurt states that his wife Sarah "kicked him out" several months ago and reports that he did not identify any warning signs or precursors to the separation. Kurt states that he has been depressed, has few friends, is in a "dead-end" career, and is unsure how to rebuild his life. He states that he attempts to contact Sarah daily, but she hangs up on him. Kurt reports not wanting to initiate contact with his daughter, resulting from his statement that the quality of the relationship with his daughter has diminished.

Strategic Treatment Plan for Individual

Early-Phase Goals

1. Join with client and note his reported interaction patterns, mood, and dynamics during the *social stage.*
   a. Engage in neutral/social conversation with Kurt while assessing general mood and dynamics.
   b. Inquire about the family's stage of development and his recent transition from a marriage and family to single status.

2. Gather information about Kurt's problem issue in the *problem stage.*
   a. Initiate a discussion of the separation/divorce, Kurt's emotional status, his relationship with his daughter, and his social/work life attending to his descriptions of relational patterns.
   b. Therapist develops hypothesis about the "voluntary" nature of depression and isolation symptoms and recognizes the "control" he tries to maintain over ex-wife and child. Explore cultural issues in relation to themes of male control.

3. Establish goals with Kurt.
   a. Design a contract defining goals associated with reducing depression and isolation related to the divorce and creating a more satisfying life as a single father.

Middle-Phase Goals

1. Interrupt covert hierarchical structure and covert alliances between Kurt and ex-wife.
   a. Apply directives to disrupt the power/hierarchy between Kurt and his spouse, such as asking Kurt to avoid contacting Sarah by telephone for a week.
   b. Assign a metaphorical task that highlights the hierarchy imbalance between Kurt and Sarah, such as having Kurt get on his knees to talk with her on the phone, in person, or in "pretend" exercise.
   c. Present a paradoxical injunction to highlight the dysfunctional hierarchical structure, such as asking Kurt to worship her with an elaborate altar in his home, being more submissive, giving her the "red carpet" treatment, and so on.

2. Alter unproductive interaction styles and patterns between Kurt and ex-wife.
   a. Introduce an ordeal, such as before Kurt calls Sarah with the intention of discussing reuniting, Kurt has to call another friend, run a mile, or so on.
   b. Use restraining techniques to paradoxically discourage Kurt to change.
   c. Utilize positioning to exaggerate the hopelessness of the case, perhaps suggesting that the best years of his life are probably over, and so on.
   d. Present a defiance-based paradoxical injunction, such as prescribing Kurt's symptoms.

Late-Phase Goals

1. Strengthen relationship between Kurt and his daughter by increasing visits and interaction.
   a. Have Kurt set up "practice" visits with daughter, where he practices being a father for short periods of time; explore cultural expectations and beliefs.
   b. Suggest the following ordeal: if he cancels a visit with his daughter, he will put $100 into a college savings account so that he can "father" her in some way.
   c. Restrain Kurt from attempting to make too many changes in the relationship, saying he might not be ready to take on the job of being a father.
   d. Utilize positioning to exaggerate hopelessness, saying it may take years to be a good father again.
   e. Consider co-parent sessions if appropriate.

2. Increase other social contacts and successfully transition to being a divorced, single father.
   a. Use ordeals to discourage isolation and encourage isolation: if he declines a social invitation, he needs to take a co-worker to lunch.
   b. Use restraining to encourage him not to change too quickly; cite cultural restraints.
   c. Identify and discuss changes Kurt made and ways to avoid problems in the future.

Vignette: Couple

Joanne, age 33, and Richard, age 34, are a Hispanic couple that has been married for 7 years. They have been in and out of couples counseling to address interrelational conflict associated with lack of communication and infidelity. Joanne and Richard state that the previous counseling was helpful and diminished the level of conflict. However, since the birth of their daughter, Joanne reports feeling anxious and depressed. Richard and Joanne state that Richard's mother has been very active in the new child's life. They state that Richard's mother is at their house from 6 in the morning to 6 in the evening. While she's at Richard and Joanne's home, she reportedly cleans up after and "waits on" Richard. Joanne states that her mother-in-law's help was useful; however, Joanne felt overwhelmed by her presence and asked her to leave. This incident has resulted in a reemergence of conflict between Joanne and Richard, as well as a decrease in intimacy.

Strategic Treatment Plan for Couple

Early-Phase Goals

1. Join with couple while beginning to assess system.
   a. Observe couple's interaction patterns while discussing neutral and/or social topics.
   b. Inquire about and assess family's adjustment to current stage of family life cycle: couple with infant child.

2. Gather information about the role of conflict in the relationship.
   a. Direct questions and conversation about current relational conflict.
   b. Conceptualize and develop preliminary hypothesis about current conflict, perhaps highlighting that mother-in-law seems to hold the "power" in the marriage.
   c. Instruct couple to discuss problem issue and observe couple's interaction, noting power moves.

3. Establish goals for the couple.
   a. Design a contract defining goals for therapy that can be used to measure change.

Middle-Phase Goals

1. Interrupt covert hierarchical structure and covert alliances between Richard and his mother with the ultimate aim of reducing Joanne's depressive symptoms and couple conflict.
   a. Apply directives that encourage hierarchy to become disrupted, such as directing Richard to limit mother's presence at his home.
   b. Assign a metaphoric task that highlights the hierarchy imbalance, such as telling Richard that he needs to ask his mother for permission to go out with friends.

   c. Present a paradoxical injunction to highlight the dysfunctional hierarchical structure, such as asking Richard to act like a child in the presence of his parents and asking Joanne to act helpless when her mother-in-law is around.
   d. Assign metaphoric task, such as having each call at least two other people to ask for advice at the start of an argument to highlight how mother-in-law has become drawn into their relationship.
   e. Recommend couple "pretend" to be helpless when mother-in-law is around.

2. Alter unproductive interaction styles and patterns between couple to reduce conflict and stress and increase productive communication and intimacy.
   a. Use restraining techniques to paradoxically discourage couple to change and to prepare for setbacks.
   b. Utilize positioning to exaggerate Richard's resistance to change to hopelessness.
   c. Assign ordeal therapy techniques, such as stating that every time they begin to have an argument, they have to do a chore together before they can start.
   d. Present a paradoxical injunction, such as prescribing the couple to fight about something once a day.
   e. Use pretend techniques to have each "pretend" to be arguing and withholding affection to highlight voluntary nature.
   f. Paradoxically forbid couple to engage in sex.

Late-Phase Goals

1. Establish new couple relational patterns that allow for sense of being loved and opportunities to love the other.
   a. Use pretend techniques to have couple practice new behaviors.
   b. Offer directives that increase and expand new ways to express and receive love.
   c. Caution to "go slow," when making these changes to prepare for setbacks.
   d. Take the "one down" position to encourage couple to take initiative in defining how best to love one another.

2. Highlight gains while focusing on the couple's ability to transition through another family life stage.
   a. Discuss problem issue and the successful transition to assist in avoiding other problems.
   b. Highlight the previous role of the symptom in the couple dyad.
   c. Discuss current distribution of power in the relationship and how it affects sense of intimacy.

Vignette: Family

Malorie, a Caucasian American single parent struggling with reported depressive symptoms, initiated counseling services. During a 20-year marriage to Doug, an African American male, she had three children; 17-year-old daughter Kristin, 15-year-old daughter Julia, and 12-year-old son Brad. Malorie reports that Kristin is highly disruptive at home and at school, and she suspects that she is using drugs and alcohol. Malorie states that Julia and Brad have become more withdrawn from the family by staying in their rooms and spending time with friends due to Kristin's adverse behavior.

Strategic Treatment Plan for Family

Early-Phase Goals

1. Join with family while observing family interaction, mood, dynamics, and organization.
   a. Begin by discussing neutral or social topic and observe interactions between family members.
   b. Assess and inquire about the family's stage of development: divorced family with adolescents preparing to launch first child.

2. Gather information about Kristin's behavior and family's response to her.
   a. Direct discussion of Kristin's disruptive behavior and other symptoms, while ensuring participation by all members.
   b. Conceptualize problem and hypothesis surrounding Kristin's behavior; perhaps Kristin is asking mother to act like a mother or asking her to prove she really cares.
   c. Encourage all members to attend, and inquire about those who do not attend and status of father(s).

3. Establish goals for the family.
   a. Design a contract defining goals as a measure of change; contract may include reduction in arguments at home, increase in joint family activities, and so on.

Middle-Phase Goals

1. Interrupt covert hierarchical structure and covert alliances between Malorie and the children to reduce depressive symptoms and disruptive behavior.
   a. Apply directives that encourage the hierarchy to become disrupted, such as asking Malorie to identify characteristics of a "strict" parental role and adapt one characteristic.
   b. Assign a metaphoric task that highlights the hierarchy imbalance between Malorie and her children, such as having Kristin determine her younger siblings' curfew.
   c. Present a paradoxical injunction to highlight the dysfunctional hierarchical structure by asking Kristin to continue her disruptive behavior every other night so that Mom can practice her parenting skills.

   d. Paradoxically direct Malorie to allow Kristin to maintain the control of the family members and allow her to make family decisions or have mother act more helpless when daughter acts up.
   e. Use pretend techniques to have family consciously experience how problem scenes are acted out.

2. Reduce Kristin's disruptive behavior and develop more cooperative interaction patterns between family members.
   a. Use restraining techniques to discourage a change in the system and prepare them for setbacks.
   b. Utilize positioning to exaggerate mother, daughter, and/or family's hopeless situation.
   c. Present an ordeal, such as directing Malorie to write a one-page reflection on parenting every time she gives into Kristin, to make the problem issues harder to maintain.
   d. Present a paradoxical injunction, such as asking mother and daughter to rotate who starts fights each day.
   e. Work with family to identify an ordeal they are willing to agree to, such as putting on matching outfits, signifying their peer relationship.
   f. Instruct younger siblings to "grade" the responses of each during the next argument or session in terms of how "mature" each response is.

Late-Phase Goals

1. Address withdrawal of younger children from family life if this is still a problem.
   a. Develop directives to have family nights or rituals.
   b. Suggest metaphoric task of having children cover ears and eyes during next argument between mother and Kristin.
   c. Employ paradox by having younger children grade performance or "keep score" for mother and Kristin during arguments.

2. Highlight gains while focusing on the family's ability to transition through another stage of life.
   a. Discuss accomplishment of the transition and gains and ways to avoid problem.
   b. Validate mother and her ability to maintain the hierarchical status appropriate to each child's needs.

References

Haley, J. (1963). *Strategies of psychotherapy.* New York: Grune & Stratton.

Haley, J. (1973). *Uncommon therapy: The psychiatric techniques of Milton H. Erickson, M.D.* New York: Norton.

Haley, J. (1976). *Problem-solving therapy: New strategies for effective family therapy.* San Francisco, CA: Jossey-Bass.

Haley, J. (1980). *Leaving home: The therapy of disturbed young people.* New York: McGraw-Hill.

Haley, J. (1981). *Reflections on therapy.* Chevy Chase, MD: The Family Therapy Institute of Washington, DC.

Haley, J. (1984). *Ordeal therapy.* San Francisco: Jossey-Bass.

Haley, J. (1996). *Learning and teaching therapy.* New York: Guilford Press.

Madanes, C. (1981). *Strategic family therapy.* San Francisco, CA: Jossey-Bass.

Madanes, C. (1984). *Behind the one-way mirror: Advances in the practices of strategic therapy.* San Francisco, CA: Jossey-Bass.

Madanes, C. (1990). *Sex, love, and violence: Strategies for transformation.* New York: Norton.

Madanes, C., & Haley, J. Dimensions of family therapy. *Journal of Nervous and Mental Disease 165*(2), 88–98.

"Therapeutic interventions in the family, as we have gradually devised, applied, and critically examined them, appear to be, at a certain point, no more than a learning process acquired by the therapists through trial and error" (Selvini Palazzoli, Cecchin, Prata, & Boscolo, 1978, p. 47).

MILAN SYSTEMIC APPROACH

CHAPTER 4

KEY THEORISTS

Luigi Boscolo
Gianfranco Cecchin
Mara Selvini Palazzoli
Giuliana Prata

HISTORICAL OVERVIEW

The "Milan group" included Mara Selvini Palazzoli, Luigi Boscolo, Gianfranco Cecchin, and Guiliana Prata who founded the Milan Group Center for the Study of the Family in 1971. The Milan group attempted to put into practice the systemic ideas of Gregory Bateson, viewing family interaction as a set of rules that is best intervened upon with paradox. In 1980, the group split, with Boscolo and Cecchin focusing on training and later exploring constructivism and Selvini Palazzoli and Prata focusing on research with the invariant prescription and anorectic families. Other contributors to the Milan approach include Lynn Hoffman, Karl Tomm, and Peggy Penn.

KEY CONCEPTS

Epistemology and Epistemological Error

The early Milan team's goal was to apply Bateson's cybernetic ideas as directly as possible to therapeutic practice. Central to Bateson's work is epistemology, which is the study of knowledge and knowing. Epistemology originates from the "Greek verb *epistamai,* which means to put oneself 'over' or 'higher' in order to better observe something" (Selvini Palazzoli, Cecchin, Prata, & Boscolo, 1978, p. 5). From a Batesonian perspective, an epistemology that does not acknowledge reciprocal cause and effect often results in runaway escalations or similar systemic "crises." Such epistemologies are examined for "errors" that cause systemic distress. An epistemological error can also be thought of as an erroneous set of beliefs or distinctions that an individual or family uses to make sense of the world. Perhaps one of the most common errors is to believe that one individual's behavior can be the *cause* of another's behavior, implying unilateral control of one over the other (e.g., a man who says his wife's nagging *causes* him to withdraw). Such epistemological errors create and maintain stress and are believed to be the root of family symptomology.

Games

"Game" is used as a metaphor to understand problem family interactions and is described as "an exchange of concrete bits of behavior among subjects" (Selvini Palazzoli, Cirillo, Selvini, & Sorrentino, 1989, p. 152). Games are unacknowledged strategies and destructive patterns of family interaction in which members attempt to control each other's behavior. The family game "touches on our very existence" (p. 161). In the Milan approach, "the power is only in the rules of the game which cannot be changed by the people involved in it" (Selvini Palazzoli et al., 1978, p. 6). Therefore, Milan therapists aim at changing the rules of the game rather than attempting to change individual game players.

Meaning Versus Action

The therapist distinguishes between meaning and action to help correct epistemological errors. For example, the interpretation of a child's behavior (child is disrespectful) is carefully separated from the act itself (the child does not follow rules). The introduction of this new distinction allows the family to create new belief patterns that are followed by new behavioral patterns.

Tyranny of Linguistics

Language is a linear construct that is used to describe reality, which is a circular construct (Palazzoli et al., 1978). People generally assume that distinctions made by language are correct. However, systemic therapists recognize the epistemological aspects of language, particularly how language shapes our reality, making it impossible for language to ever fully capture reality (Selvini Palazzoli et al., 1989). In therapy, basic linguistic forms, such as subject-predicate-object, are reworked to reveal the static, linear assumptions that underlie them. The therapist uses language to create new interpretations of the situation. In particular, the verb *to be* is replaced with *to seem, to show, to act* in order to put behavior in context. For example, he *shows* depression, *acts* depressed, or *appears* to be depressed, rather than he *is* depressed (Palazzoli et al., 1989, p. 259).

GOALS OF THERAPY

Focus of Treatment: New Meaning

The therapist and team focus on providing new meanings and distinctions that will alter unproductive rules for family behavior and the family game. The Milan team examines the family game to assist in tracing the origins of the symptoms and dysfunctional patterns (Selvini Palazzoli et al., 1978; Selvini Palazzoli et al., 1989). The team focuses on the family system and its intrinsic self-corrective nature to promote a transformation that will alleviate symptomatic patterns. Additionally, the Milan team focuses on process and relational interaction within the family game rather than the more static family structure.

Goals

In the Milan systemic approach, the goal is to maintain healthy systemic functioning to assist in the system or family's "survival" (Selvini Palazzoli et al., 1989, p. 159) and to maintain stability and cohesion (Palazzoli et al., 1978). To sustain systemic survival, the Milan therapist introduces goals, including:

- The family system will learn to accommodate and adjust to new information and beliefs to encourage "playing a different game" (Selvini Palazzoli et al., 1989, p. 248).
- New information and rules within the family game are accommodated to in a way that no family members develop symptoms (Selvini Palazzoli et al., 1978).
- Other specific goals and how they are to be achieved are left up to the family (Selvini Palazzoli et al., 1978).

STRUCTURE OF THERAPY

Long-Term Brief Therapy

In the Milan approach, therapy is highly structured. The Milan approach has traditionally been described as "long-term brief therapy" because relatively few sessions (generally 10) are held approximately once a month (Selvini Palazzoli et al., 1978; Selvini Palazzoli et al., 1989). Time between sessions is required for interventions to take effect. Once frequency is determined, no extra sessions are granted. Each session is divided into five segments: pre-session, session, intervention, intersession, intervention, and discussion. Each segment of the sessions includes discussions, observations, assessment, and interventions.

Overview of Sessions

Session One All family members are present to allow the team to observe interactional patterns and the family game and to assist in assessment and developing the hypothesis.

Session Two The family members are present, and the focus is on the children. After the second session, "the children are dismissed" from therapy (Selvini Palazzoli et al., 1989, p. 42).

Session Three The parents are present, and the therapists prescribe the invariant prescription.

Session Four Only the parents return to therapy and are promoted to the identified patients and children's "co-therapist." "No one else, not even the patient, will be summoned again" (Selvini Palazzoli et al., 1989, p. 44). Changes in the parental unit become the means of altering symptoms in the initial identified patient.

Session Five The therapist addresses the parents' "victory" or defeat in altering the system and identified patient's symptoms, while prescribing "more of the same," including a "longer absence from home" (Selvini Palazzoli et al., 1989, p. 60).

Subsequent Sessions Additional sessions involve monitoring the invariant prescription and the identified patient's progress, while highlighting the parental role. Furthermore, additional strategic techniques are applied to assist the family in accommodating to the new rules in the family game.

ASSESSMENT

Therapeutic Interview

In the therapeutic interview, the Milan therapist assesses for interactional patterns and the family games. Assessment occurs during all five segments of the therapeutic interview. The assessment or hypothesis is continually revised over the course of therapy.

Pre-Session Therapy begins with the initial phone call by a member of the family (Selvini Palazzoli et al., 1978). In the initial intake, information such as who called; who referred the family; caller expectations; family member names, ages, education, religion, profession, and attitude; and overall observations are used to assess the family. Before meeting with the family, the team has a pre-session meeting to discuss the call and formulate an initial hypothesis; or, if the session is not an initial session, the team reads and discusses the records of the previous meeting.

Session One therapist, referred to as the "conductor" of the session, interviews the family to gather information about the problem situation and family rules while the team observes. During the session, the conductor and team observe communication and behavioral transactions. Furthermore, during the session, the observation team or the conductor has the option of interrupting the session to obtain feedback and suggestions or to refocus the session.

Intersession Midway through the session, the therapist/conductor takes a break to meet with the team, a small group of observing therapists. The team validates or modifies the hypotheses, proposes an intervention, and recommends how to further proceed and conclude the session.

Intervention After the intersession, the therapist returns, presents brief comments, and prescribes the agreed-upon intervention, which is typically paradoxical (Selvini Palazzoli et al., 1978).

Discussion "When the family has left, the team unites to discuss the family's reaction to the comment or prescription, to formulate and to write the *synthesis of the session*" (Selvini Palazzoli et al., 1978, pp. 15–16).

TECHNIQUES

A Learning Process

"Therapeutic interventions in the family, as we have gradually devised, applied, and critically examined them, appear to be, at a certain point, no more than a learning process acquired by the therapists through trial and error" (Selvini Palazzoli et al., 1978, p. 47). Through the process of trial and error and the resulting feedback, additional information is acquired and used to formulate new interventions.

Team Approach

The Milan approach uses a team of therapists who plan a strategy together. The team approach is said to reflect "a collective mind" that is "self-correcting, self-reflecting, and self-appraising" (Selvini Palazzoli et al., 1989, p. xiii). One or two of the team members work directly with the family, and the others watch behind a one-way mirror. "Teamwork brought with it a number of advantages, such as direct supervision, co-therapy, the possibility of alternating the role of the therapist with that of supervisor, and a collaborative rapport that had everyone on an equal footing" (p. xiii).

Hypothesizing

The therapist continually develops hypotheses about family interaction patterns and games and modifies them as the family presents additional information (Selvini Palazzoli, Boscolo, Cecchin, & Prata, 1980). For example, a therapist may hypothesize that a child's symptoms serve to keep the parents distracted from marital difficulties. Hypotheses, all of which need to be tested by the therapist, help direct the questioning of the therapist and aid the therapist in organizing information gathered from the family (Selvini Palazzoli et al., 1989). The hypotheses about family functioning and the role of symptom are revised during and after each session and have "organic" or evolving characteristics rather than being static or stable.

Circular Questioning

Circular questions focus on family interaction and behavioral exchanges within the family game rather than symptoms (Selvini Palazzoli et al., 1980). These questions serve to undermine a family's belief system that is based on "truths" and labeling. Circular questions can take many forms, but all serve to highlight systemic interaction patterns in the family. The circular questions include:

- *Relational and interaction pattern questions:* "What does your father do when you argue with your mother?"
- *Future-oriented questions:* "If your mother stopped worrying, what would your father do?"
- *Comparisons and rankings questions:* "Who gets most upset when you fail?"
- *Before-and-after-change questions:* "What were the fights like before versus after father's heart attack?" (Selvini Palazzoli et al., 1980).

Circular questions should focus on specific behaviors rather than feelings or interpretations. This method of questioning clarifies confused messages about family relationships.

Neutrality

Neutrality in this context refers to the therapist remaining allied with all family members and avoiding involvement in family coalitions. The Milan therapists maintain "a strictly neutral manner" and attempt to "avoid blaming anyone for anything" (Selvini Palazzoli et al., 1989, p. 20). Neutrality is first initiated by avoiding aligning with the family members who typically identify and differentiate the identified patient. The potential coalition between the Milan therapists and the family members is countered by "declaring the identified patient to be the real leader" who has made sacrifices for the "good of the family, or one or more of its members" (Selvini Palazzoli et al., 1978, p. 165). Cecchin (1987) has also described this type of neutrality as a form of "curiosity" in which the therapist is equally curious and interested in each person's description of the problem rather than a form of neutrality that is distant and aloof.

Positive Connotation

Positive connotation is an intervention in which the symptomatic behavior is reframed with a positive connotation, most often as a person "sacrificing him or herself by suffering the consequences of the symptom for the greater benefit of the family" (Selvini Palazzoli et al., 1978, p. 61). A common form of positive connotation is to frame a child's symptomatic behaviors, such as tantrums or depression, as "personal sacrifices" on the part of the child to give parents someone to care for so the parents can feel good about themselves as parents. Family members' behaviors are paradoxically commended, and positive motives are assigned to the negative behavior. Positive connotations assist in establishing that all family members are on the same level, highlights the system's homeostatic tendency, and prepares the way for the paradox.

Counterparadox

A double bind is a paradoxical form of communication that involves presenting conflicting messages. A family's double-bind message can only be undone with a therapeutic double bind, which is termed *counterparadox*. Counterparadox interventions request that the family not change although they came to therapy in order to change, referring to the dysfunction as "right and legitimate" (Selvini Palazzoli et al., 1978, p. 157).

Rituals

Family rituals are "an action or series of actions, usually accompanied by verbal formulas or expressions, which are to be carried out by all family members" (Selvini Palazzoli et al., 1978, p. 95). Rituals are typically highly structured events and/or interactions that are presented by the team in detail, including the place, time, duration, frequency, and who is to say what, and so on. Family rituals are assigned as an intervention that helps provide clarity and consistency in family relationships. Selvini Palazzoli and colleagues (1978) prescribed the following ritual to a family: "Each member of the family, starting with the eldest, would have 15 minutes to talk, expressing his own feelings, impressions, and observations regarding the behavior of the other members of the clan" (p. 93). The ritual was prescribed to assist the family differentiating itself from the enmeshed, extended family, as well as strengthening the identified patient's position in the family.

Invariant Prescription

Selvini Palazzoli and colleagues (1989) proposed that a single prescription be used with all schizophrenic and anorectic families, which was therefore termed the *invariant prescription*. The invariant prescription attempts to break up a "hitherto obscure family game" (Selvini Palazzoli et al., 1989, p. 17). The prescription requires that the parents form a tight alliance and reestablish their relationship as a couple by having them engage in activities that are kept secret from the children.

The invariant prescription consists of four parts (Selvini Palazzoli et al., 1989). The first part of the prescription involves the therapist directing the parental unit to maintain a sense of secrecy about the therapy session to which the children are not invited. In the second part, the parental unit is told to go on secret "outings." The destination and activity engaged in during these "outings" are to remain secret "from everyone." The third part of the invariant prescription involves maintaining the secrecy from the children, even when asked about the outings. The last part of the prescription involves directing the parental unit to keep a personal diary or notebook that will contain a record of "every piece of verbal or nonverbal behavior" from children and others that may have resulted from the prescription (p. 22).

The invariant prescription assists in aligning the parental unit as a couple and allows the parental unit to separate from dysfunctional, interfering, cross-generational alliances. The tight parental alliance severs existing covert alliances between generations and thereby assists in achieving therapeutic goals. Furthermore, the invariant prescription attempts to send the message that "it is not the task of the children to improve the relationship between their parents or to substitute for them in their functions" (Selvini Palazzoli et al., 1978, p. 111).

MILAN SYSTEMIC TREATMENT PLANS

The following general treatment plan identifies possible goals and interventions for each stage of therapy that could be used in treating individuals, couples, and families. Not all goals and techniques are applicable to all clients.

General Milan Systemic Treatment Plan

Early-Phase Goals

1. Therapist and team form an initial hypothesis about the family game and/or purpose of the symptom.

Possible Interventions

a. Gain information from initial contact on the telephone, including person initiating services, referral source, expectations, and attitudes, if possible.
b. Meet with the team to discuss information to generate initial hypothesis.
c. Based on hypothesis, encourage all family members to attend first session and/or later sessions, if possible.

2. Session conductor joins with the system.

Possible Interventions

a. Maintain a sense of neutrality and curiosity with members to avoid coalitions. Ask each member about his/her perceptions about the problem and family situation.
b. Discuss meeting schedule with family, typically once a month.

3. Identify the presenting problem issue and assess family games by gathering information about the problem and the family rules.

Possible Interventions

a. Use circular questions to gain information about interactional functioning.
b. Address each member to gain his/her perspective about symptoms and problem.
c. Utilize team to continually modify and refine hypothesis as part of a learning process; present hypotheses to family using positive connotation.
d. Dismiss children after second session and work with parents to alter family game.

Middle-Phase Goals

1. Alter unproductive rules/games that support the presenting symptom.

Possible Interventions

a. Present a counterparadox intervention by using a positive connotation or prescribing the symptom.
b. Use the invariant prescription to sever covert generational alliances.
c. Present specific behavioral tasks to assist in creating new beliefs and meanings and/or to highlight unhelpful dynamics of the family game.
d. Identify epistemological errors within the system and present corresponding hypothesis in their language.
e. Utilize circular questioning to highlight for the family unproductive rules and interactions.
f. Design family rituals to highlight or alter unproductive dynamics of the family game.

2. Help family to identify more helpful meanings and distinctions in relation to the problem issue and games.

Possible Interventions

a. Present the problem issue using positive connotation, highlighting the sacrifice a member or members are making to maintain the symptom, balance, and cohesion.
b. Reshape meaning by attending to epistemology behind linguistic distinctions used by the family, especially attending to "is/are" statements. For example, instead of stating the person "is" depressed or "is" conflictual, reframe the statement by saying that the person "displays/shows" depression or "acts" conflictual.
c. Use circular questioning to draw new distinctions that incorporate the perspectives of multiple persons in the family system.
d. Separate actions (e.g., leaving the room during argument) from interpretation of actions (e.g., does not care, unable to communicate, etc.).

Late-Phase Goals

1. Address any new issues that arise in response to addressing presenting symptom.

Possible Interventions

a. Utilize circular questioning to identify the meanings and perceptions related to emerging problem and how it may relate to presenting problem.
b. With team input, develop and present hypotheses that account for presenting and emerging problems using positive connotation.
c. Develop rituals that address new issue and presenting issue.

2. Develop and maintain new family "game" or interaction pattern that allows the family to accommodate and adjust to the new information and beliefs without the emergence of symptoms in family members.

Possible Interventions

a. Present family rituals that support a "symptom-free" family game.
b. Use circular questioning to help family develop a richer understanding of how the new rules work in comparison to prior rules.
c. Use circular questions about future scenarios and how each might respond.
d. Attend to language used to describe family functioning, attending to use of "is/are."

Vignette: Individual

Steve is a 23-year-old single, Hispanic male and a student in an undergraduate degree program. Steve initiated counseling services to address emotional distress reported in the form of depression and lack of motivation. He resides with his father and stepmother and reports that his biological mother "left" the family when he was 10. He states that, since then, he has not seen his mother and does not have any feelings toward her. Furthermore, Steve states that 2 years ago he was involved with the legal system following a petty theft charge against him and his girlfriend. He states that since then he has felt "bad" and has withdrawn from friends and family.

Practice Milan Systemic Treatment Plan for Individual

Early-Phase Goals

1.
    a.
    b.

2.
    a.
    b.

Middle-Phase Goals

1.
    a.
    b.

2.
    a.
    b.

Late-Phase Goals

1.
    a.
    b.

2.
    a.
    b.

Vignette: Couple

Marcus, an African male, and Kim, a Chinese American female, have been married for 7 years. Marcus has three children from a previous marriage that reside with their biological mother and her husband. Kim has four children from a previous marriage. The younger children reside with the identified couple, and the older two live outside the home. Marcus and Kim state that their relationship has become "strained," and they are considering divorce due to the conflict. Marcus states that he does not feel connected to the family and often feels like an "outsider" in his own home. Kim states that she feels torn between her children and Marcus. Kim's two children who reside in the home have reportedly experienced problems in school and in other relationships. Marcus and Kim report that if they do not get help for themselves they will not be able to stay together.

Practice Milan Systemic Treatment Plan for Couple

Early-Phase Goals

1.
   a.
   b.

2.
   a.
   b.

Middle-Phase Goals

1.
   a.
   b.

2.
   a.
   b.

Late-Phase Goals

1.
   a.
   b.

2.
   a.
   b.

Vignette: Family

Maria and her 9-year-old daughter Sonia requested counseling services. Maria reported that she and her husband Gerry separated approximately 6 months ago but are trying to "work things out." Maria stated that she has become concerned about Sonia's emotional well-being since the separation. According to Maria, Sonia has witnessed several fights and arguments between her parents prior to and since the separation. Maria also reported that she thinks her husband has been drinking more since the separation. Maria also reports that she has become very depressed and has been prescribed an antidepressant by her general medical physician. Reportedly, Sonia attempts to comfort her mother but rarely discusses her emotions. Sonia reports that her mother becomes upset when she discusses her feelings and states that she feels unimportant and in the way. Sonia's grades have reportedly dropped, and her teacher has complained about behavior problems at school.

Milan Systemic Treatment Plan for Family

Early-Phase Goals

1.
   a.
   b.

2.
   a.
   b.

Middle-Phase Goals

1.
   a.
   b.

2.
   a.
   b.

Late-Phase Goals

1.
   a.
   b.

2.
   a.
   b.

Vignette: Individual

Steve is a 23-year-old single Hispanic male and a student in an undergraduate degree program. Steve initiated counseling services to address emotional distress reported in the form of depression and lack of motivation. He resides with his father and stepmother and reports that his biological mother "left" the family when he was 10. He states that, since then, he has not seen his mother and does not have any feelings toward her. Furthermore, Steve states that 2 years ago he was involved with the legal system following a petty theft charge against him and his girlfriend. He states that since then he has felt "bad" and has withdrawn from friends and family.

Milan Systemic Treatment Plan for Individual

Early-Phase Goals

1. Therapist and team form an initial hypothesis.
   a. Gain information from initial contact on the telephone, including Steve initiating services, referral source, expectations, and his attitude, if possible.
   b. Meet with team to discuss information obtained and generate initial hypothesis.
   c. Encourage Steve's father, stepmother, girlfriend, and other family member to attend first session.

2. Session conductor joins with Steve.
   a. Maintain a sense of neutrality and curiosity with Steve.
   b. Discuss meeting schedule, once a month.

3. Explore family rules while gathering information about roles of reported depression and lack of motivation.
   a. Use circular questions to gain information about family functioning, such as how do his family and friends interact and respond when he withdraws? How were things before, during, and after his mother left the family? How do father and stepmother interact?
   b. Utilize team to assist in generating a hypothesis about Steve, his symptoms, and his situation, highlighting his reported lack of feelings toward his mother and withdrawal from others.

Middle-Phase Goals

1. Alter unproductive rules/games that support Steve's acting depressed.
   a. Possibly present a counterparadox by asking Steve to act depressed.
   b. Present a ritual in which Steve will alternate days of acting depressed.
   c. Incorporate circular questioning technique to assist Steve in seeing the depression and the effects on his life and relationships, such as: How do you respond to others when you feel depressed? How do your parents react and interact with you? How does your culture view depression? What is the meaning between you, your culture, gender, and depression?

   d. Identify and uncover the epistemological errors that support hopeless outlook; look at possible ideas about perfection related to guilt about incident and mother's abandonment; consider in context of culture and gender beliefs.

2. Alter the "game" of acting unmotivated and explore function of this game in larger family context.
   a. Present lack of motivation using a positive connotation, highlighting the sacrifice Steve is making to maintain balance in his life and cohesion between Steve and his parents, as well as between father and stepmother.
   b. Alter language and utilize concept of "the tyranny of linguistics" to reshape meaning of lack of motivation. Instead of stating that Steve is unmotivated, state that he shows symptoms of acting unmotivated or acts unmotivated at certain times.
   c. Use circular questioning by exploring parents' perspectives of him. Highlight the distinction between Steve's biological mother leaving and the beliefs he has about her leaving.
   d. Explore culture and gender aspects of current games.

Late-Phase Goals

1. Address loss of biological mother; help Steve/family grieve and make sense of loss.
   a. Ask circular questions to gain a sense about how the family dealt with grief before and after biological mother left, as well as how each member reacted to her absence. Explore the connection between the loss and Steve's reported symptoms, while addressing how his culture views grief and the process of letting go.
   b. Present loss of mother with a positive connotation, highlighting strength and cohesion within family.
   c. Create a ritual that involves the family members coming together to discuss their feelings and thoughts associated with absent biological mother, as well as a ritual that encourages positive leisure activities.

2. Help Steve make more productive meaning of current life situations and the changes he has made in therapy.
   a. Utilize circular questioning to identify changes, highlighting how the family interaction has altered in the absence of depression.
   b. Explore potential obstacle that may disrupt the new game and utilize circular questions to identify how Steve will respond.
   c. Continue to address the language uses and the meaning he attributes to actions, altering when necessary.
   d. Create and maintain rituals that support communication of feelings and positive interactions with others.

Vignette: Couple

Marcus, an African American male, and Kim, a Chinese American female, have been married for 7 years. Marcus has three children from a previous marriage that reside with their biological mother and her husband. Kim has four children from a previous marriage. The younger children reside with the identified couple, and the older two live outside the home. Marcus and Kim state that their relationship has become "strained," and they are considering divorce due to the conflict. Marcus states that he does not feel connected to the family and often feels like an "outsider" in his own home. Kim states that she feels torn between her children and Marcus. Kim's two children who reside in the home have reportedly experienced problems in school and in other relationships. Marcus and Kim report that if they do not get help for themselves they will not be able to stay together.

Milan Systemic Treatment Plan for Couple

Early-Phase Goals

1. Therapist and team form an initial hypothesis about the systemic functioning of the couple and family systems.
   a. Gain information from initial contact on the telephone, including whether Kim or Marcus initiated services, referral source, and Marcus and Kim's expectations and attitudes toward counseling.
   b. Discuss information with team and generate initial hypothesis, which may address role of children in distracting couple from marriage.

2. Session conductor joins with Marcus and Kim.
   a. Maintain a sense of neutrality and curiosity while establishing a therapeutic relationship with each to avoid collations. Explore Marcus and Kim's perspectives on the problem issues and family functioning.
   b. Discuss meeting once a month.

3. Identify the presenting issues and couple/family games while gathering information about the "strain" in Kim and Marcus's relationship and family rules that support the problems in the family.
   a. Present circular questions to gain information about interactional functioning between Kim and Marcus (i.e., How would each of you characterize the relationship between the two of you? Who is most afraid of divorce? How do the ethnic differences impact the relationship?)
   b. Ask circular questions to understand role of children in couple situation, such as: How does each child interact with you? How did they interact with you before and after you married? How do you interact with the "strain" in the relationship? What about before the strain? What is the role of the ethnic differences between Marcus and the children?
   c. Utilize team to modify initial hypothesis.

Middle-Phase Goals

1. Alter the unproductive rules and games that create and support strain and conflict in the relationship.
   a. Prescribe invariant prescription to assist in severing alliances between Kim and the children.
   b. Present a positive connotation by highlighting sacrifices each is making for couple and family.
   c. Uncover and explore the epistemological errors associated with Marcus and Kim's beliefs around marriage, parenting/stepparenting, biracial couples, and the role of children.
   d. Present specific behavioral tasks to assist in creating new beliefs and meanings, such as asking Kim and Marcus to consult and discuss parenting issues without the presence of the children.
   e. Create ritual that supports couple spending time as a couple.
   f. Create rituals, such as asking Kim to take on sporting referee role (dress, actions) next time feels torn.

2. Explore possibilities for new meaning in the "strain" in their relationship related to Marcus feeling like an "outsider" and Kim feeling "torn."
   a. Discuss the "strained" relationship using a positive connotation, highlighting Marcus and Kim's sacrifices to maintain balance and cohesion, such as Marcus taking the role of outsider to create space for other relationships and Karen feeling torn in order to be a caretaker of family relationships.
   b. Identify, explore, and alter meaning Marcus and Kim attribute to each other's actions when they feel torn or like an outsider.
   c. Alter unproductive language through concept of "the tyranny of linguistics" to reshape meaning by altering language. Instead of stating "the outsider," state *acting* like outsider or *doing* emotional caretaking.
   d. Use circular questioning to highlight reciprocal patterns, such as how do they interact with one another and with the children.

Late-Phase Goals

1. Address "newly defined" couple's approach to joint parenting. Address any remaining issues with children.
   a. Identify positive connotation to reframe previous problems as increasing engagement between couple.
   b. Use circular questions to highlight the interaction before and after redefining meaning and altering unproductive patterns, as well as to highlight changes in children's interactional patterns.
   c. Present rituals that involve couple discussing parenting issues.
   d. Assist Steve in separating children's actions and behavior toward him from his beliefs about them and Kim.

2. Highlight cohesion between Kim and Marcus as a couple while emphasizing the contribution of gains and alterations in the couple/family game.
   a. Utilize circular questions to identify the new meanings and interactions by asking about before, during, and after game/rule changes.
   b. Inquire about additional problem issues and observe how Kim and Marcus define problem issues and achieve goals. Consider inviting children to attend sessions.
   c. Create and maintain couple rituals and assist the couple in creating family rituals.

Vignette: Family

Maria and her 9-year-old daughter Sonia requested counseling services. Maria reported that she and her husband Gerry separated approximately 6 months ago but are trying to "work things out." Maria stated that she has become concerned about Sonia's emotional well-being since the separation. According to Maria, Sonia has witnessed several fights and arguments between her parents prior to and since the separation. Maria also reported that she thinks her husband has been drinking more since the separation. Maria also reports that she has become very depressed and has been prescribed an antidepressant by her general medical physician. Reportedly, Sonia attempts to comfort her mother but rarely discusses her emotions. Sonia reports that her mother becomes upset when she discusses her feelings and states that she feels unimportant and in the way. Sonia's grades have reportedly dropped, and her teacher has complained about behavior problems at school.

Milan Systemic Treatment Plan for Family

Early-Phase Goals

1. Therapist and team form an initial hypothesis.
   a. Gain information from initial contact on the telephone, including, Maria initiating services, referral source, and Maria and Sonia's expectations and attitudes, if possible.
   b. Meet with team to discuss information obtained to formulate initial hypothesis about role of alcohol, depression, and Sonia's behavior.
   c. Encourage all family members to attend first session.

2. Session conductor joins with family.
   a. Maintain neutrality and curiosity when interacting with Maria, Gerry, and Sonia to avoid coalitions.
   b. Discuss meeting schedule, once a month.

3. Gather information about the family game/rules, Sonia's emotional functioning, role of alcohol and depression, and interrelational functioning while identifying family and cultural rules.
   a. Present the circular questioning technique to gain information about interactional functioning between Maria, Gerry, and Sonia, such as: Who is most upset after the parents argue? What does each person do before, during, and after an argument? Who has been most affected by the separation?
   b. Ask each person about his/her perspectives on child's behavior, mother's depression, and father's drinking.
   c. Utilize team to generate a hypothesis about role of symptoms in family, perhaps focusing on Sonia's "heroic" attempts to keep the family together.
   d. After second session, "dismiss" daughter from sessions.

Middle-Phase Goals

1. Alter unproductive rules/games that support Sonia's parenting of her mother.
   a. Present invariant prescription to sever the apparent covert generational alliance between mother and daughter.
   b. Use circular questioning to help parents see the effect of their arguing and relational difficulties on daughter.
   c. Present positive connotation of daughter's heroic willingness to sacrifice her normal childhood role (doing school work, being emotionally vulnerable, playing with friends, etc.) to parent parents.
   d. Prescribe ritual of alternating nights when daughter parents and parents parent.
   e. Prescribe rituals that support parents focusing directly on parenting and child needs, such as organizing a family game night, family meetings, and so on.

2. Alter unproductive rules/games that support wife doing depression and husband acting alcoholic.
   a. Use circular questioning to help couple recognize the connection between wife's depression and husband's drinking.
   b. Discuss depressiveness and drinking as actions rather than adjectives (e.g., when Maria is acting depressed; when Gerry is doing his drinking).
   c. Based on team's observations and recommendations, present hypothesis about the role of depression and drinking.
   d. Offer positive connotation of depressiveness and drinking as tools that each partner has developed to "not burden" the other by sharing hurt feelings.
   e. Present a counterparadox by asking Maria and Gerry not to abandon depressiveness or drinking too quickly because they might overburden the other.
   f. Identify and uncover the erroneous beliefs within the system that support the symptoms, particularly those related to cultural prescriptions for marriage, gender roles, and parenting.
   g. Based on hypothesis, develop rituals, such as having Gerry and Maria sit down to discuss feelings and thoughts about the couple relationship and the family every other evening.

Late-Phase Goals

1. Help to identify more useful distinctions that will support family communication without arguing.
   a. Use positive connotation to reframe arguing as couple's way of demonstrating commitment and connection at any cost.
   b. Use circular questions to identify interaction patterns of all family members before, during, and after arguments.

c. Separate actions (e.g., leaving room during argument) from interpretations (e.g., Gerry does not care); allow each person to share his/her interpretation of reported actions in arguments and explore differences.
d. Prescribe rituals that alter problem interactions during arguments (e.g., if Maria fears abandonment when Gerry leaves room during argument, Gerry will be asked to announce his need for a "time out," clarify that taking a time out is his way of preventing additional hurt between them, and make an "appointment" for resuming discussion).

2. Maintain new family "game" or interaction that allows for satisfying couple and family interactions without the need for Sonia to neglect her childhood "duties," Maria to act depressed, Gerry to act alcoholic, or couple to "do" arguments.
   a. Utilize circular questions to identify the new meanings gained, focusing on how relationships and roles have changed.
   b. Create and maintain family rituals that support new behaviors, such as family and couple nights.
   c. Use circular questions about future scenarios and how each might respond.

References and Suggested Readings

Boscolo, L., Cecchin, G., Hoffman, L., & Penn, P. (1987). *Milan systemic family therapy.* New York: Basic Books.

Cecchin, G. (1987). Hypothesizing, circularity, and neutrality revisited: An invitation to curiosity. *Family Process, 26*(4), 405–413.

Prata, G. (1990). *A systemic harpoon into family games: Preventive interventions in therapy.* New York: Brunner/Mazel.

Selvini, M. (Ed). (1988). *The work of Mara Selvini Palazzoli.* New York: Jason Aronson.

Selvini Palazzoli, M. (1981). *Self-starvation: From the intrapsychic to the transpersonal approach to anorexia nervosa.* New York: Jason Aronson.

Selvini Palazzoli, M., Boscolo, L., Cecchin, G., & Prata, G. (1978). *Paradox and counterparadox.* New York: Jason Aronson.

Selvini Palazzoli, M., Boscolo, L., Cecchin, G., & Prata, G. (1980). Hypothesizing-circularity-neutrality: Three guidelines for the conductor of the session. *Family Process, 19*(1), 3–12.

Selvini Palazzoli, M., Cecchin, G., Prata, G., & Boscolo, L. (1978). *Paradox and counterparadox: A new model in the therapy of the family in schizophrenic transaction.* New York: Jason Aronson.

Selvini Palazzoli, M. S., Cirillo, S., Selvini, M., & Sorrentino, A. M. (1989). *Family games: General modes of psychotic processes in the family.* New York: Norton.

". . . The target of change is the attempted solution; and the tactics chosen have to be translated into the person's own 'language'; that is, it must be presented to him [or her] in a form which utilizes his [or her] own way of conceptualizing 'reality' " (Watzlawick, Weakland, & Fisch, 1974, p. 113).

MENTAL RESEARCH INSTITUTE APPROACH

CHAPTER 5

KEY THEORISTS

Theoretical Background	*Clinical Application*
Gregory Bateson	Richard Fisch
Milton Erickson	Don Jackson
Heinz von Foerster	Paul Watzlawick
	John Weakland

HISTORICAL OVERVIEW

Don Jackson was the founding director of the Mental Research Institute (MRI), where many outstanding figures in the field developed their ideas, including Jules Riskin, Arthur Bodin, Jay Haley, Virginia Satir, Janet Beavin, Paul Watzlawick, and John Weakland. The MRI group incorporated ideas from Bateson (1979) and Milton Erickson to establish a brief-treatment approach for children and families. Watzlawick, Beavin, and Jackson (1967) outlined the seminal theoretical principles in *Pragmatics of Human Communication;* and Watzlawick, Weakland, and Fisch (1974) detailed the pragmatic approach in *Change: Principles of Problem Formation and Problem Resolution.*

KEY CONCEPTS

Problem

A problem is characterized by persistent failed attempts to change some distress; problems are "created and maintained through the mishandling of difficulties" (Watzlawick et al., 1974, p. 39). Not all life difficulties are considered to be problems. Problems are defined as those difficulties that cannot be resolved. For example, a child breaking curfew is only defined as a problem to the extent that the parents are able to manage the behavior; after repeated attempts to punish the child fail, most families would then define the situation as a problem. In the MRI approach, the therapist focuses on solving only the identified problem and does not search for underlying pathology.

The Interactional View

Regardless of the etiology and origins, the kinds of problems people bring to treatment persist only if they are maintained by the ongoing behaviors of the client and others with whom the client interacts (Watzlawick et al., 1974). If such problem-maintaining behavior can be altered, the problem will be resolved or will vanish. Therefore, the therapist focuses on current behavioral patterns and sequences.

The Problem Is the Attempted Solution

Problems arise and persist through the mishandling of normal life difficulties, and "a 'solution' may itself be the problem" (Watzlawick et al., 1974, p. 55). Problems arise and are maintained as the result of

- mistaken attempts at changing an existing difficulty,
- initiating changes when they are not necessary,
- not taking action when change is necessary, and/or
- making changes at the wrong level.

More of the Same

Attempted solutions become the problem when those interacting around the problem persist in attempts to resolve the solution or "do more of the same" because the attempted solution seems logical and necessary. In these situations, the attempt at changing by initiating more of the same solution has the potential to become the problem. For example, when one spouse begins to "pursue" the other in order to create a greater sense of closeness, this pursuit (the attempted solution) typically causes the other to distance, resulting in a more intense pursuit or more of the same. In these situations, the solutions are of the wrong order and, therefore, the therapist focuses on reversing the more-of-the-same solutions.

First- and Second-Order Change

First-order change involves a change in the system's interactional patterns and occurs when the system itself remains unchanged. *Second-order change* requires change in the organization of the system and is characterized by a change in the client's perspective and assumptions, a change in the system, and is referred to as "change of change." Furthermore, "when we talk about change in connection with problem formation and problem resolution we always mean second-order change" (Watzlawick et al., 1974, p. 11). A classic example of first-order change is when the person who was formerly the distancer in a relationship becomes the pursuer and the former pursuer becomes the distancer. Second-order change in such a system would involve a cessation of the pursuer-distancer pattern, which is replaced with an alternative interaction.

Communication

Mental Research Institute theorists maintained that "[o]ne cannot not communicate, and one cannot not behave," implying that all behavior is communication at some level (Bateson, 1991). The MRI therapists closely observe the various levels of communication between people and identify how these patterns contribute to the maintenance of problems. The interactional patterns that sustain problems are most basically communication/behavioral sequences that therapists can observe and intervene upon.

Report and Command Functions

Every communication has two aspects: report (content) and command (relationship). Bateson (1979, 1991) refers to the *report* as the literal message and the *command* as the action that cues the message recipient on how to interpret the message and thereby defines the present relationship. Therefore, communication not only conveys information but also simultaneously defines the relationship between speakers; "there is a parallel between the 'signals of state' and the signals which define the contingencies of relationship" (Bateson, 1991, p. 129). Therapists pay attention to both levels of communication. Consistent, ongoing contradictions between these two levels of communication result in a double bind.

Metacommunication

Metacommunication refers to the command aspect (or "action or behavior") of communication; it is the communication about the communication. Metacommunication includes nonverbal cues that accompany the content of the message. For example, the statement "I need your help" can be accompanied by differing nonverbal cues based on the relational context. The metacommunication in this type of situation can include the implication that the other is at fault for not helping, that the requestor is feeling unusually vulnerable, or that the two are in a partnership where help is asked for when needed. Therefore, the metacommunication essentially defines the relationship as adversarial, supportive, or an equal partnership.

Double Bind

The *double bind* is a destructive form of paradoxical communication. In this type of communication, a person simultaneously sends contradictory report and command messages (Bateson, 1979, 1991; Watzlawick et al., 1974). A double bind requires (Watzlawick, Beavin, & Jackson, 1967):

- Two or more people,
- Repeated experience and interactions (not an isolated event),
- A primary negative injunction: If you do such and such, I will punish you,
- A secondary injunction conflicting with the first at an abstract level; also enforced by punishment, and
- A tertiary negative injunction prohibiting the victim from escaping the field.

The complete set of ingredients is no longer necessary when the victim has learned to perceive the universe in double-bind patterns. Examples of simple, double-bind messages are "Be spontaneous" and the command "Love me." Other examples include a father who says he "trusts" his child but consistently acts otherwise or a mother who says, "Why don't you love me" yet rejects the child's attempts to show affection. Therapists intervene upon double binds by addressing the *metacommunication* (e.g., the father's "untrusting" acts and the mother's rejection of affection) rather than the content aspect of exchanged messages.

A *therapeutic double bind* is a form of metacommunication used to intervene on a double bind and involves instructing a symptomatic person to not change in a context where the person is expecting to be helped to change (i.e., in the therapeutic relationship) (Watzlawick et al., 1974).

Symmetrical and Complementary Relationships

In *symmetrical interactions,* the participants mirror each other's behavior. In *complementary interactions,* one person assumes a position and the other assumes the opposite position (i.e., aggressive and passive; Bateson, 1979, 1991). Symmetrical relationships risk becoming competitive, while complementary relationships can become oppressive. Symmetrical and complementary relationships "could conceivably lead to runaway and the breakdown of the system" (Bateson, 1979, p. 105). Therapists assess relationships for extremes in either form of relationship in order to formulate interventions.

GOALS OF THERAPY

The goals of therapy are established by highlighting attempted solutions to the problem issue(s). However, "not infrequently we find that our original goal has to be revised as more information becomes available or partial change occurs during treatment" (Watzlawick et al., 1974).

Focus

In the MRI approach, the focus is on interrupting attempted solutions that are maintaining the problem (Watzlawick et al., 1974).

Five Questions in Case Planning

The following five questions are used to focus case planning:

1. What is (are) the attempted solution(s)? What command (metacommunication) is common to the solutions used by the client and anyone else involved in the problem? What are the minefields to avoid ("more-of-the-same" behaviors)?
2. What would be a 180-degree shift from the attempted solution?
3. What specific behavior would operationalize this shift?
4. Given the family's position, how can the therapist "sell" the behavior?
5. What might the client report that would signal that the intervention has been successful and the case is ready for termination?

Small, Concrete Steps

The therapist breaks the operationalized goals into small, concrete steps to help the family achieve a sense of confidence and progress as early as possible. To define these steps, the therapist asks, "At minimum, what change would indicate to you that a definite step forward has been made?"

STRUCTURE OF THERAPY

In the MRI approach, therapy is structured into four stages (Watzlawick et al., 1974, p. 118):

1. Identify and explore the problem.
2. Identify attempted solutions and the results of such solutions.
3. Formulate a concrete goal.
4. Intervene utilizing MRI techniques and the client's language.

ASSESSMENT

Four-Step Procedure

Watzlawick et al. (1974) identified a four-step procedure to be utilized in approaching a problem:

1. Define the problem and identify how it is a problem.
2. Determine which solutions have been tried and identify the outcome of such attempts. Look for "more-of-the-same" patterns and identify family rules that support the unsuccessful solutions.
3. Obtain a clear description of the concrete change to be achieved.

4. Formulate and implement a plan to produce change. The target of change is the attempted solution. Solutions can be mishandled in four general ways:
   a. Attempting to be deliberately spontaneous
   b. Seeking a no-risk method when some risk is inevitable
   c. Attempting to reach interpersonal accord through opposition
   d. Confirming the accuser's suspicions by defending oneself

TECHNIQUES

Initial Interview Questions

Initial interview questions that can be utilized to explore the problem and attempted solutions include:

- What is the problem that brings you here today?
- How is it a problem?
- What does it stop you from doing or make you do that you do not want to do?

Reframing

Reframing "means to change the conceptual and/or emotional setting or viewpoint in relation to which a situation is experienced and to place it in another frame which fits the 'facts' of the same concrete situation equally well or even better, and thereby changes its entire meaning" (Watzlawick et al., 1974, p. 95). The therapist redefines the meaning of implications of the problem or attempted solution behavior. Mental Research Institute therapists emphasize the importance of using the client's language when reframing the problem for the reframe to have significance to the client. For example, depression can be a way of "honoring" the loss of a loved one, or "tantrums" can be framed as a child's attempt to give the parent someone to parent.

Prescribing the Symptom: "Do More of the Same"

In this therapeutic double bind, the therapist encourages the client to engage in symptomatic behavior (Watzlawick et al., 1974). Engaging consciously in previously spontaneous behavior renders resistance unnecessary. The symptomatic interactive pattern no longer serves its purpose of maintaining homeostasis, and the family must establish new interactive patterns. Examples of prescribing the symptom include asking couples to fight at 7:00 P.M. for 20 minutes each night or having someone engage in worrying for 20 minutes each morning.

Relabeling

Language is used to redescribe the pattern and thereby change the interpretation of the symptom (Watzlawick et al., 1974). For example, "withdrawal" can be relabeled as "needing personal space" or "needing time to think." The situation does not change, but the meaning attributed to it changes, allowing for new action and consequences.

Dangers of Improvement: "Go Slow"

Clients are paradoxically instructed to "go slow" so that assignments are carried out carefully (Watzlawick et al., 1974, p. 135). This injunction also helps clients adjust to ups and downs in their progress. If a client is overly optimistic about change, small setbacks can be discouraging. The therapist's pessimism can reduce the negative effects of setbacks and become a reinforcement to continued change.

Making the Covert Overt

In this type of intervention, the therapist prescribes various behaviors, which may or may not be the symptom, in such a way that covert processes are highlighted. For example, to highlight a silent father-daughter coalition, a therapist may prescribe the father to give the daughter a dime in front of the mother each time the daughter is arrogant toward the mother (Watzlawick et al., 1974).

Advertising Rather than Concealing the Problem

This type of prescription involves having clients advertise a socially inhibiting or embarrassing handicap, which has the paradoxical effect of reducing anxiety (Watzlawick et al., 1974). For example, advertising at the beginning of a speech that one is petrified often serves to reduce anxiety. "This behavior prescription amounts to a complete reversal of the solution attempted so far; instead of trying to conceal his symptom, he is made to advertise it" (Watzlawick et al., 1974, p. 125).

Bellac Ploy

This type of prescription involves complimenting another with the paradoxical result of making that person so. It is the idea that "reality is what we have come to call 'reality' " (Watzlawick et al., 1974, p. 131). The technique highlights that "a very small change may be all that is needed to effect a change of the entire pattern" (p. 133). The classic example is that by complimenting a stranger about his/her kindness, that person is more likely to act in that way.

MENTAL RESEARCH INSTITUTE TREATMENT PLANS

The following general treatment plan identifies possible goals and interventions for each stage of therapy that could be used in treating individuals, couples, and families. Not all goals and techniques are applicable to all clients.

General Mental Research Institute Treatment Plan

Early-Phase Goals

1. Define the problem and identify how it is a problem.

Possible Interventions

a. Ask initial interview questions, such as, What is the problem that brings you here today? How is it a problem? What does it stop you from doing or make you do that you do not want to do? What keeps things from getting worse?

2. Identify previous attempts to solve the problem (attempted solutions) and the outcome.

Possible Interventions

a. Identify family rules, more-of-the-same patterns, and communication styles that support the unsuccessful solutions.
b. Explore metacommunication around the problem situation.

3. Assess the family system.

Possible Interventions

a. Identify the current behavior that is assisting in maintaining problem through interactional view.
b. Identify first- and second-order processes within family system, as well as in the therapy session.
c. Explore communication in terms of metacommunication and report and command congruencies/incongruencies.
d. Examine symmetrical and complementary relationships.
e. Identify more-of-the-same patterns in resolving problem issue.

4. Identify specific, behavioral goals.

Possible Interventions

a. Assist client in defining behaviorally defined, clear goals.
b. Direct system to "go slow" to assist in successful completion of tasks, to prepare for "ups and downs" of the treatment process, and to present a paradoxical approach.

c. Ask, "What change would indicate that progress has been made?"
d. Instruct the family to take small, concrete steps and ask, "At minimum, what change would indicate to you that a definite step forward has been made?"

Middle-Phase Goal

1. Interrupt more-of-the-same attempted solutions to assist in identifying solutions to the identified problem issue.

Possible Interventions

a. Discuss the problem by relabeling the symptom.
b. Prescribe a 180-degree shift from attempted solution.
c. Present a therapeutic double bind by prescribing the symptom.
d. Reframe the problem.
e. Use paradoxical directives.
f. Intervene at higher order of system to facilitate second-order shift.
g. Comment on metacommunication verbally or nonverbally.
h. Modify directives each week based on family response, noting which solutions work and which do not work.
i. Initiate and assign specific behavioral changes to assist in second-order changes.
j. Make covert overt with directives or comments.
k. Advertise the symptom.
l. Utilize bellac ploy to solicit preferred behaviors from others.

Late-Phase Goals

1. Interrupt any new problems that are identified/created by addressing the presenting issue.

Possible Interventions

a. Identify attempted solution and prescribe a 180-degree shift.
b. Reframe the problem, possibly in relation to presenting problem.
c. Present a therapeutic double bind by prescribing the symptom.

2. Highlight successful solutions to the problem issue.

Possible Interventions

a. Compliment the system on resolving the problem issue while highlighting the successful solution.
b. Identify and discuss second-order changes.

Vignette: Individual

Greg is a 43-year-old male who reports past relationship issues. Greg states that his ex-wife was emotionally and mentally abusive throughout their 5-year relationship. He states that she would often leave for long periods of time, and he was unaware of where she was or whom she was with. Greg states that he is struggling with "going back," since he reports that he has "taken her back" after conflict and abusive situations several times in the past. He reports feeling very empty and sad and states that he has nowhere to go and no one to talk to. Furthermore, Greg states that the reported sadness results in his missing several days of work at a time.

Practice Mental Research Institute Treatment Plan for Individual

Early-Phase Goals

1.
    a.
    b.

2.
    a.
    b.

Middle-Phase Goals

1.
    a.
    b.

2.
    a.
    b.

Late-Phase Goals

1.
    a.
    b.

2.
    a.
    b.

Vignette: Couple

Mary and Jason have been divorced for 3 years, and Mary is remarried. Jason and Mary have a child together and have decided to initiate postrelationship couple counseling to address their continual conflict and the parenting of their son. Both report that their relationship began like many others, with genuine love and concern, but was "rocky" for the years following. Their arguments typically involved Mary complaining that Jason did not follow through on her requests and was too lenient in parenting. Mary and Jason report that their son is experiencing difficulty in transitioning from one house to another, is not excelling in school, and is often quiet and withdraw. Despite that reported conflict, Jason and Mary state that they are concerned about their son and would like to work together to parent him.

Practice Mental Research Institute Treatment Plan for Couple

Early-Phase Goals

1.
   a.
   b.

2.
   a.
   b.

Middle-Phase Goals

1.
   a.
   b.

2.
   a.
   b.

Late-Phase Goals

1.
   a.
   b.

2.
   a.
   b.

Vignette: Family

Shirley (divorced mother), Danielle (daughter), and Mark (grandson) report conflictual relationships at home. Danielle is a single parent living with her mother. She states that she is a recovering alcoholic in the process of "rebuilding her life." Mark is a third-grade student experiencing emotional and behavioral conflict and reports feeling torn between his mother and his grandmother. Shirley states that she feels that her daughter is not a responsible parent. Both report that Danielle's past alcohol abuse has "torn the family apart" and state that they have both been hurt by one another. Shirley and Danielle also state that they are ready to "move forward."

Practice Mental Research Institute Treatment Plan for Family

Early-Phase Goals

1.
   a.
   b.

2.
   a.
   b.

Middle-Phase Goals

1.
   a.
   b.

2.
   a.
   b.

Late-Phase Goals

1.
   a.
   b.

2.
   a.
   b.

Vignette: Individual

Greg is a 43-year-old male who reports past relationship issues. Greg states that his ex-wife was emotionally and mentally abusive throughout their 5-year relationship. He states that she would often leave for long periods of time, and he was unaware of where she was or whom she was with. Greg states that he is struggling with "going back," since he reports that he has "taken her back" after conflict and abusive situations several times in the past. He reports feeling very empty and sad and states that he has nowhere to go and no one to talk to. Furthermore, Greg states that the reported sadness results in his missing several days of work at a time.

Mental Research Institute Treatment Plan for Individual

Early-Phase Goals

1. Define the effects of the termination of the relationship and identify how it is a problem.
   a. Ask Greg initial interview questions, such as, What is the problem that brings you here today? How is your sadness a problem? What does the sadness stop you from doing or make you do that you do not want to do? What keeps things from getting worse?
   b. Identify complementary or symmetrical relationship between Greg and ex-spouse.

2. Identify previous attempts to solve the problem (attempted solutions) and the outcome.
   a. Inquire about previous solutions, such as going back after abuse, trying to "keep the peace," forgiving, and so on.
   b. Identify Greg's more-of-the-same patterns that sustain his sadness.

3. Assess the relationship to identify the patterns that maintain the symptoms.
   a. Examine symmetrical and complementary aspects of the relationship between ex-wife and Greg, noting the current pursuer-distancer situation that sustains his current complaints.
   b. Explore the couple's communication and interactional patterns, noting report and command congruencies/incongruencies.
   c. Identify Greg's current behavior that maintains his inability to let go of the relationship.
   d. Identify more-of-the-same patterns in Greg's attempts to resolve his sadness and termination of the relationship.

4. Identify specific behavioral goals.
   a. Assist Greg in defining clear behavioral goals, such as not calling or improved work attendance.
   b. Direct Greg to "go slow" and take small, concrete steps to assist in successful completion of tasks, to prepare him for "ups and downs" of the treatment process, and to present a paradoxical task.
   c. Ask Greg, "What small change would indicate that you have made some progress?"

Middle-Phase Goals

1. Interrupt more-of-the-same attempted solutions that sustain Greg's sadness about the termination of the relationship.
   a. Prescribe a 180-degree shift from Greg's attempted solutions, which would involve distancing rather than pursuing behavior.
   b. Present a therapeutic double bind by prescribing the symptom and asking Greg to schedule social withdrawal and directly asking others to define who he is.
   c. Reframe the termination of the relationship by redefining the meaning; highlight how Greg has been presented with the opportunity to regain a sense of control over self, while highlighting Greg's ability to relinquish contact from the reported abuse.
   d. Discuss the problem by relabeling Greg's sadness as a process of rediscovering himself, who had been "lost" in the relationship.
   e. Modify directives each week based on Greg's response, noting which solutions work and which do not work.
   f. Offer straightforward directives to attend one social event each week.
   g. Have Greg advertise his difficulty talking to strangers when he meets someone.
   h. Initiate and assign specific behavioral changes to assist in second-order changes, targeting his willingness to let others define him and determine his self-worth.

Late-Phase Goals

1. Highlight Greg's successful solutions and accomplishment of middle-phase goal.
   a. Compliment Greg on resolving his sadness and withdrawal while highlighting the successful solution.
   b. Identify and discuss Greg's second-order changes, particularly noting the change in how he defines his relationship with others via metacommunication.

Vignette: Couple

Mary and Jason have been divorced for 3 years, and Mary is remarried. Jason and Mary have a child together and have decided to initiate postrelationship couple counseling to address their continual conflict and the parenting of their son. Both report that their relationship began like many others, with genuine love and concern, but was "rocky" for the years following. Their arguments typically involved Mary complaining that Jason did not follow through on her requests and was too lenient in parenting. Mary and Jason report that their son is experiencing difficulty in transitioning from one house to another, is not excelling in school, and is often quiet and withdrawn. Despite that reported conflict, Jason and Mary state that they are concerned about their son and would like to work together to parent him.

Mental Research Institute Treatment Plan for Couple

Early-Phase Goals

1. Define problem and identify how their conflictual relationship is a problem in co-parenting their son.
    a. Ask initial interview questions, such as, What is the problem that brings you here today? How is it a problem? What does the relational conflict stop you from doing or make you do that you do not want to do? What keeps things from getting worse?
    b. Identify more-of-the-same patterns related to parenting their son.

2. Identify previous attempts to solve son/postdivorce family problems.
    a. Inquire about attempted solutions on the part of both.
    b. Identify Jason and Mary's family rules and communication styles that support the unsuccessful solutions.

3. Assess postdivorce family system to identify interactional patterns that support the conflict.
    a. Inquire about current behavior that maintains their conflictual relationship.
    b. Examine symmetrical and complementary patterns in the relationship, attending to possibility of extreme complementary patterns in parenting (e.g., mother strict; father lenient).
    c. Attend to possible double-bind messages from parents to son.
    d. Examine and comment on metacommunication and report and command congruencies/incongruencies that define current relationship.
    e. Identify Mary and Jason's more-of-the-same patterns in resolving their conflictual relationship.

4. Identify specific behavioral goals.
    a. Assist Jason and Mary in defining clear goals and what they would like to see change in their postdivorce relationship.
    b. Direct Mary and Jason to "go slow" to assist in successful completion of tasks and to prepare for "ups and downs" of the treatment process.
    c. Ask couple, What small change or changes would indicate that a definite step has been made?

Middle-Phase Goals

1. Interrupt more-of-the-same attempted solutions to assist in identifying effective solutions to current conflict and son's behavior.
   a. Discuss the conflict by relabeling it as maintaining engagement between couple.
   b. Prescribe a 180-degree shift from attempted solutions, such as complimenting any minor aspect of the other in situations when each would prefer to correct the other's style of parenting.
   c. Present a therapeutic double bind by prescribing the symptom and asking them to schedule arguments.
   d. Instruct couple to first comment on the likelihood of having an argument when each brings up topics that would typically cause an argument, thus disrupting the pattern with a metastatement.
   e. Make covert overt by highlighting interactional moves and metacommunication.
   f. Use Bellac ploy and have each compliment aspects of the other before anticipated problem interaction.
   g. Reframe Jason and Mary's attempts to resolve the conflict as steps toward change or as each person's best attempt to parent the child.
   h. Intervene on metacommunication by highlighting Mary's attempts to parent Jason.
   i. Modify directives each week based on Mary and Jason's response, noting which solutions work and which do not work.

Late-Phase Goals

1. Highlight successful solutions to the problem issues.
   a. Compliment Mary and Jason on resolving the problem issue while highlighting the successful solution.
   b. Highlight that the couple worked together to solve the problem and the connection to how they will handle future issues with son.
   c. Identify and discuss second-order changes.

Vignette: Family

Shirley (divorced mother), Danielle (daughter), and Mark (grandson) report conflictual relationships at home. Danielle is a single parent living with her mother. She states that she is a recovering alcoholic in the process of "rebuilding her life." Mark is a third-grade student experiencing emotional and behavioral conflict and reports feeling torn between his mother and his grandmother. Shirley states that she feels that her daughter is not a responsible parent. Both report that Danielle's past alcohol abuse has "torn the family apart" and state that they have both been hurt by one another. Shirley and Danielle also state that they are ready to "move forward."

Mental Research Institute Treatment Plan for Family

Early-Phase Goals

1. Define problem and identify how the interrelational conflict between Shirley and Danielle is a problem that affects the child and the family.
   a. Ask each member in the system the initial interview questions, such as, What is the problem that brings you here today? How is the conflictual relationship a problem? What does it stop you from doing or make you do that you do not want to do? What keeps things from getting worse?
   b. Identify complementary or symmetrical relationships between Shirley and Danielle. Who is the parent when?
   c. Identify more-of-the-same patterns around parenting and conflict.

2. Identify previous attempts to solve the problem (attempted solutions) and the outcomes.
   a. Directly inquire about what each has done to solve the problem and how it failed.
   b. Explore metacommunication around the attempted solutions, highlighting Shirley and Danielle's covert messages to each other and to Mark.

3. Assess Shirley, Danielle, and Mark's family system.
   a. Identify behavioral sequences that maintain the familial conflict.
   b. Attend to communication, listening for report and command congruencies/incongruencies, implicit defining of relational roles, and double binds.
   c. Examine symmetrical and complementary relationships between family members, particularly Shirley and Danielle.
   d. Identify more-of-the-same patterns in resolving the conflict.

4. Identify specific behavioral goals.
   a. Assist family in defining clear behavioral goals.
   b. Direct family to "go slowly" to assist in successful completion of tasks and to prepare for "ups and downs" of the treatment process.
   c. Ask about what change would indicate that they have made progress.

Middle-Phase Goals

1. Interrupt more-of-the-same attempted solutions to assist in identifying solutions to the familial conflict.
   a. Relabel the familial conflict as "too much good parenting."
   b. Prescribe a 180-degree shift from attempted solutions, such as having Danielle ask for more help in parenting her child, exaggerating her helplessness.
   c. Paradoxically prescribe Shirley and Danielle to have an argument every other day or have Danielle act more like a helpless child.
   d. Reframe the problem as sustaining communication and a connection between Shirley and Danielle.
   e. Reframe Mark's behavior as an attempt to create enough problems so that both the grandmother and the mother will have enough "parenting work."
   f. Address metacommunication and make covert overt by highlighting the multiple levels of parenting in the system.
   g. Instruct them to "advertise" concern that a particular situation will turn into conflict over parenting before/as the problem topic is brought up, thus interrupting the automatic conflict pattern.
   h. Modify directives each week based on family's response, and note which solutions work and which solutions do not work.
   i. Direct each to use the Bellac ploy by complimenting each other on parenting before anticipated problem encounters.

Late-Phase Goals

1. Address any remaining child behavior problems, particularly between child and mother.
   a. Prescribe a 180-shift in how mother responds to child's behavioral problems.
   b. Reframe child's behavior as her child providing her an opportunity to "practice" her new role as primary parent, allowing her to make up for lost time.
   c. Paradoxically prescribe the symptom, having the child act out at preset times so that the mother can improve her parenting skills.
   d. Address metacommunication about parent-child relationship and prescribe directives that highlight when the child acts more like the parent.
   e. Have mother use Bellac ploy by stating that she anticipates the child is going to behave well in particular situations.

2. Highlight successful solutions to the family conflict.
   a. Compliment family on resolving the problem issue while highlighting the successful solution.
   b. Identify and discuss second-order changes in the family system.

References and Suggested Readings

Bateson, G. (1972). *Steps to an ecology of mind.* San Francisco: Chandler.

Bateson, G. (1979). *Mind and nature: A necessary unity.* New York: Dutton.

Bateson, G. (1991). *A sacred unity: Further steps to an ecology of mind.* New York: Harper/Collins.

Fisch, R. (1978). Review of problem-solving therapy, by Jay Haley. *Family Process, 17,* 107–110.

Fisch, R., Weakland, J., & Segal, L. (1982). *The tactics of change.* San Francisco: Jossey-Bass.

Jackson, D. D. (1967). The myth of normality. *Medical Opinion and Review, 3,* 28–33.

Watzlawick, P., Beavin, J., & Jackson, D. (1967). *Pragmatics of human communication.* New York: Norton.

Watzlawick, P., Weakland, J., & Fisch, R. (1974). *Change: Principles of problem formation and problem resolution.* New York: Norton.

Weakland, J., Fisch, R., Watzlawick, P, & Bodin, A. (1974). Brief therapy: Focused problem resolution. *Family Process, 13,* 141–168.

Weakland, J., & Ray, W. (Eds.). (1995). *Propagations: Thirty years of influence from the Mental Research Institute.* Binghamton, NY: Haworth Press.

"What she was doing was helping people find what she called their wisdom box—their sense of self-worth, hope, acceptance of self, empowerment, and ability to be responsible and make choices" (Satir, Banmen, Gerber, & Gomori, 1991, p. 4).

6 CHAPTER SATIR'S COMMUNICATIONS APPROACH

KEY THEORISTS

John Banmen
Jane Gerber
Maria Gomori
Virginia Satir

HISTORICAL OVERVIEW

Virginia Satir believed that therapy and change involve warmth, genuineness, and congruent communication, and she is best known for her sincere and enthusiastic belief in every person's potential. Satir was trained as a social worker and began her clinical career in 1951. She joined Don Jackson and the MRI group in Palo Alto until 1955, when she left to set up a training program in Illinois. In 1966, Satir became the director of the Escalon Institute. Later in her career, she worked with larger social systems and entire communities toward community and international peace. Satir published extensively on her approach to families (Satir, 1967a & b, 1972, 1988; Satir & Baldwin, 1983; Satir, Banmen, Gerber, & Gomori, 1991; Satir, Stachowiak, & Taschman, 1975). During her career, Satir argued that the power of warmth and love was essential in therapy. Her work is continued by the Avanta Network.

KEY CONCEPTS

Four Primary Assumptions

Satir communications therapists have four primary assumptions that inform their work (Satir et al., 1991, pp. 14–15):

1. *People naturally tend toward positive growth.* Satir maintained, "People have an internal drive to become more fully human" (p. 19). Thus, they strive toward positive growth and the actualization of this human potential. From this perspective, discomfort and pain are viewed as a signal that change is needed to realize one's potential.
2. *All people possess the resources for positive growth.* Satir believed that each person was unique with inherent value and that all people possess an "inborn spiritual base." These characteristics assist in the recognition of individual resources necessary for positive growth.
3. *Every person and every thing or situation impact and are impacted by everyone and everything else.* This assumption is informed by cybernetic systemic theory and refers to circular reciprocity and the acknowledgment that "any event is the outcome of many variables and events."
4. *Therapy is a process, which involves interaction between therapist and client; and, in this relationship, each person is responsible for him/herself.* This reflects Satir's assumption that individuals and relationships are equal and "roles and status are distinct from identity" (p. 14).

Primary Survival Triad

The *primary survival triad,* or triangle, consists of the child and both parents (Satir, 1967a, 1972; Satir et al., 1991; Satir et al., 1975). This relationship serves as the primary source of an infant's "social interaction." It is also one's initial "gratifying relationship" (Satir, 1967a) and the foundation for an internal sense of being within oneself and in relation to others. Within the primary survival triangle, the parental figures provide input, approval, punishment, and expectations that assist in forming a child's identity. "So the infant whose survival depended on others becomes the child whose identity depends on others" (Satir et al., 1991, p. 22). As a result, the primary survival triad has a significant impact on both self-worth and survival stances.

Body, Mind, and Feelings

An individual's body, mind, and feelings are methods of communication and form the second triad in Satir's theory (Satir et al., 1975). Satir believes that the mind, body, and feelings interact and influence communication processes verbally and nonverbally. Satir et al. (1991) stated, "We receive information through sound, sight, and touch, movement, and people's tone of voice (p. 31)." We also communicate and respond with our body, mind, and feelings. According to Satir, body parts can become metaphors for psychological meaning and, thus, physical symptoms are often an expression of emotional distress. Satir encourages increasing self-awareness to assist in recognizing the body, mind, and feelings connection (Satir et al., 1975). Furthermore, the body, mind, feelings triad is also conveyed in Satir's concept of survival stances.

Communication

In Satir's approach, all forms of behavior, such as the movements of the body, use of sense organs, and words, are considered communication (Satir, 1972; Satir et al., 1991; Satir et al., 1975). Discrepancies between verbal and nonverbal cues contribute to interpersonal dysfunction and are referred to as "incongruent communication" (Satir et al., 1991, p. 32). For example, an individual may verbalize the comment "I feel great," yet the individual's affect and nonverbal communication may incongruently communicate a sad tone and facial expression. On the other hand, "congruent communication" reflects an awareness and congruence between an individual's mind, body, and feelings, as well as self, other, and context (p. 77).

Self-Worth

Self-worth or self-esteem is a person's "picture of individual worth" and is influenced by internal processes and interrelational interaction (Satir, 1972). Self-worth stems from the premise that everyone has intrinsic and equal self-worth. Satir maintained that self-worth is determined by one's family of origin and that it is something that is "learned." Self-worth is shaped by overt and covert messages that are evident in the words, expressions, gestures, and actions of others (Satir, 1972; Satir et al., 1991; Satir et al., 1975). Satir believes that everyone has self-worth, although it is manifested differently in different persons; each individual is distinct and unique. Satir's therapy strives to acknowledge and validate each person's inherent worth.

Survival Stances

Satir believed that people adopt survival stances to "protect their self-worth against verbal and nonverbal, perceived and presumed threats" (Satir et al., 1991, p. 31). In the four survival stances, an imbalance exists between acknowledging the (a) self, (b) other, and (c) context. The fifth alternative is congruence, in which the person is equally able to acknowledge self, other, and context.

Placater Satir et al. (1991) wrote, "When we placate, we disregard our own feelings of worth, hand our power to someone else, and say yes to everything" (p. 36). Context and other are acknowledged, while self is not. When sculpting or modeling the placating stance, the body is in a kneeling position with one hand extended upward and the other placed over the heart.

Blamer When assuming the blaming stance, a person often displays tyrannical, domineering, loud, and/or violent behavior in order to ward off a perceived threat. Self and context are acknowledged, but others are not. When sculpting the blamer stance, the body is tight with one hand on the hip and the other outstretched with finger pointed at someone.

Superreasonable An individual who assumes the superreasonable stance is typically characterized as computerlike, rigid, and devoid of feelings, yet is also viewed as extremely logical and intellectual. In this stance, only context is acknowledged; self and other are not. In the superreasonable stance, the body is sculpted as "stiffly erect and immobile, with both arms at our sides or folded symmetrically in front of us" (Satir et al., 1991, p. 45).

Irrelevant The irrelevant stance is characteristic of one who reflects unrelated and distracting behaviors and does not consider self, others, or context in the process of communicating. People assuming this stance can sometimes be viewed as entertaining but can also have significant difficulty functioning in relational, school, and work contexts. When sculpting, the irrelevant body is in constant, purposeless motion in an attempt to serve as a distraction.

Congruence Congruence, Satir's fifth communication stance, differs in that it reflects an individual that is able to send "level" messages in which words and feelings match; therefore, the stance is also sometimes referred to as the "level" stance. When congruently communicating, self, context, *and* other are acknowledged (Satir et al., 1991; Satir et al., 1975; Satir, 1972). Congruent communication and the attainment of a higher level of human wholeness are the ideal goals in therapy. To assist in reaching the established goal associated with congruent communication, the therapist should model such communication. In the congruent stance, the body is erect with arms comfortably at the body's side and eyes and head facing the other (Satir et al., 1991).

GOALS OF THERAPY

Focus of Treatment

The focus of the therapeutic experience is *growth* at the individual and systemic levels based on the assumption that growth will result in symptom reduction.

Three Goals for Improved Communication in the Family System

Congruence, high self-esteem, and personal growth are major goals in the Satir approach (Satir et al., 1991). These three goals assist in the process of improving communication and growth within the family system, while contributing to high self-esteem and self-worth in the individuals.

Congruent Communication The first goal of Satir's communications approach is associated with becoming aware of conflicting messages to ensure a shift toward congruence (Satir et al., 1991). Each person should be able to communicate congruently on what he/she sees, hears, feels, and thinks about self and others while in the presence of others.

Self Esteem The second goal involves an individual's uniqueness. Each person should be related to and addressed in terms of his/her uniqueness so that decisions are made in terms of exploration and negotiation rather than in terms of power (Satir et al., 1991). Self-esteem is evidenced by the ability to confidently make decisions and take proactive action in one's life.

Growth The third goal is associated with the open acknowledgment and recognition of differentness, which is used to actualize each person's growth potential (Satir 1972; Satir et al., 1991).

STRUCTURE OF THERAPY

Satir et al., (1991) identified six stages of change that outline the structure of the therapeutic process.

Stage One: Status Quo

In the first stage, the family members operate in a manner that reflects their patterns and beliefs and can be referred to as homeostasis or "status quo" (Satir et al., 1991, p. 99). As the therapist begins to "*make contact*" and emotionally connect with the family, the family's homeostatic pattern begins to be disrupted, thus creating a space for change.

Stage Two: Introduction of a Foreign Element

During Stage Two, the family initiates contact with a "foreign element" (or therapist) to assist in the process of change. The first interview involves the establishment of rapport and hope, while determining treatment focus and goals (Satir, 1967; Satir et al., 1991). During this process, expectations and potential barriers are explored. If resistance is apparent, it is addressed and reframed.

Stage Three: Chaos

The therapeutic process proceeds by exploring expectations, patterns, and dynamics and results in a state that the family experiences as "chaos." During this process, the therapist explores conflict, normalizes associated feelings, examines family of origin and family rules, and attempts to uncover unexpressed feelings and thoughts.

Stage Four: New Possibilities/New Options and Integration

Satir et al. (1991) describe Stage Four as a process of "developing new possibilities, using dormant resources, integrating our parts, and reevaluating past and present expectation" (p. 114). This process uncovers the possibilities for change and more adaptive ways of communicating.

Stage Five: Practice/Implementation

Stage Five is considered the "implementation" or "practice" stage. This stage involves the family system experiencing the changes and exploring feelings and thoughts concerning the shift in communication and self. Furthermore, Stage Five allows the therapist and family system to explore the increased awareness regarding change within self and the system.

Stage Six: Goal Attainment/The New Status Quo

Stage Six reflects the changes and the successful attainment of the therapeutic goals. This stage reflects a new status quo, a sense of equality, wholeness, and an openness to possibilities.

ASSESSMENT

Satir's communications approach involves the assessment of (a) the family system's symptomatic behavior, (b) communication patterns and stances, and (c) the influence and exploration of family-of-origin issues. These areas of assessment create a foundation for conceptualizing the family system.

Symptomatic Behavior

The symptomatic behavior serves as the system's homeostatic mechanism and attempts to maintain homeostasis or the status quo (Satir et al., 1975; Satir et al., 1991). The behavior reflects the systemic pain that all members experience. Context is an important consideration when identifying symptomatic behavior because it provides an opportunity for the specifics of the symptomatic behavior to become apparent.

Communication and Survival Stances

The assessment process involves an exploration of the family's congruent/incongruent communication patterns and each person's survival stance. A complete assessment of these issues provides a detailed and intimate glance into the perception and reality of each individual and the family as a whole. The identification of the system's survival stances provides the family and the therapist with the opportunity to experience the dysfunction in terms of mind, body, and feelings within each member.

Family of Origin

The therapist reviews and assesses family-of-origin issues for a better understanding of the current situation and may create a *family life fact chronology* to record information. The exploration of family-of-origin rules, patterns, values, beliefs, myths, and themes assists in creating a sense of the family's worldview (Satir et al., 1991). In addition to exploring family-of-origin issues, assessing the family's developmental history is also an important aspect of evaluation. Overall, the assessment of family-of-origin information provides valuable information regarding history and rituals and also serves as the structure for various treatment techniques.

TECHNIQUES

"Instead of developing a set of simple techniques that were easy to learn, Virginia Satir developed what she called vehicles for change" (Satir et al., 1991, p. 121).

Note: To gain a sense of the affective feel of Satir's techniques and her work in general, you may want to read *Satir's Step by Step: A Guide to Creating Change in Families* (Satir & Baldwin, 1983). This book includes a complete transcript of a case. You can also view one of her tapes; a list is provided in the appendix of video and Internet resources at the end of the text.

Role of Therapist

In Satir's approach, the therapist is an equal, unique individual whose role is to assist in the process of facilitating change. Satir et al., (1976) describe the therapist as a "change agent" (p. 37). Therefore, therapists must be aware of their own responses to clients and use them to produce change in the family through personal involvement. This personal involvement requires the therapist to be congruent and genuine while engaged in the therapeutic process. Furthermore, the therapist's role is to create a safe environment, be competent, remain honest, avoid judgment, build self-esteem, determine interactional structure and guidelines, maintain accountability, and ensure appropriate communication from self and others. The therapist must be aware of his or her role as a teacher and a model of congruent communication.

Modeling Communication

One of the key components of Satir's approach is the therapist's modeling of congruent communication (Satir, 1967a, 1972; Satir et al., 1975; Satir et al., 1991). The therapist demonstrates congruent communication by using the following three guidelines (Satir, 1967a).

1. The therapist must speak in the first person by communicating and responding with "I" messages.
2. The therapist must express thoughts and feelings directly while avoiding statements or declarations about what others may think or feel.
3. The therapist must be honest with others.

This modeling of congruent communication should be evident at all times in the therapy process and, therefore, is a component of all other techniques.

Family Life Fact Chronology

The *family life fact chronology* depicts important events in the life of the family. It is a charting technique that involves three complete generations of the family system, including birth dates, dates of important family events, and dates of important historical events (Satir et al., 1991; Satir, 1967a). The establishment of a family life fact chronology allows the therapist to get a sense of the context in which symptoms emerge as well as the characteristic intergenerational family patterns. This process is used as preparation for family sculpting and family reconstruction.

Family Sculpting

Family sculpting, also known as *family choreography* or *spatial metaphor,* was established to help "people learn to take responsibility for themselves relative to other people or situations in a given context" (Satir et al., 1991, p. 283). In the process, family members are asked to silently place each person in a position that symbolizes his or her role in the family system from the sculptor's perspective; typically, each family member has a chance to sculpt the family from his or her viewpoint. The placement of each person highlights the family's strengths, dysfunctions, possibilities for change, and new meanings, as well as each member's unique perspective of the family system. For example, an uninvolved father may be placed at a distance with his back toward the family or an overly involved mother might be portrayed by grasping after or clinging to her children or spouse.

The process may also begin with the therapist physically positioning each member in a composite living sculpture. The positioning reflects Satir's survival stances and distance and proximity from individual members and the family system. Members may also be directed to include verbal statements that reflect their positioning in the family as part of the sculpting process. After the initial sculpting, the family members share thoughts and feelings. The process proceeds by each member's sculpting the members "to show his or her desired picture of these relationships" (Satir et al., 1991, p. 284). The family-sculpting technique is applied to assist in shifting dysfunctional patterns to more adaptive, supportive relationships and interactions.

Metaphors

Satir et al., (1991) considered *metaphors* "powerful tools for promoting change" (p. 259). Metaphors are used to communicate ideas that language cannot directly describe or to introduce threatening material. Sometimes metaphors are used to help clients understand the interconnections between their roles in the system, such as "martyr," "hero," "entertainer," and "scapegoat." Storytelling is also considered a form of applying metaphors with families. In addition, Satir integrates metaphors in other techniques, including coping stances, parts parties, and ropes, to assist in externalizing internal processes and identifying relational dynamics.

Self-Mandala

The *self-mandala* consists of an innermost circle with the phrase "I am" and eight concentric circles arranged in the following order: physical, intellectual, emotional, sensual, interactional, nutritional, contextual, and spiritual (Satir et al., 1991). The self-mandala technique is a tool that is used to represent a person's resources and demonstrate that person's systemic, interconnected nature. The mandala is presented to clients and used to discuss their strengths, resources, and challenges. In addition, the self-mandala serves as a powerful metaphor for concepts and therapeutic goals such as connection and congruence.

Parts Party

The *parts party* is a technique that "identifies, transforms, and integrates inner resources" (Satir, 1991, p. 175) and assists in the process of identifying and acknowledging one's wholeness and parts. The process acknowledges the various "good" and "bad" or acceptable and unacceptable parts of a person. The parts party is typically done in a group format with 15 to 40 people. Five steps are involved in the process including: identifying and preparing the *host* (primary client), presenting and describing the parts, developing conflict between the parts, integrating resolution from the conflict, and integrating the parts. Furthermore, the process is elaborated and expanded with various interventions to highlight themes, conflicts, strengths, and other pertinent issues. For example, role plays are used to resolve inner conflicts between the parts, such as the "fearful child" and the "responsible adult." "This is a useful way for clients to make contact with and integrate their parts and inner process" (Satir et al., 1991, p. 204). Variations of this technique can be used in individual therapy by identifying parts and exploring them through talk therapy, written exercises, role plays, puppet play, or other art mediums.

Ingredients Intervention

"The *ingredients intervention* focuses on the pattern or sequence of our internal mental and emotional steps through which we process messages" (Satir et al., 1991, p. 121). In this process, the client explores his/her internal process when interacting with others to assist in altering coping patterns, strengthening self-worth, and reducing defensiveness. Six questions increase awareness and address exploration of one's interaction with others (Satir et al., 1991, p. 124):

1. What do I hear and see?
2. What meaning do I make of what I hear and see?
3. What feelings do I have about the meaning I make?
4. What feelings do I have about these feelings?
5. What defenses do I use?
6. What rules for commenting do I use?

Transforming Rules

Relational rules are learned from childhood and are deeply embedded into every individual. "At least one rule always underlies a behavior" (Satir et al., 1991, p. 306). Three steps are involved in *transforming* a rule into a more functional guideline (p. 307):

1. Change the *should* to a *can* (i.e., from I *should* never ask questions, to I *can* (never) ask questions).
2. Expand from *never* to *sometimes* (i.e., I *can sometimes* ask questions).
3. Identify possibilities of *I can* (i.e., I can ask questions when I am in school, when I am not understanding, and when I want to know something).

Temperature Reading

Temperature reading explores thoughts and feelings while improving communication and self-worth (Satir et al., 1991). It can be implemented in session or assigned as an out-of-session task. In the temperature-reading process, the client and/or family share specific (as opposed to general) information about:

- Appreciations and excitements
- Worries, concerns, and puzzlements
- Complaints and possible solutions
- New information
- Hopes and wishes

The therapist can present the technique by pictorially representing the topics as layers on a thermometer. The therapist facilitates the process by encouraging discussion of topics as layers, beginning with hopes and wishes and ending with appreciations and excitements. Each member shares specific information related to the layers of their experiences and perception, thus referring to layers on the thermometer. Furthermore, the therapist and members of the family are able to gain insight into each member's "temperature." Each component of the reading opens up communication and encourages support by members in the family.

Family Reconstruction

Family reconstruction is classically implemented in a large-group setting that takes several hours to complete (Satir et al., 1991); however, alterations to the structure can be made to accommodate the family. In the first phase of the reconstruction process, the family shares its "life story" (p. 212). This is followed by:

- Sculpting the family of origin
- Sculpting mother and father's family of origin
- Sculpting parents' meeting and marriage
- Resculpting the family of origin

SATIR'S COMMUNICATIONS TREATMENT PLANS

The following general treatment plan identifies possible goals and interventions for each stage of therapy that could be used in treating individuals, couples, and families. Not all goals and techniques are applicable to all clients.

General Satir Communications Treatment Plan

Early-Phase Goals

1. "Make contact": Establish rapport, a sense of equality, and hope.

Possible Interventions

a. Speak genuinely and honestly as therapist.
b. Allow for all voices to be heard.
c. Attempt to make emotional contact with all members by establishing a warm, supportive environment.
d. Model congruent communication by speaking in the first person and refraining from speaking for others.

2. Assess family's communication patterns, stances, and concerns.

Possible Interventions

a. Encourage all members to attend initial session.
b. Conduct a family life fact chronology to obtain history of significant family-of-origin issues that may be affecting the current situation.
c. Assess each member's survival stance and level of self-esteem.
d. Assess the homeostatic function of the presenting problem/symptom, focusing on what the symptom helps communicate.
e. Use sculpting to assist in the assessment of communication stances and patterns.
f. Use family art and conjoint family drawings to assess communication patterns and concerns in families with young children. May have family members draw self in relation to others in a large circle.
g. Construct self-mandala(s) to assess areas of strength and challenge.
h. Use ingredients intervention to ask, explore, and process answers to questions, such as "What do I hear and see?" "What meaning do I make of what I hear and see?" "What feelings do I have about the meaning I make?" "What feelings do I have about these feelings?" "What defenses do I use?" "What rules for commenting do I use?"

3. Identify treatment focus and goals for (a) the family and (b) individuals.

Possible Interventions

a. Identify specific communication and relational goals for the family; goals should address the role the symptom plays in family communication.
b. Identify individual growth needs for each member, attending to self-esteem issues and survival stances.

Middle-Phase Goals

1. Increase the family's congruent communication, especially in contexts related to the presenting problems/symptoms and issues of power.

Possible Interventions

a. Model communication by using I statements, expressing thoughts and feelings, and remaining honest.
b. Discuss the family's rules for communication and modify to address problem patterns.
c. Use family sculpting to explore current patterns and possible alternatives to family communication patterns.
d. Discuss significant events in family life fact chronology, how they are affecting the current situation, and possibilities for making new life choices.
e. Use metaphors to introduce new ideas or to help family to reframe problem; metaphors that describe each person's role, such as "martyr," "hero," "entertainer," and "scapegoat," can be particularly helpful.
f. Use parts party technique and variations to help family see how their parts interact with each other.

2. Support and strengthen each individual's sense of uniqueness and self-esteem.

Possible Interventions

a. Encourage each member to speak for him/herself.
b. Construct a self-mandala to highlight individual resources and to identify areas needed for growth.
c. Have each person explore his/her strengths and difficulties in terms of recognizing (a) self, other, and context in communication; and (b) body, mind, and feelings.
d. Use parts party to help each person explore various parts of self; may be modified for family intervention or may be done in larger-group setting.
e. Transform individual and/or family rules into guidelines by altering language, that is, from "I can never ask questions" to "I can sometimes ask questions" to "I can ask questions when I am in a school-related situation, when I do not understand, and when I want to explore things."
f. Use "temperature reading" to allow all family members to share their (1) "appreciations and excitements"; (2) "worries, concerns, and puzzles"; (3) "complaints and possible solutions"; (4) "new information"; and (5) "hopes and wishes."
g. Use individual therapy to address a family member's personal areas of concern.
h. Identify (1) expectations, (2) perceptions, (3) feelings and feelings about those feelings, and (4) behaviors related to the primary survival triad.

Late-Phase Goals

1. Help family to practice, implement, and integrate changes and increase awareness of problem issue and larger familial patterns.

Possible Interventions

a. Sculpt newly emerging family interactional patterns; compare to previous sculptings and scultpings of family of origin.
b. Readdress family life fact chronology and identify family-of-origin patterns that are helpful and unhelpful.
c. Help family to develop "family life story"; may be told by therapist or family.
d. In family or larger-group sessions, have family members "reconstruct" family.
e. Identify new metaphors to describe family functioning and family roles.
f. Establish new guidelines for family communication.

2. Solidify new status quo that is characterized by a sense of equality, wholeness, and openness to possibilities.

Possible Interventions

a. Discuss and compliment growth and changes in each individual and the family as a whole.
b. Discuss the family's and each individual's specific resources and skills for positive growth.
c. Sculpt changes that have been achieved in the system and anticipated future changes as children grow and/or situations change.
d. Identify and name new roles for each family member.
e. Use metaphors and stories to help family envision using their skills to address future challenges.

Vignette: Individual

James is a single, gay male in his mid-thirties. He reports that he feels a sense of anxiety and often participates in self-destructive behaviors. He states that for the last year he pulls his hair out of his head to feel "normal." Furthermore, James reports that his thoughts represent "catastrophic tendencies."

Practice Satir's Communications Treatment Plan for Individual

Early-Phase Goals

1.
   a.
   b.

2.
   a.
   b.

Middle-Phase Goals

1.
   a.
   b.

2.
   a.
   b.

Late-Phase Goals

1.
   a.
   b.

2.
   a.
   b.

Vignette: Couple

Lawrence and Joan, a Filipino couple, were previously in other relationships and have been married for 3 years. Joan has one daughter from a previous marriage, and they have no other children in the home. Lawrence and Joan work full-time and spend time participating in different activities. The couple reports dissimilar interests and hobbies, as well as a lack of intimacy. Lawrence reports that Joan "pushes too much," while Joan states that Lawrence is very distant. Both deny past and present infidelity and state that they want to repair the relationship.

Practice Satir's Communications Treatment Plan for Couple

Early-Phase Goals

1.
   a.
   b.

2.
   a.
   b.

Middle-Phase Goals

1.
   a.
   b.

2.
   a.
   b.

Late-Phase Goals

1.
   a.
   b.

2.
   a.
   b.

Vignette: Family

A 40-year-old, Hmong woman who recently immigrated to the United States, Anne, and her 14-year-old son, Raymond, sought treatment because he has received several suspensions from school this year and they have been told by school officials that one more infraction will result in expulsion. Anne reported that Raymond's teachers complain that he does not do his schoolwork, is often disrespectful of authorities, and is frequently aggressive with other students. This is the first year that Raymond has been mainstreamed, having been in special education until this year due to a partial hearing loss from birth. Anne does not have any noteworthy complaints about Raymond's behavior at home.

Practice Satir's Communications Treatment Plan for Family

Early-Phase Goals

1.
   a.
   b.

2.
   a.
   b.

Middle-Phase Goals

1.
   a.
   b.

2.
   a.
   b.

Late-Phase Goals

1.
   a.
   b.

2.
   a.
   b.

Vignette: Individual

James is a single, gay male in his mid-thirties. He reports that he feels a sense of anxiety and often participates in self-destructive behaviors. He states that for the last year he pulls his hair out of his head to feel "normal." Furthermore, James reports that his thoughts represent "catastrophic tendencies."

Satir's Communications Treatment Plan for Individual

Early-Phase Goals

1. Make contact: Establish rapport, equality, and a sense of hope.
   a. Speak genuinely and honestly as a therapist.
   b. Allow for James's voice to be heard by actively listening, and encourage him to freely discuss his sexuality and discrimination he may have experienced.
   c. Attempt to make emotional contact with James by establishing a warm, supportive environment.

2. Identify James's communication pattern and stance and those of pertinent people in his life, while addressing interrelated thoughts, feelings, and behaviors.
   a. Conduct a family life fact chronology.
   b. Use a metaphoric story reflecting James's familial dynamics and his reported symptoms.
   c. Identify James's primary survival triad and the critical dynamics in these relationships. Assess how these relationships may be affecting his self-esteem.
   d. Explore effects of social messages about homosexuality.
   e. Create a self-mandala to explore strengths and resources and identify areas for growth.
   f. Use ingredients questions: "What do I hear and see?" "What meaning do I make of what I hear and see?" "What feelings do I have about the meaning I make?" "What feelings do I have about these feelings?" "What defenses do I use?" "What rules for commenting do I use?"
   g. Assess James's verbal and nonverbal communication patterns and survival stance.
   h. Draw self in reference to others within a circle representing family.

3. Identify treatment focus and goals.
   a. Identify specific goals, such as reducing anxiety and self-destructive behaviors, while exploring James's expectations and the potential barriers to progress.
   b. Identify James's growth needs.

Middle-Phase Goals

1. Help James become more aware of conflicts and incongruencies in communication and between mind, body, and feelings to develop congruence to reduce anxiety symptoms and self-destructive behaviors.
   a. Model communication by using I statements, expressing thoughts and feelings, and remaining honest.
   b. Help James to identify and congruently express his thoughts and feelings regarding the issues that trigger anxiety and self-destructive behaviors.
   c. Allow James to sculpt his family and explore messages from his family of origin.
   d. Use parts party intervention to identify parts that are anxious and self-destructive and those that are not.
   e. Use metaphors to explore and facilitate communication and emotional expression.

2. Identify and support individual uniqueness, attending to how he and others measure his worth based on his sexual orientation and the issues of power associated with this.
   a. Invite James to sculpt himself in relation to others, particularly family and friends, as well as society, highlighting the social issues related to his sexual orientation.
   b. Recognize and utilize James's differences; identify strengths.
   c. Identify James's (1) "expectations," (2) "perceptions," (3) "feelings and feelings about those feelings," and (4) "behavior" related to the primary survival triad.
   d. Transform James's family rules into guidelines by altering his language.
   e. Use temperature reading to allow James to share his (1) "appreciations and excitements"; (2) "worries, concerns, and puzzles"; (3) "complaints and possible solutions"; (4) "new information"; and (5) "hopes and wishes."

Late-Phase Goals

1. Increase and strengthen sense of growth and development and invite James to participate in a group reconstruction process.
   a. Readdress James's family life fact chronology and family map.
   b. Introduce an audience.
   c. Therapist retells James's "life story," while James listens.
   d. Audience members are sculpted and role-play James's life situations.
   e. Audience and participants of the reconstruction process share their experiences.

2. Solidify newly established sense of equality, wholeness, and openness to possibilities and change.
   a. Discuss James's growth and changes, and compliment him.
   b. Reiterate that James possesses resources and skills for positive growth.
   c. Sculpt changes in James and his relationships.

3. Highlight the decrease in anxiety, catastrophic thinking, and hair-pulling tendencies.
   a. Compliment growth and changes.
   b. Utilize meditation to assist in decreasing anxiety.
   c. Identify James's resources to assist in positive growth.

Vignette: Couple

Lawrence and Joan, a Filipino couple, were previously in other relationships and have been married for 3 years. Joan has one daughter from a previous marriage, and they have no other children in the home. Lawrence and Joan work full-time and spend time participating in different activities. The couple reports dissimilar interests and hobbies, as well as a lack of intimacy. Lawrence reports that Joan "pushes too much," while Joan states that Lawrence is very distant. Both deny past and present infidelity and state that they want to repair the relationship.

Satir's Communications Treatment Plan for Couple

Early-Phase Goals

1. Make contact: Establish rapport, equality, and a sense of hope.
   a. Speak genuinely and honestly with Lawrence and Joan.
   b. Allow for both of their voices to be heard in the session by inquiring about information from both.
   c. Attempt to make emotional contact with both by establishing a warm, supportive environment.

2. Identify couple's communication patterns, survival stances, and problem issues while addressing interrelated thoughts, feelings, and behaviors.
   a. Construct a family life fact chronology, including histories from families of origin.
   b. Initiate a metaphoric story reflecting Joan and Lawrence's dynamics and problem issue.
   c. Assist Lawrence and Joan in family sculpting, including families of origin and present relationship.
   d. Encourage to create a couple drawing, highlighting relational dynamics.
   e. Construct a family map for each, exploring communication and relational patterns.
   f. Have Lawrence and Joan create a self-mandala, identifying areas of strength and areas for development.
   g. Identify Joan's and Lawrence's verbal and nonverbal communication patterns.

3. Identify treatment focus and goals.
   a. Identify specific goals, such as increasing intimacy and common activities, while exploring Joan's and Lawrence's expectations and potential barriers to the goals.
   b. Identify individual growth needs for Lawrence and Joan.

Middle-Phase Goals

1. Help couple to reduce incongruent communication and pursuer/distancer pattern to increase sense of intimacy and connection.
   a. Model communication by using I statements, expressing thoughts and feelings, and remaining honest.
   b. Direct couple in how to congruently communicate in session.
   c. Explore cultural issues and expectations that may be inhibiting congruent communication.
   d. Invite Joan and Lawrence to participate in a parts party to assist in identifying different parts of each other to better understand inner conflicts.
   e. Use ingredients questions to explore communication in greater depth: "What do I hear and see?" "What meaning do I make of what I hear and see?" "What feelings do I have about the meaning I make?" "What feelings do I have about these feelings?" "What defenses do I use?" "What rules of commenting do I use?"
   f. Discuss couple rules openly, including those pertaining to parenting, and renegotiate to create rules that support desired intimacy.
   g. Sculpt Joan's and Lawrence's present family and families of origin, focusing on couple and parenting issues.

2. Identify and support Joan's and Lawrence's individual uniqueness and address the issues of power that are making intimacy difficult for the couple.
   a. Allow each to speak for him/herself, while remaining sensitive to the cultural expectations and issues.
   b. Have Lawrence and Joan construct a self-mandala to highlight individual resources and areas for individual and couple development.
   c. Use temperature reading to allow Joan and Lawrence to share their (1) "appreciations and excitements"; (2) "worries, concerns, and puzzles"; (3) "complaints and possible solutions"; (4) "new information"; and (5) "hopes and wishes".
   d. Invite each to sculpt him/herself in relation to others, particularly family and friends, as well as society.
   e. Recognize and explore Lawrence's and Joan's differentness, as well as that of other family members. Identify ways to support each other's unique needs.
   f. Identify Joan's and Lawrence's (1) "expectations," (2) "perceptions," (3) "feelings and feelings about those feelings," and (4) "behavior" related to the primary survival triad.

3. Alter the unproductive communication stances and patterns to reflect more congruent selves capable of intimacy.
   a. Sculpt Lawrence as distant/superreasonable and Joan as a blamer; speak from positions, and process experience.
   b. Role-play a situation in the sculpted positions.

c. Allow Joan and Lawrence to switch positions and process.
d. Invite Joan and Lawrence to scuplt selves how they would like it to be.

Late-Phase Goals

1. Increase and strengthen couple's sense of growth and development to assist in group family reconstruction.
   a. Review family map and chronology.
   b. Therapist tells the couple "life story" while couple and group listen.
   c. Other members are sculpted into current relationship, couple's family of origins, each of their parents' families of origins, and the process of couple engaging in relationship; current relationship is then resculpted in present and hoped-for future.
   d. Members of family reconstruction process share their experiences.

2. Solidify newly established sense of equality, wholeness, and openness to possibilities and change.
   a. Discuss growth and changes in Joan and Lawrence, and compliment them.
   b. Reiterate that the couple possesses resources and skills for positive growth.
   c. Sculpt changes.

Vignette: Family

A 40-year-old, Hmong woman who recently immigrated to the United States, Anne, and her 14-year-old son, Raymond, sought treatment because he has received several suspensions from school this year and they have been told by school officials that one more infraction will result in expulsion. Anne reported that Raymond's teachers complain that he does not do his schoolwork, is often disrespectful of authorities, and is frequently aggressive with other students. This is the first year that Raymond has been mainstreamed, having been in special education until this year due to a partial hearing loss from birth. Anne does not have any noteworthy complaints about Raymond's behavior at home.

Satir's Communications Treatment Plan for Family

Early-Phase Goals

1. Make contact: Establish rapport, equality, and a sense of hope.
    a. Speak genuinely and honestly as therapist.
    b. Allow for Anne's and Raymond's voices to be heard; address translation issues.
    c. Attempt to make emotional connection with Anne and Raymond by establishing warm, supportive environment.

2. Identify communication patterns and stances, as well as problem issues, while addressing interrelated thoughts, feelings, and behaviors.
    a. Initiate a family life fact chronology, addressing cultural and immigration issues.
    b. Identify Anne's and Raymond's verbal and nonverbal communication stances and patterns, remaining sensitive to cultural expectations.
    c. Use a metaphoric story reflecting the family dynamics and problem issue.
    d. Assist Anne and Raymond in family sculpting, including Anne's family of origin and family with father (if relevant).
    e. Anne and Raymond draw family, exploring metaphors and relational patterns.
    f. Anne and Raymond create a self-mandala to identify strengths and areas for development, particularly ethnic identification issues.

3. Identify treatment focus and goals.
    a. Identify goals associated with decreasing Raymond's disruptive behavior while exploring expectations and potential barriers. Address immigration, acculturation, and identification issues and create appropriate goals
    b. Refer for medical and educational needs assessment.
    c. Identify individual growth needs for Anne and Raymond.

Middle-Phase Goals

1. Help family become more aware of conflicts and incongruencies in communication and between mind, body, and feelings to increase congruent communication and create a strong emotional bond.
   a. Explore cultural beliefs about mind, body, and feelings, highlighting Anne's and Raymond's individual experiences of the culture. Remain sensitive to how they have been experiencing the transition from their country of origin to the United States and beliefs about disability.
   b. Model communication by using I statements, expressing thoughts and feelings, and remaining honest.
   c. Direct mother and son in congruent communication.
   d. Introduce and initiate a parts party to allow Anne and Raymond to identify the different parts within each other, especially those relating to school problems and disability.
   e. Use ingredients questions about general communications and problem communication at school: "What do I hear and see?" "What meaning do I make of what I hear and see? "What feelings do I have about the meaning I make? "What feelings do I have about these feelings?" "What defenses do I use?" "What rules for commenting do I use?"
   f. Use family sculpting to explore communication and relational patterns at home and at school.
   g. Sculpt Anne and Raymond to represent the challenges of immigrating to a new country and explore/identify associated thoughts and feelings.

2. Identify and support individual uniqueness while addressing issues of power as they relate to school authorities and peers.
   a. Allow each to speak for him/herself while being respectful of others.
   b. Explore acculturation and ethnic identification issues as they may relate to Raymond's behavior.
   c. Anne and Raymond construct self-mandalas to highlight individual resources.
   d. Discuss family rules for communication and relating and identify more productive rules that support Raymond in being more cooperative at school.
   e. Use temperature reading to allow Anne and Raymond to share their (1) "appreciations and excitements"; (2) "worries, concerns, and puzzles"; (3) "complaints and possible solutions"; (4) "new information"; and (5) "hopes and wishes."
   f. Invite each to sculpt him/herself in relation to others, including family, friends, school personnel as well as to society.
   g. Recognize and utilize Anne's and Raymond's differentness, as well as that of others.

   h. Identify Anne's and Raymond's (1) "expectations," (2) "perceptions," (3) "feelings and feelings about those feelings," and (4) "behavior" related to the primary survival triad.

3. Support Raymond's individual growth by facilitating transition to mainstream classroom.
   a. Sculpt Raymond's behavior and stance at school, while comparing it to Raymond at home. Be aware of the influence of cultural differences.
   b. Sculpt and role-play alternative ways to assist Raymond in identifying possibilities for change.
   c. Allow Raymond to share his worries and concerns, as well as hopes and wishes, in the school environment.

Late-Phase Goals

1. Solidify newly established sense of equality, wholeness, and openness to possibilities and change.
   a. Discuss growth and changes in Anne and Raymond, and compliment them.
   b. Reiterate that family possesses resources and skills for positive growth.
   c. Sculpt changes and process.

2. Highlight and maintain Raymond's improvements at school.
   a. Identify how Raymond has made changes.
   b. Invite him and mother to sculpt new relationships at school.
   c. Discuss possibilities for continued growth, utilizing culture resources.

Suggested Readings

Jackson, D., Riskin, J., & Satir, V. (1961). A method of analysis of a family interview. *Archives of General Psychiatry, 5*, 321–339.

Satir, V. (1967a). *Conjoint family therapy.* Palo Alto, CA: Science and Behavior Books.

Satir, V. (1967b). Family systems and approaches to family therapy. *Journal of the Fort Logan Mental Health Center, 4*(2), 81–93.

Satir, V. (1972). *Peoplemaking.* Palo Alto, CA: Science and Behavior Books.

Satir, V. (1987). *The therapist story: The use of self in therapy.* Binghamton, NY: Haworth Press.

Satir, V. (1988). *The new peoplemaking.* Palo Alto, CA: Science and Behavior Books.

Satir, V., & Baldwin, M. (1983). *Satir's step by step: A guide to creating change in families.* Palo Alto, CA: Science and Behavior Books.

Satir, V., Banmen, J., Gerber, J., & Gomori, M. (1991). *The Satir model: Family therapy and beyond.* Palo Alto, CA: Science and Behavior Books.

Satir, V., Stachowiak, J., & Taschman, H. A. (1975). *Helping families to change.* New York,: Jason Aronson.

"From the symbolic-experiential view, every couple and family has a unique organization that serves both to aid adaptation and to block needed change" (Roberto, 1991, p. 446).

SYMBOLIC-EXPERIENTIAL FAMILY THERAPY

CHAPTER 7

KEY THEORISTS

David Keith
Walter Kempler
Thomas Malone
August Napier
Laura Roberto
John Warkentin
Carl Whitaker

HISTORICAL OVERVIEW

The symbolic-experiential approach grew out of humanistic psychology and Gestalt therapy and focused on change occurring through the growth process. Carl Whitaker, an influential figure in this experiential approach, was psychodynamically trained and worked in psychiatry. Frustrated with limited effects of medication to create change, Whitaker began experimenting with *listening* to clients. Whitaker discovered that, in the process of listening, the client was able to explore the self and problem issues, thus growing and healing (Whitaker & Malone, 1953). Another influential figure in the field was Kempler, who trained in Gestalt therapy under Fritz Pearls. Symbolic-experiential therapists, such as Carl Whitaker, John Warkentin, Thomas Malone, and Richard Felder, formed the Atlanta Psychiatric Clinic. Other influential figures identifying with this approach include August Napier, Laura Roberto, and David Keith.

KEY CONCEPTS

Person of the Therapist

Whitaker's symbolic-experiential approach is not a theory-driven approach in the traditional sense. Instead of strictly adhering to theory, therapists are encouraged be spontaneous and fully themselves—to be "real" people. Whitaker believed that therapists should focus on authentically "being" with families and their anxieties rather than aloofly applying predetermined techniques. The therapist's own emotional response to what is happening in the room is the primary source of inspiration for interventions. Furthermore, when the therapist is fully present and communicating spontaneously, clients are encouraged to be "real" and authentic people themselves.

Existential Encounter

The *existential encounter* is the critical change factor in symbolic-experiential therapy. This encounter involves an authentic meeting of the therapist and client in the present moment without the customary social pretenses. Such encounters touch on our deepest emotions, evoking despair, laughter, anger, love, and fear. Through this process, both the client and the therapist are transformed. To allow for such moments, the therapist stays closely attuned to the family's spoken and unspoken emotions in the "here and now" of each session and then directly responds to these emotions.

Therapy of the Absurd

The symbolic-experiential approach is sometimes referred to as the *therapy of the absurd,* because, to the uninitiated eye, there appears to be a "craziness" to the approach. This craziness can be a reflection of the spontaneity of the therapist, or it may be the therapist's way of reflecting back to the family members their own absurdity. This "absurdity" may be expressed in many forms—playfulness, mimicking, challenging remarks, and so on.

Individuation

Individuation is one of the primary goals in this growth-oriented approach. "Differentiation and individuation in functioning families distinguish members from one another" (Roberto, 1991, p. 448). Each member is allowed his/her own perceptions and treatment as an individual. Furthermore, the degree of individuation within the family depends on the individuation of the couple.

Family Interaction

Symbolic-experiential therapists use several concepts for conceptualizing healthy family interaction, most of which include a sense of flexibility and openness to life experiences.

Flexible Roles "Role flexibility allows individuals to express differences and to change behavior or beliefs without disqualification, making use of their own life experiences, familial legacies, and developing preferences" (Roberto, 1991, p. 447). In healthy families, roles are flexible. This accounts for the "rotating scapegoat" phenomena in which each member experiences problems and success. In addition, healthy family members demonstrate gender-role flexibility.

Permeable Boundaries *Permeable boundaries* characterize functional relations and imply a clear sense of identity while also allowing others "in." The two types of boundaries are external and internal. External boundaries separate the family and environment; internal boundaries distinguish generations and subsystems.

Flexible Coalitions In well-functioning systems, coalitions are available for support when problems arise; these dyads are neither permanent nor threatening to others. When these coalitions become permanent aspects of family life, symptoms are likely to develop.

Intimacy Needs Intimacy and trust are characteristic of well-functioning families. "Bonding and intimacy exist between parent and child, between marital partners, and between siblings" (Roberto, 1991, p. 448).

Maintaining Commitment Healthy families also demonstrate an underlying commitment, which provides a sense of family identity and cohesion.

Resolving Conflict "The healthy family shows tolerance for conflict that allows disagreement to become overt and explicit" (Roberto, 1991, p. 448). A tolerance for conflict is present in healthy families, and disagreement is overt and can be resolved in many ways including agreement and compromise.

GOALS OF THERAPY

Focus

Therapy focuses on the "growth" of all individuals involved and completion of developmental tasks.

Goals

Symptom Relief The initial goals focus on the presenting problem; focusing on these goals helps collaboration efforts and gains relief from symptoms.

Cohesion Cohesion increases the sense of belonging within the nuclear family and encourages connection with the extended family and the family of origin.

Creating Transgenerational Boundary Sex, passion, and playfulness are acknowledged within and/or between generations, and this process allows for both separation of generations and transcendence of generation boundaries.

Growth Growth is the "natural orderly emergence of potential forms and capacities of the total individual organisms through maturation, differentiation, and integration" (Whitaker & Malone, 1953, p. 232). Rather than stability, the overall goal of experiential therapy is growth and the completion of developmental tasks. This includes consideration of existential and emotional issues. Whitaker believes this could be achieved by expanding a person's range of experience, especially through creative activities.

STRUCTURE OF THERAPY

Frequency and Duration of Treatment

In the symbolic-experiential approach, therapy is structured into weekly sessions; however, in the late phase, frequency may be altered to once a month. "The length of symbolic-experiential family or marital therapy is time-unlimited and could be best described as growth-oriented and intermediate in term" (Roberto, 1991, p. 459). Duration of therapy is from 6 months to 2 years for most families.

Phases of Treatment

Therapy is structured into early-, middle-, and late-stage sessions. In early sessions, therapists "must convey that they are in charge of the therapy's structure" (Roberto, 1991, p. 458). In the middle phase, there is "reorganization around the interpersonally expanded symptom" (p. 462). In the middle phase, therapists use the following four central strategies:

1. Creating alternative interactions
2. Replacing key players in certain conflicts with one's self
3. Increasing the focus on others besides the scapegoat
4. Avoiding blaming the caretaking parent or spouse (p. 462)

In the late phase, "the family operates as a mobile milieu therapy unit within the family-co-therapist suprasystem" (Roberto, 1991, 462).

ASSESSMENT

"In symbolic-experiential therapy, families are assessed using an explicit theory of healthy functioning" (Roberto, 1991, p. 452).

Competency-Based Assessment

Symptom and dysfunction are measured "in the context of intact competencies and resources for change"; therefore, assessment focuses on competencies rather than problems (Roberto, 1991, p. 452). The therapist is vigilant against reifying symptoms and creating an iatrogenic effect. When assessing families, the therapist considers the family's stage in the life cycle and its transgenerational belief system.

Shells of Context

Assessment considers the variable contexts from the outermost shell (extended family and or community) to the innermost shell (identified patient).

"Trial of Labor"

The assessment interview is conducted in the earliest sessions, and this period is referred to as a "trial of labor" (Whitaker & Keith, 1981). During this period, therapists work toward understanding of roles, beliefs, history, and developmental patterns. They also observe the family's reaction to therapeutic interventions.

When assessing a family, symbolic-experiential therapists consider the following characteristics.

Disorganized Boundaries Problems can occur with internal and external boundaries:

- *Internal:* Overly rigid or overly fused boundaries produce symptoms that result in triangulation.
- *External:* Overly rigid or overly permeable boundaries result in isolation or overdependency.

Coalitions to Avoid Conflict Poor boundaries result in triads and tetrads rather than dyads seen in healthier families:

- *Pathological triad:* Similar to triangulation, a third person is used to stabilize a two-person subsystem.
- *Tetrad:* A tetrad is similar to a triad, but both members of the dyad turn to another person to stabilize the subsystem; this results in a four-person system, which is used to stabilize the volatile dyad.

Conflict Conflict is perceived as dangerous in dysfunctional families and is avoided. The three types of conflict are (a) chronic tension, (b) conflict avoidance, and (c) premature closure:

- *Chronic tension:* Chronic tension results because conflict is not allowed and constant tension exists between family members.
- *Conflict avoidance:* In conflict avoidance, the family denies the existence of problems.
- *Premature closure:* Premature closure is associated with open conflict that is not sustained long enough to resolve a situation. Premature closure is a means of avoiding conflict.

Role Rigidity Role rigidity is another structural characteristic of dysfunctional families. Role rigidity restricts the family members' behaviors and potential solutions to difficulties; a common example of this is sex role stereotyping.

Delegates Children are often pressured to adopt certain roles to maintain family structure in overly fused families. If children are able to carry out these roles without overt symptoms, they are considered "white knights" (as in the Type A personality) and are praised (Whitaker & Keith, 1981). Members who develop observable symptoms become the family "scapegoats."

Pseudomutuality/Emotional Cutoff Families with poor internal boundaries develop either an artificial congeniality (pseudomutuality) or overt emotional cutoff, such as hostility or isolation.

Parental Empathy "Failure of parental empathy is a process dysfunction that is highly resistant to present-focused interventions" (Roberto, 1991, p. 450). Lack of parental empathy for children results in difficulty responding to children's needs.

TECHNIQUES

Battle for Structure

The *battle for structure* refers to the therapist's responsibility to establish the rules and working atmosphere at the beginning of treatment (Napier & Whitaker, 1978; Whitaker & Malone, 1953). This battle often addresses the need for the entire family to be in treatment. The battle for structure is a battle the therapist must "win." This battle requires the therapist to be firm and even unyielding regarding what he or she believes is the necessary structure for treatment.

Battle for Initiative

Napier and Whitaker (1978) emphasize the importance of the family taking initiative for change after structure is established. The *battle for initiative* must be "won" by the family. Symbolic-experiential therapists believe that families have a natural tendency for growth that needs to be nurtured; therefore, the motivation to change must come from them. If the therapist is more motivated to change than the client, things are not likely to change because the therapist cannot "grow" for the client. Practically, the battle for initiative may involve encouraging the family to state the agenda for each session, not forcing the therapist's agenda for change on the family, waiting in silence for the family to take the initiative, not working harder than the family, or allowing the family to determine how change is to happen.

Expanding Distress to Include Each Member

Expanding the distress and problem issue to each member shifts the tension and anxiety. This process encourages cohesion, avoids blame, and demands group solution (Whitaker & Keith, 1981). Augmenting distress forces members to break from covert ultimatums.

Activating Constructive Anxiety

Symbolic-experiential therapists identify two forms of anxiety: positive anxiety and negative anxiety (Whitaker & Ryan, 1989). "Symbolic-experiential therapy tends to focus more on positive anxiety [i.e., fear of failing to accomplish what one is capable of] by positively reframing symptoms as efforts toward competence and by overtly addressing the life-cycle transitions each family member is facing" (Roberto, 1991, p. 454). The focus on positive anxiety is more likely to stimulate growth than negative anxiety, or the fear of harm.

Redefining Symptoms

Symptoms are redefined as efforts toward growth in order to expand the family's sense of freedom. Often, metaphors or stories are used to redefine symptoms or to help families view symptoms in a new perspective. For example, a teen's desire for more independence can be redefined as an attempt to "try on" adult roles.

Fantasy Alternatives

Whitaker and Malone (1953) define *fantasy* as "non-reality bound intrapsychic experiences" (p. 231). The therapist can work with fantasy in two ways. In the first, actual stressful situations are discussed in fantasy or "what if . . ." terms, thus breaching the silence taboo. An alternative use of fantasy would de-emphasize stressful events by suggesting absurd fantasy alternatives. "For example, a father may be told, 'Maybe if you took your son's clothes, he couldn't go out and buy drugs' " (Roberto, 1991, p. 463).

Separating Interpersonal and Intrapersonal Stress

In separating interpersonal and intrapersonal stress, the therapist and client distinguish actual relational problems from individual reactivity to these problems. For example, a working husband would be encouraged to separate work stresses from family life.

Affective Confrontation

The therapist confronts the family with the therapist's subjective emotional experience of working with the family (i.e., bored, angry, etc.). "By speaking intimately and subjectively at times, the therapists induce family members to allow their own subjectivity to emerge for examination" (Roberto, 1991, p. 460). Examples of affective confrontation include "When did you divorce your husband and marry your son?" or "It must be easier on you to have your son parent his sisters."

Co-Therapist

"One method of management is to utilize a second person as an administrator" (Whitaker & Malone, 1953, p. 197). Since intense personal involvement is advocated, co-therapists can be useful in maintaining and broadening perspective. Often one therapist takes the role of the nurturer so the other can be more confrontational. The use of the co-therapist has also been referred to a "multiple therapy" (Whitaker & Malone, 1987).

The family and co-therapists combine to create a therapeutic system. Meaning is shared and intermember alliances are formed. "It is the new dynamic interaction of each co-therapist with each family member, along with the co-therapists' ability to separate, that will allow the couple or family to evolve new positions and renegotiate intimacy and authority" (Roberto, 1991, p. 455).

"Craziness," Play, and Humor

Symbolic-experiential therapists "seek to make a person's irrational, 'crazy,' or affective side more available since it is this irrational side that promotes change" (Roberto, 1991, p. 461). Craziness may take the form of play, humor, drama, or any other form that makes sense with the family. This type of interaction is encouraged as a means to discovering solutions and promoting growth.

SYMBOLIC-EXPERIENTIAL TREATMENT PLANS

The following general treatment plan identifies possible goals and interventions for each stage of therapy that could be used in treating individuals, couples, and families. Not all goals and techniques are applicable to all clients.

General Symbolic-Experiential Treatment Plan

Early-Phase Goals

1. Provide safe environment and join with system to begin discussing presenting problems.

Possible Interventions

a. Engage family as an authentic, real person.
b. Battle for structure by establishing rules and a therapeutic atmosphere.
c. Present total/real person as a therapist to model communication and interaction with others.
d. Encourage all members to attend.
e. Involve humor and spontaneity.
f. Invite co-therapist when possible and appropriate.

2. Gain information about systemic boundaries, coalitions, roles, empathy, and level of conflict—also referred to as a "trial of labor."

Possible Interventions

a. Actively listen and involve all members in the system.
b. Utilize affective confrontation to assess.
c. Assess shells of context.
d. Explore competencies.
e. Identify level of conflict, whether chronic tension, conflict avoidance, and/or premature closure.
f. Use symbolic drawing of the family life space; draw a circle that represents the family, instruct family members to represent themselves in the circle, and comment and reflect on observations.
g. Use conjoint family drawings.
h. Identify role rigidity.
i. Assess level of parental empathy and pseudomutuality/emotional cutoff.
j. Assess for disorganized boundaries.

3. Establish goals and strengthen family initiative.

Possible Interventions

a. Family should win the battle for initiative. Therapist must allow the system to determine the pace and course of therapy.
b. Challenge family to determine each session's agenda, tolerating silence and anger.

c. Therapist avoids working harder than client in and out of session.
d. Engage family in fantasy alternatives to identify "what if . . ." situations.

Middle-Phase Goals

1. Develop sense of cohesion with nuclear family, extended family, and family of origin in order to relieve presenting symptoms.

Possible Interventions

a. Redefine symptom as a step toward growth and/or to expand freedom.
b. Focus on activating constructive anxiety by encouraging positive anxiety rather than negative anxiety; may use affective confrontation.
c. Use "craziness": Spontaneously interact with family, responding to what is happening in session.
d. Use affective intensity to address unacknowledged feelings and issues.
e. Present fantasy alternative to the symptoms and stress.
f. Expand the distress to each member in the system.
g. Role-play a situation or problem issue to call the "bluff."
h. Use empty chair to dialogue with family members not in session.

2. Create and maintain appropriate generational boundaries.

Possible Interventions

a. Present affective confrontation statements to highlight coalitions.
b. Point out areas of role rigidity and/or delegated child roles.
c. Encourage parents to directly communicate with each other.
d. Use craziness, humor, and metaphors to help family/parents see the absurdity of their interactional dance.
e. Seize moments in session to highlight inappropriate boundaries as they occur.

Late-Phase Goals

1. Promote growth of individuals by achieving developmental tasks.

Possible Interventions

a. Remain total/real person to encourage individual family members to do so.
b. Use "craziness" and fantasy alternatives to explore "what if . . ." situations to encourage growth and identify new options for thinking, feeling, and responding.
c. Separate interpersonal and intrapersonal stress to increase individuation.
d. Activate constructive anxiety to encourage addressing developmental tasks.

2. Highlight accomplishment of goals, while addressing relief of symptom, growth, and completion of developmental task.

Possible Interventions

a. Encourage each member to acknowledge self and family growth.
b. Discuss and redefine problem issue to reflect growth.
c. Identify possible blocks to continued development and growth of family and individual members.
d. Role-play current/future scenarios in the family and discuss implications.
e. Allow each member to express feelings about his/her *experience* of therapy.

Vignette: Individual

Andrew is a 53-year-old male who was court mandated to attend 24 individual sessions for domestic violence. Andrew states that he verbally and physically abused his ex-wife for several years. He reports that as a child he was physically abused by his father and states that occasionally he has nightmares of the abuse. Andrew states that he is court ordered to address the domestic violence issues and does not want to address his past abuse issues, stating that they "are not relevant."

Practice Symbolic-Experiential Treatment Plan for Individual

Early-Phase Goals

1.
   a.
   b.

2.
   a.
   b.

Middle-Phase Goals

1.
   a.
   b.

2.
   a.
   b.

Late-Phase Goals

1.
   a.
   b.

2.
   a.
   b.

Vignette: Couple

Virginia and Gary, working professionals in their mid-forties, initiate counseling to address lack of intimacy in their relationship. Virginia and Gary report that they never have time to engage in leisure activities and that their sexual life is nonexistent. Gary states that he would like to spend more time with Virginia; however, Virginia often works long hours at work. Virginia reports that she lacks the desire to spend time with Gary and admits that she does not fully understand the problem. Virginia and Gary state that they are committed to their relationship and would like to improve and establish a sense of intimacy.

Practice Symbolic-Experiential Treatment Plan for Couple

Early-Phase Goals

1.
    a.
    b.

2.
    a.
    b.

Middle-Phase Goals

1.
    a.
    b.

2.
    a.
    b.

Late-Phase Goals

1.
    a.
    b.

2.
    a.
    b.

Vignette: Family

Lynn and Frank have been married for 20 years and have four children. Lynn initiated counseling to address her 8-year-old daughter Hannah's reported anxieties. Lynn reports that Hannah is very nervous in social situations and often refrains from family activities. Lynn states that her other children—Molly, age 12; Jesse, age 14; and Jack, age 16—present no anxious symptoms; however, Lynn reports a generalized anxiety disorder as a child. Lynn denies couple conflict; however, the children report that their parents often "yell and argue."

Practice Symbolic-Experiential Treatment Plan for Family

Early-Phase Goals

1.
   a.
   b.

2.
   a.
   b.

Middle-Phase Goals

1.
   a.
   b.

2.
   a.
   b.

Late-Phase Goals

1.
   a.
   b.

2.
   a.
   b.

Vignette: Individual

Andrew is a 53-year-old male who was court mandated to attend 24 individual sessions for domestic violence. Andrew states that he verbally and physically abused his ex-wife for several years. He reports that as a child he was physically abused by his father and states that occasionally he has nightmares of the abuse. Andrew states that he is court ordered to address the domestic violence issues and does not want to address his past abuse issues, stating that they "are not relevant."

Symbolic-Experiential Treatment Plan for Individual

Early-Phase Goals

1. Provide safe environment for Andrew to begin discussing past and present violence.
   a. Remain open and authentic as a therapist.
   b. Battle for structure by establishing rules and a therapeutic atmosphere, highlighting the court order to address domestic violence issues and clarifying frequency of meetings and fee.
   c. Present total/real person as a therapist to model communication and interaction with Andrew.
   d. Challenge client to explore childhood abuse and how it relates to present.
   e. Utilize humor and spontaneity.

2. Obtain information about Andrew's boundaries, coalitions, roles, empathy, and level of conflict to determine why violence has become vehicle for emotional expression.
   a. Actively listen and involve Andrew in discussing violence.
   b. Assess shells of context; consider extended family members, immediate family members, and self.
   c. Explore and identify conflict pattern in relationships, attending to the specific role of violence in relationship; also explore abuse in family of origin.
   d. Identify role rigidity regarding gender roles and marital roles.
   e. Assess for boundaries and coalitions in families of origin and procreation.
   f. Identify client's competencies and strengths.
   g. Assess for level of empathy toward wife and family of origin.
   h. Use symbolic drawing of the family life space; therapist draws a circle that represents family, instructs Andrew to represent himself and family members in the circle, and comments and reflects on observations.

3. Work with client to establish goals and initiative.
   a. Challenge client to assume the initiative for change; use court as leverage if needed; refrain from lecturing and educating about abuse until client has assumed initiative for change.
   b. Challenge client to determine each session's agenda, tolerating silence and anger if necessary.
   c. Therapist avoids working harder than Andrew in and out of session.
   d. Engage client in fantasy alternatives to identify "what if . . ." situations, such as, What if the authorities were not involved in the case?

Middle-Phase Goals

1. Increase Andrew's awareness of emotional inner life and the related need for violence, with the ultimate aim of ending the violence.
   a. Utilize affective confrontation by disclosing therapist's sincere response to the violence.
   b. Explore the need for violence in his families; why do emotions need to be expressed this way? Which emotions are not being expressed? Do all emotions get expressed as anger?
   c. Attend to emotional content of client's words and stories and reflect back.
   d. Focus on Andrew's fear of failing to remain "violence free" rather than more negative forms of anxiety.
   e. Redefine involvement in the legal system as a step toward growth by accepting consequences "like an adult."
   f. Present fantasy alternatives to the symptoms and stress, such as, What if you could go back in time and make choices to not be violent?
   g. Role-play stressful situation with various responses to reduce Andrew's role rigidity.
   h. Use empty chair to dialogue with ex-spouse and/or father.

2. Address unacknowledged feelings regarding childhood abuse and relationship with father to address reported trauma symptoms.
   a. Use affective confrontation statements to disclose the therapist's subjective emotional experience of the process.
   b. Use play interventions to facilitate experiencing of childhood feelings.
   c. Use empty chair role play to dialogue with father, mother, himself as child, and so on.
   d. Redefine nightmares as a signal that part of him is still hurting from abuse.
   e. Encourage expression of feelings related to abuse, particularly more vulnerable feelings; relate to current pattern of his abusing others.

Late-Phase Goals

1. Increase ability to fully experience emotions and learn how to express emotion in an appropriate manner.
   a. Remain total/real person to encourage Andrew to do so.
   b. Use fantasy alternatives to explore "what if . . ." situation associated with Andrew moving forward with his life without any barriers.
   c. Separate Andrew's interpersonal and intrapersonal stresses, especially as they relate to violence.
   d. Activate constructive anxiety by focusing on Andrew's fear of moving past current situation.

2. Highlight accomplishment of goals, while addressing Andrew's progress in terms of remaining violence free, personal growth, and completion of developmental task.
   a. Present affective confrontation by disclosing emotions associated with Andrew's accomplishments.
   b. Discuss and redefine violence to reflect growth and "violence-free" status.
   c. Discuss, draw, and experience new range of emotions.
   d. Allow Andrew to discuss *experience* of therapy; therapist may share personal reactions also.

Vignette: Couple

Virginia and Gary, working professionals in their mid-forties, initiate counseling to address lack of intimacy in their relationship. Virginia and Gary report that they never have time to engage in leisure activities and that their sexual life is nonexistent. Gary states that he would like to spend more time with Virginia; however, Virginia often works long hours at work. Virginia reports that she lacks the desire to spend time with Gary and admits that she does not fully understand the problem. Virginia and Gary state that they are committed to their relationship and would like to improve and establish a sense of intimacy.

Symbolic-Experiential Treatment Plan for Couple

Early-Phase Goals

1. Establish a safe environment and join with couple.
   a. Remain open and authentic as a therapist.
   b. Battle for structure by establishing rules and a therapeutic atmosphere; require that both attend sessions.
   c. Present total/real person as a therapist to model communication.
   d. Utilize humor and spontaneity.

2. Gather information about systemic boundaries, coalitions, roles, empathy, and level of conflict to explore role of intimacy.
   a. Actively listen and involve each partner.
   b. Assess couple's shells of context, immediate family, extended family, friends, and community.
   c. Identify individual and couple competencies.
   d. Explore couple's conflict avoidance patterns.
   e. Use symbolic drawing of the couple's life space; draw a circle that represents the couple, instruct Virginia and Gary to represent themselves in the circle, and comment and reflect on observations.
   f. Assess for role rigidity patterns, including gender and work roles.
   g. Assess emotional cutoff; explore history and emotions they are avoiding or are unable to directly express.
   h. Assess level of mutual empathy, warmth, affection, and intimacy.

3. Work with couple to establish goals and assert initiative.
   a. Allow couple to assert initiative and determine the agenda for therapy—may involve tolerating silence and anger.
   b. Therapist avoids working harder than couple in and out of session.
   c. Engage couple in fantasy alternatives to identify "what if . . ." they spent time together, had a weekend away, away so on.

Middle-Phase Goals

1. Develop sense of cohesion between couple, including an emotional and intimate connection.
   a. Use affective intensity to bring unexpressed emotions into the room; encourage each to share what they have been avoiding.
   b. Expand husband's distress to include wife.
   c. Focus on activating constructive anxiety by framing as fear of intimacy rather than fear of failure.
   d. Use play, humor, stories to highlight absurdity of distance in marriage and role of work in the marriage.
   e. Discuss work roles, gender roles, and other sources that may have caused them to become "stuck."
   f. Present fantasy alternative: "What if each had a great assistant at work and had too much 'free time'?"
   g. Increase couple's sense of mutual empathy and expression of love by allowing for free exchange of genuine emotions.

Late-Phase Goals

1. Promote ability of each to be real and authentic in and outside the marriage.
   a. Remain total/real person to encourage individual family members to do so.
   b. Use fantasy alternatives to explore "what if . . ." situation, thus de-emphasizing stressful events and encouraging growth.
   c. Separate couple's interpersonal and intrapersonal stress resulting from professional careers versus home life.
   d. Address emotions as they arise in session.

2. Highlight accomplishment of goals, while addressing increase of intimacy in the relationship, growth, and completion of developmental task.
   a. Allow Virginia and Gary to express their feelings about their *experiences* of therapy.
   b. Discuss potential blocks to continued growth and identify ways to mitigate.
   c. Use play and humor to reflect on where they started and how far they have come.

Vignette: Family

Lynn and Frank have been married for 20 years and have four children. Lynn initiated counseling to address her 8-year-old daughter Hannah's reported anxieties. Lynn reports that Hannah is very nervous in social situations and often refrains from family activities. Lynn states that her other children—Molly, age 12; Jesse, age 14; and Jack, age 16—present no anxious symptoms; however, Lynn reports a generalized anxiety disorder as a child. Lynn denies couple conflict; however, the children report that their parents often "yell and argue."

Symbolic-Experiential Treatment Plan for Family

Early-Phase Goals

1. Establish a safe environment and join with the family system.
    a. Remain open and authentic as a therapist.
    b. Battle for structure by establishing rules and a therapeutic atmosphere; require all family members to attend.
    c. Present total/real person as a therapist to model communication with the family.
    d. Utilize humor and spontaneity.

2. Gather information about systemic boundaries, coalitions, roles, empathy, and level of conflict to determine role of anxiety.
    a. Actively listen and involve all members in the system; use play with younger family members.
    b. Assess family's shells of context, including extended family and community.
    c. Explore each member's competencies and strengths.
    d. Identify the system's conflict avoidance patterns; obtain a good description of each member's role with Hannah being symptom bearer.
    e. Use symbolic drawing of the family life space; draw a circle that represents the family, instruct family members to represent themselves in the circle, and comment and reflect on observations.
    f. Identify role rigidity, especially youngest as scapegoat.
    g. Assess for the internal and external overly fused boundaries, particularly between mother and youngest.
    h. Explore and challenge the youngest daughter's role as *scapegoat* and symptom bearer.

3. Establish goals and assert family initiative.
    a. Family should win the battle for initiative; therapist must allow the family to provide the motivation for change.
    b. Challenge family to determine each session's agenda, while tolerating silence and anger.
    c. Therapist avoids working harder than the family in and out of session.
    d. Engage family in fantasy alternatives to identify "what if . . ." situations, such as, What if the anxiety was gone. Who would be the most relieved? What would Hannah be doing?

Middle-Phase Goals

1. Develop sense of cohesion with the nuclear family with clear boundaries that do not support the daughter's symptoms.
   a. Expand anxiety to each member by tracing the patterns around the symptom.
   b. Interrupt the pathological triad between parents and younger daughter by extending the anxiety to the other children.
   c. Focus on activating constructive anxiety by encouraging positive anxiety, such as the family's desire to not live in the "shadow of fear."
   d. Use affective intensity to highlight coalitions and address parents' denial of their problems.
   e. Redefine daughter's anxiety as a way to take care of her mother and father by keeping them from fighting.
   f. Use family drawings to assess how each sees family and how each would like family to be.
   g. Increase parental empathy to ensure daughter's needs are met.
   h. Role-play a situation in which the family is not able to leave the house due to daughter's anxiety issues. Once the situation is enacted, introduce the incident of a house fire and observe how the family negotiates and solves the dilemma.
   i. Suggest children rotate who serves as a distracter from marital conflict each week.

2. Create and maintain generational boundary to reduce marital conflict to reduce need for daughter's symptoms.
   a. Use affective confrontation to address marital conflict.
   b. Encourage couple to share here-and-now feelings about each other in session.
   c. Activate positive anxiety about marriage.
   d. Encourage expression of feelings of love and intimacy; explore blocks.
   e. Use humor to confront how they avoid even acknowledging there is a problem.
   f. Present a fantasy alternative: "What if your children were not here, what would you do together?"

Late-Phase Goals

1. Promote growth of all family members and new family structure that does not require symptomatic child.
   a. Remain total/real person to encourage individual family members to do so.
   b. Use fantasy alternatives to explore "what if . . ." situations that encourage personal growth by exploring how to handle future challenges.
   c. Separate interpersonal and intrapersonal stress, highlighting that marital conflicts do not need to involve children.
   d. Activate constructive anxiety to highlight family members' fears of not living up to capabilities/dreams.

2. Highlight accomplishment of goals, while addressing relief of symptoms, growth, and completion of developmental task.
   a. Allow each member to express feelings about his/her *experience* of therapy, perhaps using drawings to involve all members.
   b. Share therapist's personal responses to family and termination.
   c. Identify possible blocks to continued development and growth of family and individual members.
   d. Discuss and redefine Hannah's anxiety to reflect growth as a family, as well as growth in each individual.

Suggested Readings

Ferber, A., Mendelsohn, M., & Napier, A. (1972). *The book of family therapy.* New York: Jason Aronson.

Gurman, A. S., & Kniskern, D. P. (1978b). Deterioration in marital and family therapy: Empirical, clinical, and conceptual issues. *Family Process 17*(1), 3–20.

Malone, T. P., Whitaker, C. A., Warkentin, J., & Felder, R. E. (1961). Rational and nonrational psychotherapy. *American Journal of Psychotherapy, 15,* 212–220.

Napier, A. Y., & Whitaker, C. (1978). *The family crucible: The intense experience of family therapy.* New York: Harper.

Roberto, L. G. (1991). Symbolic-experiential family therapy. In A. S. Gurman, & D. P. Kniskern (Eds.), *Handbook of family therapy, volume 2* (pp. 444–476). New York: Brunner/Mazel.

Whitaker, C. A. (1975). Psychotherapy of the absurd: With a special emphasis on the psychotherapy of aggression. *Family Process, 14,* 1–15.

Whitaker, C. A., & Bumberry, W. M. (1988). *Dancing with the family.* New York: Brunner/Mazel.

Whitaker, C. A., Felder, R. E., & Warkentin, J. (1965). Countertransference in the family treatment of schizophrenia. In I. Boszormenyi-Nagy and J. L. Framo (Eds.), *Intensive family therapy.* New York: Harper & Row.

Whitaker, C. A., & Keith, D. V. (1981). Symbolic-experiential family therapy. In A. S. Gurman, & D. P. Kniskern (Eds.), *Handbook of family therapy* (pp. 187–224). New York: Brunner/Mazel.

Whitaker, C. A., & Malone, T. P. (1953). *The roots of psychotherapy.* New York: Blakiston.

Whitaker, C. A., & Napier, A. Y. (1977). Process techniques of family therapy. *Interaction, 1,* 4–19.

Whitaker, C. A., & Ryan, M. D. (Eds.). *Midnight musings of a family therapist.* New York: Norton.

Whitaker, C. A., Warkentin, J., & Malone, T. P. (1959). The involvement of the professional therapist. In A. Burton (Ed.)., *Case studies in counseling and psychotherapy.* Englewood Cliffs, NJ: Prentice Hall.

"Sharing a family's history is a sacred relationship, not a matter of technical fact-gathering" (McGoldrick, Gerson, & Shellenberger, 1999, p. 13).

CHAPTER 8

INTERGENERATIONAL FAMILY THERAPY

KEY THEORISTS

Murray Bowen
Betty Carter
Thomas Fogarty
Edwin Friedman
Philip Guerin
Michael Kerr
Monica McGoldrick
Daniel Papero

HISTORICAL OVERVIEW

Intergenerational family therapy, also referred to as *Bowen family systems,* evolved from psychoanalytic principles. Murray Bowen was a psychoanalytically trained psychiatrist who worked with persons with schizophrenia, often focusing on the individual; however, he began to recognize the importance of the parent/child relationship and involved the mother and father in treatment. Bowen eventually shifted from his individual focus to treat the family as an "emotional unit" and highlighted the influence of extended family members, even across generations. Bowen's prominent students and colleagues include Philip Guerin, Thomas Fogarty, Michael Kerr, Betty Carter, Monica McGoldrick, Daniel Papero, Peggy Papp, and Edwin Friedman. James Framo, who is generally considered an independent practitioner, also incorporated many of Bowen's ideas in his work.

KEY CONCEPTS

Togetherness and Individuality

Togetherness and *individuality* are the two counterbalancing life forces that the differentiated person is able to successfully balance. Togetherness refers to a person's ability to engage in meaningful connection with another; individuality refers to a person's ability to maintain a clear sense of self and identity. The dynamics of individuality and togetherness are central to all emotionally significant relationships (Kerr & Bowen, 1988, p. 64). If an individual within a family system is unable to balance togetherness and individuality and reach a state of appropriate differentiation, the relationship may become polarized, such as pursuer-distancer, overfunctioning-underfunctioning, and overachieving-underachieving.

Differentiation of Self

"*Differentiation* [italics added] is the lifelong process of striving to keep one's being in balance through the reciprocal external and internal processes of self-definition and self-regulation" (Friedman, 1991, p. 140). It is a process that can never be fully achieved. Furthermore, the "interconnection between dreams, fantasies, and the relationship process means that the intrapsychic and interpersonal processes are interlocking systems" (Kerr & Bowen, 1988, p. 73). Differentiation involves both (a) interpersonal and (b) intrapsychic processes, which are interrelated.

Intrapsychic Aspect of Differentiation At one level, differentiation refers to the separation of feelings and thinking. Undifferentiated people have difficulty distinguishing thoughts and feelings, whereas more highly differentiated people are capable of both strong emotion and logical thought.

Interpersonal Aspect of Differentiation Differentiation also refers to a person's ability to clearly distinguish self from others. Undifferentiated people have difficulty distinguishing their thoughts and feelings from those of others; differentiated people are better able to be simultaneously autonomous and relational.

One's level of differentiation is believed to be significantly impacted by the general level of differentiation in one's family of origin and one's role in the family. Children who are more actively involved in family conflict are more likely to be less differentiated than those who remove themselves. Furthermore, it is generally believed that people marry others with a similar level of differentiation. Finally, lower levels of differentiation are generally accompanied by high levels of anxiety, both personally and interpersonally.

Triangles

"*Triangles* [italics added] describe a natural process that has multiple effects" (Kerr & Bowen, 1988, p. 148). Triangles are influenced by the level of anxiety; when anxiety is low, there is little tension in the relationship. When relationships become distant and anxiety increases, a third person (or thing) is introduced to stabilize the relationship (Friedman, 1991; Kerr & Bowen, 1988). Triangles commonly involve introducing a third person, such as a child, parent, or friend, into the dynamics of the troubled dyad. Triangles reduce immediate anxiety but decrease the chance the original dyad will resolve the problem. For example, when a couple argues it is very common for one or both parties to turn to a friend or family member to discuss the situation. Such triangulation becomes problematic when it is chronic and the original dyad never resumes communication to resolve its difficulties. Sometimes triangles become so habitual that little communication exists between the original dyad about difficulties as they arise. Symptomatic children are often involved in a triangle with the parents.

Nuclear Family Emotional Process

"*Nuclear family emotional process* [italics added] defines the flow of emotional process or patterns of emotional functioning in a nuclear family" (Kerr & Bowen, 1988, p. 317). Emotional processes of individual family members are interdependent with the entire family's emotional process. The emotional forces in families operate in recurrent patterns and are highly influenced by the overall level of differentiation in the family.

Undifferentiated Family Ego Mass

Undifferentiated family ego mass refers to a nuclear family emotional process that is highly *fused*. The less differentiated a family is, the more the children from this family will "fuse" in their parents' marriage. This fusion may result in (a) reactive emotional distance in the marriage, (b) physical or emotional dysfunction, (c) marital conflict, and/or (d) projection of the problem onto children.

Family Projection Process

The *family projection process* refers to a process by which parents transmit or "project" their immaturity and lack of differentiation to their children. This process often involves the replication of one's family-of-origin processes in one's family of procreation, including similar patterns of triangulation, fusion, and distancing. For example, a family may have a pattern of women colluding against men in the family that is replicated across generations.

Multigenerational Transmission Process

Multigenerational transmission of the emotional process involves "individual differences in functioning and multigenerational trends in functioning [that] reflect an orderly and predictable relationship process that connects the functioning of family members across generations" (Kerr & Bowen, 1988, p. 224). In every generation, the child most involved in the family's fusion moves toward a lower level of differentiation of self; the least-involved child moves toward a higher level of differentiation. Problems are actually the result of relational patterns across multiple generations (Kerr & Bowen, 1988). For example, a child who has difficulty verbalizing his/her thoughts and feelings is likely to have a family in which some members have "all the say" and others have "no say" or a similar pattern in which certain members are denied voice. Therefore, parents and children are not to blame; but, rather, problems result from a complicated history.

Sibling Position

"The concept of functioning position in family systems theory predicts that every family emotional system generates certain functions" (Kerr & Bowen, 1988, p. 315). Bowen posited that there are fixed personality characteristics based on sibling position, which can be helpful in determining a child's role in the family's emotional process.

- Firstborn children tend to be characterized by power, authority, and self-confidence.
- Later-born children tend to identify with the oppressed and tend to be rebellious explorers and iconoclasts.

Sibling position can also provide therapists with information about marital issues.

Emotional Cutoff

"People cut off from their families of origin to reduce the discomfort generated by being in emotional contact with them" (Kerr & Bowen, 1988, p. 271). When a person is undifferentiated, he or she may manage emotional intensity by "cutting self off" from the family of origin. Cutoff is sometimes misrepresented as "maturity" because the person appears to be no longer dependent on the family, but emotional cutoff is often a sign of unresolved issues and lower levels of differentiation. A common example is a young or middle-aged adult who refuses to communicate with his or her family because that person sees the family as "bringing me down," "irrelevant," or "immature."

Societal Emotional Process

Emotional process in society influences the emotional process of the family. "The concept of societal emotional process describes how a prolonged increase in social anxiety can result in a gradual lowering of the functional level of differentiation of a society" (Kerr & Bowen, 1988, p. 334). Sexism, classism, racism, war, and other forms of oppression are prolonged social stressors that can affect one's level of functioning.

GOALS OF THERAPY

"Symptoms can be generated by an anxiety-driven togetherness process characterized by people's pressuring one another to think, feel, and act in specific way" (Kerr & Bowen, 1988, p. 256). However, the goals of therapy are not directed toward simple reduction of symptoms but, rather, address the underlying processes that support the symptoms: low levels of differentiation and chronic anxiety.

Therefore, the goals for therapy include:

- Decrease anxiety.
- Increase differentiation in one or more family members, which is generally evidenced by an ability to objectively reflect on intense emotional situations. Increasing differentiation reduces symptoms (Kerr & Bowen, 1988).

No other goals are thought to last.

STRUCTURE OF THERAPY

Intergenerational therapy is structured into three phases that incorporate Bowen's theoretical concepts and conceptualization of families.

Phase One: Initial Assessment

"The evaluation of a symptomatic family begins with the first contact with a family member" (Kerr & Bowen, 1988, p. 282). In the first phase, the history and background information associated with the problem issue are explored, including each member's perspective of what causes and maintains the presenting problem. Additionally, the therapist also inquires about each member's intentions of participating in therapy. A history of the nuclear family is gathered, including

- "the nature of the patterns of emotional functioning in a nuclear family,"
- "the level of anxiety a family has experienced in the past and level it is presently experiencing," and
- "the amount of stress a family has experienced and is experiencing" (Kerr & Bowen, 1988, p. 295).

Significant changes in the nuclear family are important. The final part in the initial evaluation process involves assessing the broader context of the extended family systems.

Phase Two: Genogram

In the second phase, the therapist and client(s) construct a family diagram or genogram. This information is evaluated in terms of (a) symptom, (b) sibling position, (c) nuclear family emotional process, (d) stress, (e) emotional reactivity, (f) adaptiveness, (g) stability and interactiveness, (h) emotional cutoff, (i) therapeutic focus, and (j) prognosis.

Phase Three: Differentiation

In the third phase of therapy, individuality, togetherness, and differentiation are highlighted. The therapeutic focus is on the reduction of anxiety and then shifts to differentiation. In this phase, the therapist intervenes with techniques and methods to assist in the reduction of anxiety. For example, with an anxious, emotional family, the therapist "has a systemic way of reviewing all the areas that may be contributing to the problem . . . It not only helps him [her] stay out of the family's frenzy, but can also help family members step back from the problems and be a little less reactive" (Kerr & Bowen, 1988, p. 327). Furthermore, techniques that assist in attaining differentiation may involve shifting the focus of a triangle to other family members, altering the structure to include other members (i.e., conjoint couple sessions), exploring resources within extended family, and establishing appropriate emotional involvement with other members (i.e., levels of emotional cutoff).

ASSESSMENT

"The evaluation and treatment of a family may include one family member, a husband and wife, an entire nuclear family, or some other combination of nuclear and extended family members" (Kerr & Bowen, 1988, p. 286). The intergenerational therapist assesses togetherness and individuality through (a) family of origin, (b) triangles, and (c) level of differentiation.

> During the evaluation [and assessment process], a therapist addresses ten basic questions:
>
> 1. Who initiated therapy?
> 2. What is the symptom and which family member or family relationship is symptomatic?
> 3. What is the immediate relationship system (this usually means the nuclear family) of the symptomatic person?
> 4. What are the patterns of emotional functioning in the nuclear family?
> 5. What is the intensity of the emotional process in the nuclear family?
> 6. What influences that intensity—an overload of stressful events and/or a low level of adaptiveness?
> 7. What is the nature of the extended family systems, particularly in terms of their stability and availability?
> 8. What is the degree of emotional cutoff from each extended family member?
> 9. What is the prognosis?
> 10. What are the important directions for therapy? (Kerr & Bowen, 1988, p. 290)

TECHNIQUES

Intergenerational theorists generally focus more on articulating theory than on developing techniques with the assumption that, if one understands the theory, then one will know how to intervene. Therapists are encouraged to explore their own family-of-origin processes before trying to employ these ideas with others.

Detriangulate

"*Detriangulation* [italics added] is probably the most important technique in family systems therapy" (Kerr & Bowen, 1988, p. 150). To detriangulate, the therapist uses him/herself in the face of the family projection process to dissolve dysfunctional triangles and reduce fusion. "The process of detriangulating depends on the subtle as well as the more obvious ways in which one is triangulated by others and on which one attempts to triangle others" (p. 149). How a therapist detriangulates depends on the emotional processes within the family. Common ways to detriangulate include avoiding taking sides, making a judgment, or speaking for a client.

Nonanxious Presence

The therapist must maintain a *nonanxious presence* when engaging with the family. This presence is not emotionally reactive to family anxiety and stress, even in the face of heated conflict. To achieve such a presence, the therapist must work through his/her family-of-origin issues, which is typically facilitated in the supervision process and/or individual therapy.

Genogram

Genograms are used as an assessment tool and as a technique (see McGoldrick & Gerson, 1985). When used as a technique, genograms provide insight and introduce the possibility for a calm, rational discussion. Genograms can be used to map the nuclear and extended family processes and provide a means of identifying intergenerational patterns that might otherwise be difficult to see. Particular attention is given to patterns of conflict (indicated by jagged lines), distance (dotted lines), cutoff (broken lines), fusion (tripled lines), and close relationships (double lines), as well as to processes related to the presenting problem.

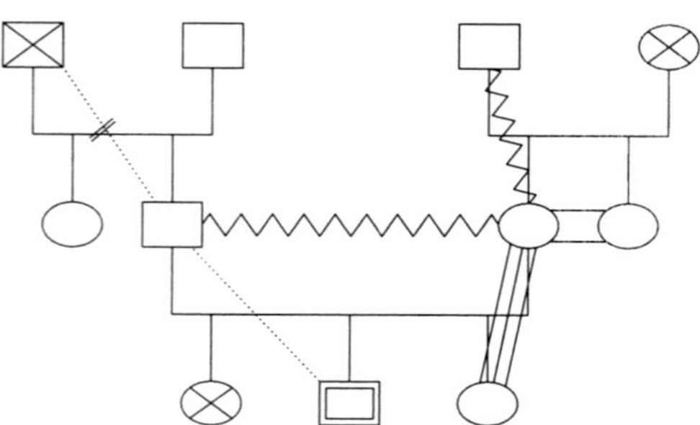

Process Questions

Process questions involve exploring family emotional processes and are designed to decrease reactive anxiety and help people think rationally about their situation. The questions highlight looking at one person's behavior and how it affects others, emphasizing personal responsibility. For example, a therapist may ask the wife of a couple, "When John has a bad day, do you believe you must also have a bad day? What makes you responsible for his day?"

Supporting Differentiation

Supporting differentiation involves focusing on the family member who is most motivated to work toward differentiation. This may involve individual sessions with this person to effect change in the larger family system. Differentiation can be supported by highlighting how the person conflates thoughts/feelings and self/others.

"Going Home Again"

"*Going home again*" encourages clients to go home and re-experience their nuclear family without emotional reactivity. Clients can do so by researching emotional cutoffs, finding lost relatives, identifying triangles, and identifying habitual family interactions.

Displacement Stories

Displacement stories are stories about other families with similar problems that therapists share with clients in order to help the family gain a clearer understanding of its own process. This technique is grounded in the idea that when one is in a highly emotional situation it is often easier to understand the situation if one can get some distance from it. Films, books, and other media sources can also be used to help clients gain a better understanding of their situation.

Coaching

The therapist often works as a "coach" or "consultant" in regard to teaching families about family process. Informational sessions are most appropriate in the middle and late phases, once the family's level of anxiety has decreased.

INTERGENERATIONAL TREATMENT PLANS

The following general treatment plan identifies possible goals and interventions for each stage of therapy that could be used in treating individuals, couples, and families. Not all goals and techniques are applicable to all clients.

General Intergenerational Treatment Plan

Early-Phase Goals

1. Establish a therapeutic relationship with client(s).

Possible Interventions

a. Maintain a nonanxious and neutral presence.
b. Role-model a clear sense of differentiation of self.
c. Attend to therapist's reaction to family, particularly reactions that relate to therapist's own family-of-origin issues.

2. Explore family-of-origin and intergenerational issues.

Possible-Interventions

a. Construct a genogram to identify intergenerational patterns.
b. Identify sibling position of those within the system and consider how these affect the current situation.
c. Explore possible emotional cutoffs in the family.
d. Assess for multigenerational patterns.
e. Identify triangles.

3. Identify level of differentiation and anxiety by inquiring about the problem issue.

Possible Interventions

a. Present process questions that focus on emotional processes.
b. Determine to what extent members separate thoughts from feelings and self from others.
c. Assess for level of fusion in the family by inquiring about family interactions and general level of anxiety.

Middle-Phase Goals

1. Address sources of anxiety and begin to decrease the anxiety that underlies symptoms.

Possible Interventions

a. Use process questions to identify the nuclear and extended family processes that maintain the anxiety.
b. Use a genogram to explore the patterns that sustain familial and individual anxiety.
c. Inquire about and discuss the sources of anxiety.

d. Identify generational transmission of anxiety and other symptoms.
e. Coach family members on how to manage anxiety.
f. Use displacement stories to help family better understand family processes that support anxiety.
g. Therapist can detriangulate by avoiding taking sides and helping family to directly address anxiety when it arises.
h. Help family members separate thoughts from feelings and self from others to help defuse sources of anxiety.

2. Increase differentiation of family members.

Possible Interventions

a. Use a genogram to explore intergenerational patterns, family transactions, and so on.
b. Present process questions to assist in identifying personal responsibility.
c. Use nonanxious presence to detriangulate and help family to more assertively address concerns.
d. Coach clients on how to respond to problem situations in a more differentiated way.
e. Use displacement stories to encourage a more objective view of situations.
f. Encourage "going home again" to help family members engage family of origin as a differentiated adult.
g. Address gender-inequality issues that may decrease ability to differentiate and maintain an equal status in relationship.
h. Support differentiation and possibly initiate individual sessions.

Late-Phase Goals

1. Facilitate change in family process brought on by increasing differentiation in family member(s).

Possible Interventions

a. Coach members on how to respond to invitations to return to previous process and triangles.
b. Use displacement stories to help family members understand responses of others.
c. Coach members on how to maintain a nonanxious presence in response to family reactions.

2. Highlight newly established differentiation and ability to balance individuality and togetherness.

Possible Interventions

a. Identify and discuss gains and decreased levels of anxiety.
b. Identify ways to interrupt dysfunctional generational processes.
c. Encourage additional "going home again" visits to key family members.

Vignette: Individual

Sandra, a 25-year-old, single, African American female has requested counseling services. She is seeking treatment to address her anxiety issues. Sandra reports feeling anxious during most of her life, beginning in elementary school. She reports recent "panic" attacks in which she feels like things are closing in on her and that she might die. Sandra reports having a fear of driving and states that she can no longer drive for long distances, as the fear is too great. She also reports that she becomes extremely anxious when speaking with friends and close relatives. Sandra reports a family history of anxiety disorders and believes that her brother and mother report similar symptoms. Her father died 6 months ago.

Practice Intergenerational Treatment Plan for Individual

Early-Phase Goals

1.
    a.
    b.

2.
    a.
    b.

Middle-Phase Goals

1.
    a.
    b.

2.
    a.
    b.

Late-Phase Goals

1.
    a.
    b.

2.
    a.
    b.

Vignette: Couple

David and Martha, a Hispanic couple in their mid-thirties who recently immigrated to the United States, sought out treatment to discuss issues and concerns pertaining to reunification with their 13-year-old son. Up until 2 years ago, the couple and their three children resided in a cult. While in the cult system, the couple reportedly signed over custody of their oldest son to his grandparents, due to the son being labeled as "deviant" in the cult society. However, while the son was in the custody of the grandparents, his uncle sexually abused him. Since then, the son has been placed in seven foster homes and has been labeled by the foster care system as "defiant" and "disruptive."

Practice Intergenerational Treatment Plan for Couple

Early-Phase Goals

1.
   a.
   b.

2.
   a.
   b.

Middle-Phase Goals

1.
   a.
   b.

2.
   a.
   b.

Late-Phase Goals

1.
   a.
   b.

2.
   a.
   b.

Vignette: Family

Allison is a 12-year-old female living in a single-parent household with her mother and her 17-year-old sister Stephanie. Allison was recently assessed at a crisis center after she stated that she wanted to kill herself. This was her second visit to the crisis center for the same reason. Allison, reportedly, refuses to go to school, is often irritable, and regularly argues with her mother. Allison states that she has no friends and sometimes refuses to leave the family home. Her mother, Beth, states that client has cut herself in the past. Beth states that Allison has always been "overly dramatic" but has gotten worse since they moved back to the area following the breakup of her brief and unhappy marriage. Beth states that she (mother) is on medication for bipolar disorder.

Intergenerational Treatment Plan for Family

Early-Phase Goals

1.
   a.
   b.

2.
   a.
   b.

Middle-Phase Goals

1.
   a.
   b.

2.
   a.
   b.

Late-Phase Goals

1.
   a.
   b.

2.
   a.
   b.

Vignette: Individual

Sandra, a 25-year-old, single, African American female has requested counseling services. She is seeking treatment to address her anxiety issues. Sandra reports feeling anxious during most of her life, beginning in elementary school. She reports recent "panic" attacks in which she feels like things are closing in on her and that she might die. Sandra reports having a fear of driving and states that she can no longer drive for long distances, as the fear is too great. She also reports that she becomes extremely anxious when speaking with friends and close relatives. Sandra reports a family history of anxiety disorders and believes that her brother and mother report similar symptoms. Her father died 6 months ago.

Intergenerational Treatment Plan for Individual

Early-Phase Goals

1. Establish a therapeutic relationship with Sandra.
    a. Maintain a nonanxious and neutral presence.
    b. Role-model a clear sense of differentiation of self.
    c. Attend to therapist's reaction to client, particularly reactions that relate to cultural issues and the therapist's own family-of-origin issues.

2. Explore family-of-origin and intergenerational issues.
    a. Construct a genogram to identify intergenerational patterns, highlighting the role of anxiety in the family across generations.
    b. Identify Sandra's sibling position within the system.
    c. Assess for possible emotional cutoffs in the family.
    d. Identify triangles and highlight possible triangulation into her parents' marriage during childhood or as an adult.

3. Identify Sandra's level of differentiation and anxiety by inquiring about reported anxiety.
    a. Present process questions that focus on emotional processes. For example, inquire about the impact of father's death on family members; explore mother's reported anxiety and how it affected Sandra and her brother.
    b. Determine to what extent Sandra differentiates her thoughts from her feelings; remain mindful of cultural issues when assessing.
    c. Assess Sandra's ability to separate her self from others, particularly in regard to the memory of her father.

Middle-Phase Goals

1. Address Sandra's sources of anxiety and begin to decrease anxiety.
   a. Use process questions; encourage Sandra to objectively explore her anxiety in the past and present.
   b. Inquire about and discuss source of anxiety, both before and since father's death. Rationally discuss family and intergenerational patterns that sustain anxiety.
   c. Coach client in specific ways to manage anxiety when talking with others, in situations involving panic attacks, and so on.
   d. Identify generational transmission of anxiety and other symptoms, while exploring culture and father's role.
   e. Encourage Sandra to delineate between her thoughts and feelings and between self and others.
   f. Use displacement stories to help Sandra more clearly see how anxiety is maintained in her family.
   g. Explore how triangulation into her parents' marriage has affected her sense of anxiety.

2. Increase differentiation and help her detriangulate from family relations and process loss of father.
   a. Present process questions to assist in identifying how Sandra's behavior affects others and her sense of personal responsibility.
   b. Encourage Sandra to "go home again" to identify unproductive coping patterns in relation to mother and brother.
   c. Coach Sandra in how to assert herself in family process.
   d. Address culture and gender inequality issues that may decrease her ability to differentiate and maintain an equal status in relationships.
   e. Offer displacement stories to help Sandra understand how to differentiate.

Late-Phase Goals

1. Encourage differentiation and the ability to balance individuality and togetherness to facilitate resolution of grief.
   a. Identify ways to interrupt dysfunctional generational processes.
   b. Coach Sandra on how to respond to invitations to return to previous process and triangles.
   c. Use displacement stories to help her understand responses of others.
   d. Coach on how to maintain a nonanxious presence in response to family reactions.
   e. Encourage Sandra to visit father's grave and/or write him letters.
   f. Identify and discuss gains and decreased levels of anxiety.

Vignette: Couple

David and Martha, a Hispanic couple in their mid-thirties who recently immigrated to the Untied States, sought out treatment to discuss issues and concerns pertaining to reunification with their 13-year-old son. Up until 2 years ago, the couple and their three children resided in a cult. While in the cult system, the couple reportedly signed over custody of their oldest son to his grandparents, due to the son being labeled as "deviant" in the cult society. However, while the son was in the custody of the grandparents, his uncle sexually abused him. Since then, the son has been placed in seven foster homes and has been labeled by the foster care system as "defiant" and "disruptive."

Intergenerational Treatment Plan for Couple

Early-Phase Goals

1. Establish a therapeutic relationship with David and Martha.
   a. Maintain a nonanxious and neutral presence.
   b. Role-model a clear sense of differentiation of self.
   c. Attend to therapist's reaction to family, particularly reactions that relate to therapist's own family-of-origin issues.

2. Explore David's and Martha's family-of-origin, cultural, intergenerational, and cult contexts.
   a. Construct a genogram to identify intergenerational patterns of sexual abuse, defiance, and other issues.
   b. Identify each spouse's sibling position within the family systems.
   c. Identify emotional cutoff between the couple and families-of-origin, particularly in relation to the decision to join the cult.
   d. Explore multigenerational patterns of abuse and cutoff, highlighting impact of family members in their country of origin.
   e. Identify triangles between the couple, families-of-origin, and the cult system.

3. Identify level of differentiation and anxiety by inquiring about the stress and family's level of anxiety.
   a. Present process questions that focus on emotional processes, such as how the sexual abuse and the other members in the cult impacted Martha and David.
   b. Determine to what extent Martha and David separate thoughts from feelings.
   c. Assess Martha's and David's ability/inability to separate him/herself from others, particularly in relation to cult and children.
   d. Determine Martha's and David's levels of cutoff and anxiety related to separation from family in their country of origin, as well as transitional and any prejudicial issues.

Middle-Phase Goals

1. Address intergenerational and historical sources of anxiety and begin to decrease anxiety regarding reunification and abuse.
    a. Present process questions such as, How does your behavior influence and affect others? while highlighting each person's personal responsibility in marriage and family.
    b. Inquire about and discuss sources of anxiety, exploring historical patterns that support these family processes, separation from family, and issues related to living in a new environment.
    c. Coach couple on alternative ways to reduce anxiety caused by family patterns of interaction.
    d. Use displacement stories to help Martha and David better understand their situation.
    e. Identify generational transmission of anxiety and other symptoms.
    f. Detriangulate by remaining neutral and encouraging couple to resolve conflicts in the marital dyad.
    g. Coach couple in ways to separate thoughts from feelings and self from others.
    h. Work with the most individuated member with the aim of lowering the system's anxiety.

2. Increase Martha's and David's differentiation by detriangulating from families-of-origin and cult.
    a. Present process questions related to each member's behavior and how each member is affected to assist in identifying each person's personal responsibility.
    b. Coach couple in ways to calmly and rationally make decisions without undo influence from families-of-origin or cult.
    c. Encourage each to "go home again" and interact with families of origin and country-of-origin traditions as differentiated adults, especially if abuse has caused cutoff.
    d. Address gender-inequality issues that may decrease wife's ability to differentiate and maintain an equal status in relationship, while exploring cultural expectations.
    e. Support differentiation and possibly initiate individual sessions with most differentiated member.

Late-Phase Goals

1. Emotionally prepare couple and family for reunification with son.
    a. Coach couple on how to respond to invitations to return to previous process and triangles in nuclear, extended, and cult family systems.
    b. Use displacement stories to help couple understand their actions and responses of others.
    c. Coach on how to maintain a nonanxious presence in response to new family challenges.

2. Highlight Martha's and David's newly established differentiation and ability to balance individuality and togetherness.
   a. Identify and discuss gains and decreased levels of anxiety.
   b. Identify ways to interrupt dysfunctional generational processes.
   c. Encourage couple to visit key family or cult members, as well as country-of-origin, as differentiated adults.

Vignette: Family

Allison is a 12-year-old female living in a single-parent household with her mother and her 17-year-old sister Stephanie. Allison was recently assessed at a crisis center after she stated that she wanted to kill herself. This was her second visit to the crisis center for the same reason. Allison, reportedly, refuses to go to school, is often irritable, and regularly argues with her mother. Allison states that she has no friends and sometimes refuses to leave the family home. Her mother, Beth, states that client has cut herself in the past. Beth states that Allison has always been "overly dramatic" but has gotten worse since they moved back to the area following the breakup of her brief and unhappy marriage. Beth states that she (mother) is on medication for bipolar disorder.

Intergenerational Treatment Plan for Family

Early-Phase Goals

1. Establish a therapeutic relationship with the family.
   a. Maintain a nonanxious and neutral presence.
   b. Role-model a clear sense of differentiation of self.
   c. Attend to therapist's reaction to family, particularly reactions that relate to therapist's own family-of-origin issues.

2. Explore family-of-origin and intergenerational issues in general and in relation to crisis.
   a. Construct a genogram to identify intergenerational patterns related to suicide, defiant behavior, dramatic tendencies, and other mental health issues.
   b. Identify each member's sibling position and determine how this has affected family process.
   c. Assess for emotional cutoff between Beth, Allison, and Stephanie, as well as other members, including father(s).
   d. Identify multigenerational patterns of parenting, rebellion, and abuse.
   e. Identify triangles between members of present family and/or with extended family members.

3. Identify each member's level of differentiation and anxiety by inquiring about interactional processes.
   a. Present process questions that focus on emotional processes, such as, How has Allison's behavior and Beth's role affected each member?
   b. Determine to what extent family members are able to distinguish thoughts from feelings.
   c. Assess family members' abilities to separate themselves from others, particularly mother from her daughters; explore intergenerational patterns for mother-and-daughter relations in mother's family-of-origin.

Middle-Phase Goals

1. Reduce anxiety that supports the patterns of the family drama, including Allison's attempts at self-harm.
   a. Ask process questions to help family assume a more rational perspective on family situation while highlighting each member's personal responsibility.
   b. Inquire about and discuss sources and history of anxiety and drama, while referring to genogram.
   c. Identify generational transmission of anxiety, suicidality, defiant behavior, and other symptoms.
   d. Maintain a neutral presence to reduce triangulation in family.
   e. Coach members on how to more rationally respond and interact.
   f. Offer displacement stories about how other families have dealt with similar problems.
   g. Coach family in separating thoughts from feelings and self from others.

2. Increase differentiation in members to reduce self-destructive behaviors and unproductive family interactions.
   a. Present process questions to assist in identifying each member's personal responsibility to differentiate.
   b. Encourage mother to "go home again" and interact with family-of-origin as a differentiated adult; encourage daughters to do the same with father(s).
   c. Coach members on how to address family problems while allowing each person to be an autonomous self with her own thoughts and feelings.
   d. Address gender inequality issues that may decrease ability to differentiate and maintain an equal status in extended family relationships.
   e. Support differentiation and possibly initiate individual sessions with each member, particularly Beth.

Late-Phase Goals

1. Facilitate change in family process brought on by increasing differentiation.
   a. Have family discuss vision of family as daughters become autonomous adults; discuss in light of processes in mother's family-of-origin.
   b. Coach family on how to respond to invitations to return to previous process and triangles in extended and blended family systems.
   c. Use displacement stories to help family members understand their actions and responses of others.
   d. Coach on how to maintain a nonanxious presence in response to family reactions.

2. Highlight newly established differentiation and the family members' ability to balance individuality and togetherness.
   a. Identify and discuss gains and decreased levels of anxiety.
   b. Identify ways to interrupt dysfunctional generational processes.
   c. Encourage members to visit with key family members to discuss changes.

Suggested Readings

Bowen, M. (1966). The use of family theory in clinical practice. *Comprehensive Psychiatry 7*, 345–374.

Bowen, M. (1972). Being and becoming a family therapist. In A. Ferber, M. Mendelsohn, & A. Napier (Eds.), *The book of family therapy*. New York: Science House.

Bowen, M. (1975). Family therapy after twenty years. In S. Arieti (Ed.), *American handbook of psychiatry, Volume 5*. New York: Basic Books.

Bowen, M. (1976). Theory in practice of psychotherapy. In P. J. Guerin (Ed.), *Family therapy: Theory and practice*. New York: Gardner Press.

Bowen, M. (1985). *Family therapy in clinical practice*. New York: Jason Aronson.

Carter, B., & McGoldrick, M. (1999). *The expanded family life cycle: Individual, family, and social perspectives* (3rd ed). Boston: Allyn & Bacon.

Fogarty, T. F. (1975). The family emotional self system. *Family Therapy*, 2(1), 79–97.

Fogarty, T. F. (1976). Systems concepts and dimensions of self. In P. J. Guerin (Ed.), *Family therapy: Theory and practice*. New York: Gardner Press.

Friedman, E. H. (1991). Bowen theory and therapy. In A. S. Gurman and D. P. Kniskern (Eds.), *Handbook of family therapy*, vol. 2 (pp. 134–170). Philadelphia, PA: Brunner/Mazel.

Guerin, P. J., Fogarty, T. F., Fay, L. F., & Kautto, J. G. (1996). *Working with relationship triangles: The one-two-three of psychotherapy*. New York: Guilford Press.

Kerr, M., & Bowen, M. (1988). *Family evaluation*. New York: Norton.

McGoldrick, M., Gerson, R., & Shellenberger, S. (1999). *Genograms: Assessment and intervention* (2nd ed.). New York: Norton.

Walter, M., Carter, B., Papp, P., & Silverstein, O. (1988). *The invisible web: Gender patterns in family relationships*. New York: Guilford Press.

There are many "variables that constitute human functioning—behavior, biology, cognition, emotion—" that "influence each other and interact with the environment" (Craighead, Craighead, Kazdin, & Mahoney, 1994, p. ix).

9 CHAPTER COGNITIVE-BEHAVIORAL THERAPY

KEY THEORISTS

Albert Bandura
Aaron Beck
Albert Ellis
Norman Epstein
Neil Jacobson
Gerald Jones
Arnold Lazarus
Robert Liberman
Donald Meichenbaum
Gerald Patterson
Ivan Pavlov
B. F. Skinner
Richard Stuart
Joseph Wolpe

HISTORICAL OVERVIEW

The *cognitive-behavioral approach* was developed as a reaction to the psychodynamic approach. It has been influenced by Ivan Pavlov's classical conditioning, John B. Watson's work with phobias and "Little Albert," Joseph Wolpe's concept of systematic desensitization, and B. F. Skinner's operant conditioning. Other influential figures include Albert Bandura, Gerald Patterson, Robert Liberman, Ed Katin, and Richard Stuart. These approaches have included behavioral techniques for families (Falloon, 1988), couples (Jacobson, 1981), children and adolescents, (Reincke, Dattilio, & Freeman, 1996) and sexual dysfunctions (LoPiccolo & LoPiccolo, 1978).

KEY CONCEPTS

Classical Conditioning

Classical conditioning, developed by Ivan Pavlov, is the process by which an *unconditioned stimulus* (presentation of food) is associated with an *unconditioned response* (salivation) and is paired with a *conditioned stimulus* (ringing a bell). With repetitions, the conditioned stimulus (ringing a bell) will produce an unconditioned response (salivation) without the presentation of the unconditioned stimulus (presentation of food). This concept is used in behavioral interventions either to elicit desired behavior or to end unwanted behavior.

Operant Conditioning

B. F. Skinner's *operant conditioning* involves shaping a desired behavior by selectively rewarding that behavior so that it will occur more frequently (Falloon, 1991). Unlike classical conditioning, the desired behavior is *voluntarily* performed and is controlled by reinforcement. Often, *shaping* is used, whereby small steps toward the desired behavior are reinforced in stages until the desired behavior is elicited. For example, a parent wanting a child to clean his/her room may initially reward making the bed, then reward for making the bed and picking up the floor, and finally only reward for the entire room being picked up.

Reinforcement

Reinforcement is an event or behavior designed to increase or decrease a specific response. The more *consistent* the reinforcement, the more quickly the behavior is shaped.

- *Positive reinforcement* aims at increasing the frequency of a behavior and is also referred to as a *reward,* such as an allowance or display of positive affection.
- *Negative reinforcement* increases the frequency of a desired behavior by removing adverse stimuli when the desired behavior is elicited, such as when a parent stops nagging once a child cleans up his/her room.
- *Punishment* distinguishes itself from negative reinforcement in that it decreases undesirable behavior. Punishment can take the form of (a) aversive consequences, such as yelling or spanking, or (b) the removal of positive consequences, such as losing television privileges.
- *Intermittent reinforcement* refers to not consistently reinforcing a behavior. Behaviors that are intermittently reinforced are the most difficult to extinguish.
- *Contingencies of reinforcement* are when and how behaviors are reinforced.
- *Reciprocal reinforcement* refers to family situations in which the behaviors of each member serve as the stimuli and reinforcements for the others, resulting in a complex series of interlocking behaviors.

Primary and Secondary Reinforcements and Punishments

Primary and secondary reinforcements and punishments describe a difference between what is biological and what is learned. Primary reinforcement and punishment refer to biologically determined reinforcements, such as food and sex. Secondary reinforcement and punishment refer to a learned association and may include praise, criticism, and attention.

Extinction

Extinction is the process in which a behavior is diminished by not reinforcing it. Without the reinforcement, the person has no motivation for continuing the behavior. A common example of this is to ignore a child's tantrum and not reinforce it by "giving in," lecturing, or offering other forms of attention.

Premack Principle

The *Premack principle* is used to increase desired behaviors. Unlike prior reinforcement theories that assumed rewards must satisfy some basic drive, the Premack principle proposes that a person's preferred or *high-probability behavior* can be used to reinforce *low-probability behaviors* that one would like to change. This principle is commonly used in parenting when parents make the high-probability behaviors (e.g., watching television, playing video games, or going out) contingent upon low-probability behaviors (e.g., completing homework, doing chores, or following curfew).

Social-Exchange Theory

Social-exchange theory states that in interpersonal interactions people attempt to maximize "rewards" and minimize "costs." Two people rewarding each other at equitable rates is called *reciprocity,* and the relationship is relatively stable and satisfying. However, when one or both people do not believe that the rewards and costs are balanced, one or both will be dissatisfied with the relationship and will seek some form of change.

Social-Learning Theory

Social-learning theory highlights the process of vicarious learning. People learn new behaviors from the behavior modeled by others; the witnessed consequences of those modeled behaviors may provide incentive or disincentive for the observer to mimic those behaviors. This theory highlights that people learn not just from consequences they personally experience but also from witnessing others' actions and the resulting consequences. This theory recognizes the influence of feelings and cognitions on behavior.

A-B-C Theory

Albert Ellis's *rational-emotive-behavioral therapy* is based on the A-B-C theory. This theory posits that the activating events (A) do not cause the problem consequence (C) but, rather, the intermediary belief (B) about A causes C. For example, when a person's invitation to lunch is rejected (A), the feeling of worthlessness (C) is not the direct result of the rejection but, rather, is mediated by the person's belief (B) about having the lunch invitation turned down. The therapist rationally explores the beliefs about not having the lunch invitation accepted. Rather than assuming that one is unlikable because an invitation is rejected, the therapist would work with the client to consider the possibility that the other person may have had other prior commitments or may not be a good person to choose as a friend, which results in a different feeling about the situation. Through this process, the therapist works with clients to rationally analyze their beliefs to change the resulting consequences.

Family Schema

Family schema is a set of similarly held beliefs about family and life. The family schema provides the "template" or set of rules that organize a family's behaviors and interactions. Cognitive family therapists work to alter the family schema in an effort to alter problematic behaviors and interactions.

Parent-Skills Training

In *parent-skills training,* the therapist provides educational information to parents in either individual or group formats and often serves as a consultant to the parents (Falloon, 1991). Once a baseline of problematic behaviors has been established, the therapist provides specific procedures for changing the targeted behaviors, which are modified and adjusted as necessary.

Behavioral Marital Therapy

Instead of linear punctuation, *behavioral marital therapy* recognizes that the behavior of each is the antecedent and consequence of the other (Holtzworth-Munroe & Jacobson, 1991). The therapist aims at increasing rewarding behaviors, decreasing negative behaviors, and bettering communication and problem-solving skills.

Conjoint Sex Therapy

In *conjoint sex therapy,* the therapist serves as an educator on sexual physiology and techniques (Mason, 1991). Interventions address maladaptive behavior patterns and cognitions, and direct methods are used to reduce anxiety and improve performance. Improved communication is an important component of conjoint sex therapy, and relationship factors are also considered and addressed when necessary.

Functional Family Therapy

Functional family therapy aims at achieving cognitive and behavioral changes in the family system by challenging negative traits attributed to others in the family. This approach focuses on the underlying cognitions, beliefs, and attributions that maintain the problem situation. "The functional analysis of a marital relationship involves pinpointing the ways in which spouses simultaneously, mutually, and reciprocally act toward each other to affect their behavior toward each other and their degree of mutual satisfaction" (Holtzworth-Munroe & Jacobson, 1991, p. 97).

GOALS OF THERAPY

The goal in the cognitive-behavioral approach is cognitive-behavioral change, that is, to alter unproductive behavior and cognitive patterns to alleviate the problem and maladaptive symptoms. Little emphasis is placed on "growth" or "insight." Possible general goals follow:

- Increase desired behavior/cognitions.
- Decrease undesirable behavior/cognitions.
- Improve problem-solving skills.

STRUCTURE OF THERAPY

Early Phase: Baseline Assessment

Cognitive "behavioral family therapy is not constrained by any formal structures that define therapeutic content" (Falloon, 1991, p. 78). However, in the initial phases of therapy, a specified number of sessions is contracted between the therapist and family. Cognitive-behavioral therapy proceeds by assessing each individual in the family and gaining information about the undesired behavior while establishing a baseline of functioning. This is followed by assessing family interaction and functioning (Falloon, 1991).

Middle Phase: Intervention

In the middle stages of therapy, the cognitive-behavioral therapist initiates treatment by implementing cognitive-behavioral techniques to assist in alleviating the undesired behavior. Techniques generally include problem-solving skills, psychoeducation, and communication enhancement (Falloon, 1991).

Late Phase: Extinction

In the late phase of the therapy, the therapist highlights the elimination of the undesired behavior and explores identified problem-solving skills.

ASSESSMENT

In the cognitive-behavioral approach to therapy, therapists assess for the relational dynamics in relation to the problem issue by doing the following:

- *Behaviorally define the problem:* The problem is defined, and the targeted behavior is analyzed and described in concrete terms.
- *Functional analysis:* The therapist performs a functional analysis of the problem behavior, noting the antecedents and consequences of the behavior, the context of the behavior, and reinforcement patterns.
- *Baseline:* When assessing a problem behavior, the therapist begins by assessing "baseline" behavior, which refers to the frequency, intensity, and duration of the problem behavior before intervention.
- *Contract:* Finally, the therapist and client make a contract that specifies desired behavioral changes in measurable terms.

TECHNIQUES

"Behavioral family therapy aims to change specific targeted family problems or goals through the application of specific strategies" (Falloon, 1991, p. 86).

Therapeutic Contracts

Therapeutic contracts are usually written and specify the goals of therapy and obligations of the client and therapist. Contracts are commonly used in behavioral family therapy as a means of setting goals and focusing therapy on specific issues.

Contracting

"Contracts are usually based on increasing mutually rewarding behaviors, but on occasion, a contract may be made that concerns setting specific limits on undesirable behavior" (Falloon, 1991, p. 84). *Contingency contracting* is a variation of operant reinforcement that is used in relational counseling and involves negotiating desirable behavior change between two parties. These contracts define explicit rules for interaction and specify circumstances under which one is to do something for another. Generally, two types of contingency contracts are used:

- *Quid pro quo contracts* are contracts in which one person agrees to make a change after the other has made a requested change.
- *Good-faith contracts* involve two people mutually agreeing to make changes that the other wants without the contingency that the other changes first. Ideally, this type of contract is mutually reinforcing. These contracts are especially useful in relationships clouded by mistrust.

Functional Analysis

"The *functional analysis* of problem behavior extends the problem analysis to a systemic level" (Falloon, 1991, p. 75). Functional analysis involves figuring out what stimulus conditions control the targeted behavior while identifying "the precise contexts in which the problem is likely to be most and least prominent" (p. 75). During this process, hypotheses are tested and treatment is adjusted accordingly.

Modeling

Modeling is a process in which new behaviors are learned by observing the behavior of others and by witnessing the consequences of these actions. Although this process happens in everyday interactions, it can also be used by the therapist to promote behavioral change.

Systematic Desensitization

Joseph Wolpe (1969) introduced *systematic desensitization* as a procedure to address various forms of anxiety and phobias. This process involves altering a person's physiological response to a specific stimulus and is based on classical conditioning. Typically, a person is slowly exposed to the feared stimulus in incremental stages. *Reciprocal inhibition* is often part of this process and involves pairing the anxiety-arousing stimulus with a relaxation response. This process may culminate in *in vivo desensitization,* where a person gradually approaches the actual feared object or situation.

Reinforcement Schedule

A *reinforcement schedule* defines the contingencies for reinforcement of a behavior and establishes the relationship between a behavior and its consequences. Parents are often encouraged to specify a reinforcement schedule to ensure that each parent has a shared understanding of the limits and consequences that both will use regarding a child's undesired behaviors.

Shaping

Shaping is a technique based on operant conditioning and refers to the process in which a complex behavior is divided into subparts; contingencies of reward and punishment are provided to these subparts until all the behaviors comprising the whole are elicited.

Charting

Charting refers to asking the client to keep a record of the targeted problem behavior between sessions. Charting can be used early in treatment to obtain a baseline and later in treatment to monitor progress and to identify triggers or precipitating stimuli.

Time Out

Time outs are used to alter problem behaviors either by extinguishing a behavior by eliminating the reinforcing consequences or by interrupting unwanted behavioral sequences between people. When used as a punishment, "a time out may mean taking the child to his or her room or placing the child in a specific place, such as a chair, for a brief period" (Falloon, 1991, pp. 83–84). Time outs may also be used to interrupt escalating behavioral sequences, such as arguments and fights, by having each person agree to disengage from the other as early as possible in the chain of escalating behaviors.

Token Economy

A *token economy* is a system of rewards using points, which can be exchanged for reinforcing items or behaviors. "A list of desired behaviors is drawn up for one or more family members," and a specified number of points or tokens are assigned to each behavior (Falloon, 1991, p. 84). The points can be accumulated and exchanged for a range of rewards. However, if an undesired behavior is displayed, points or tokens can be taken away.

Disputing Irrational Beliefs

Using techniques based in cognitive theory, therapists actively work with clients to challenge their "irrational" beliefs about the problem situation that may be causing or exacerbating the situation. For example, a therapist may challenge a couple's belief that they "should" be able to make each other happy.

Psychoeducation

Cognitive-behavioral therapists often educate clients on various topics in individual or group contexts. *Psychoeducation* is often used regarding parenting, communication, problem solving, assertiveness, sexuality, and rational thinking.

Sensate-Focus Technique

The *sensate-focus technique* is an early-phase sex therapy technique that involves teaching couples to focus on enjoying basic touch without the pressure of having to perform sexually. Couples are instructed to take turns touching and caressing the other and eventually communicate about what touch is most pleasurable.

COGNITIVE-BEHAVIORAL TREATMENT PLANS

The following general treatment plan identifies possible goals and interventions for each stage of therapy that could be used in treating individuals, couples, and families. Not all goals and techniques are applicable to all clients.

General Cognitive-Behavioral Treatment Plan

Early-Phase Goals

1. Maintain a sense of respect for client(s) while establishing a therapeutic relationship.

Possible Interventions

   a. Model appropriate communication.
   b. Positively reinforce desired behaviors in and out of session.
   c. Begin process of shaping desired behaviors.

2. Identify problem and obtain a baseline of individual and family functioning.

Possible Interventions

   a. Work with clients to behaviorally and measurably define problem, including duration and frequency.
   b. Ask clients to track baseline functioning by using a daily chart of problem behavior, including triggers, intensity, and frequency.
   c. Use functional analysis to identify the antecedents, consequences, and contexts of problem behavior; identify current reinforcement schedule.
   d. Observe individual behavior and family interaction in session to assess problem behavior.
   e. Identify the current family schema, listening for dysfunctional qualities that may be contributing to undesirable behavior.
   f. Develop a therapeutic contract that specifies goals and therapist/client roles and responsibilities.

Middle-Phase Goals

1. Take steps to eliminate undesired behavior(s) while increasing desired behaviors.

Possible Interventions

   a. Shape desired behavior by identifying specific positive and negative reinforcements for targeted behaviors that can be easily integrated into existing contexts and routines; educate clients about the importance of consistent reinforcement.
   b. Initiate token system, rewarding and punishing the undesired behavior.
   c. Dispute irrational beliefs that sustain the problem behavior.

d. Explore family schema, negative attributions, and related assumptions that support problem behavior.
e. Negotiate quid pro quo and good-faith contingency contracts to increase the frequency of desired behaviors.
f. Identify and explore social models of problem and targeted behavior.
g. Have clients chart the frequency of problem and/or targeted behaviors between sessions.
h. Identify a consistent, appropriate reinforcement schedule for targeted behavior.
i. Identify times and strategies for using time outs.
j. Use psychoeducation to provide client with educational information about the source, maintenance, and elimination of the undesired behavior.
k. Use systematic desensitization techniques to address anxiety and phobias.
l. Use sex therapy techniques to address sexual dysfunction.

Late-Phase Goals

1. Address remaining couple and family issues.

Possible Interventions

a. Use psychoeducation to address relationship and/or parenting issues, including parent-skill and communication training.
b. Identify ways family schema needs to change or has changed; identify irrational beliefs that sustain(ed) problem behaviors.
c. Encourage parents to model desired behaviors for children.
d. Renegotiate relational contract between intimate partners and/or parents and children, including specific behaviors.
e. Have family clarify rules for behaviors and the corresponding privileges and consequences for following and breaking rules.

2. Extinguish undesired behavior and maintain satisfying level of desired behavior.

Possible Interventions

a. Contract for specific length of time that symptoms must be under control before terminating therapy.
b. Use charting of problem and desired behaviors to track improvements.
c. Refer to psychoeducation or support groups to support symptom reduction.
d. Use contingency contracting to help sustain gains.
e. Identify symptoms that would signal a return of symptoms and devise a plan to address.
f. Identify which reinforcements are most likely to help maintain changes.

Vignette: Individual

Michael, age 7, has three younger siblings and is being seen individually with monthly family sessions. Michael was potty trained at age 3 and has been wetting the bed at night for 3 weeks, since his seventh birthday. His physician has ruled out biological causes. Michael states that his father is always at work and his mother is busy with the younger children. His academic and social functioning is normal, and the enuresis is only at home. Michael's mother states that they have tried "everything" and does not know what else to do.

Practice Cognitive-Behavioral Treatment Plan for Individual

Early-Phase Goals

1.
    a.
    b.

2.
    a.
    b.

Middle-Phase Goals

1.
    a.
    b.

2.
    a.
    b.

Late-Phase Goals

1.
    a.
    b.

2.
    a.
    b.

Vignette: Couple

Alexis and Chris have been married for 3 years and initiated counseling to address lack of sexual intimacy in the relationship. Chris and Alexis report that, in the beginning of their relationship, they had an active sex life, having intercourse at least five times a week. However, for the last 3 months "things have changed." Chris and Alexis state that they have not been sexually intimate for 2 months and that they would like to increase frequency.

Practice Cognitive-Behavioral Treatment Plan for Couple

Early-Phase Goals

1.
    a.
    b.

2.
    a.
    b.

Middle-Phase Goals

1.
    a.
    b.

2.
    a.
    b.

Late-Phase Goals

1.
    a.
    b.

2.
    a.
    b.

Vignette: Family

Eddie initiated counseling for his 17-year-old daughter Roxanne, his 15-year-old son Robert, and his 12-year-old son Derek. Eddie states that, since his wife's death (6 months ago), Roxanne has been leaving without telling him and Robert has been talking back to him. Eddie states that the family received grief-counseling services immediately following the death; however, he terminated services after 3 months.

Practice Cognitive-Behavioral Treatment Plan for Family

Early-Phase Goals

1.
    a.
    b.

2.
    a.
    b.

Middle-Phase Goals

1.
    a.
    b.

2.
    a.
    b.

Late-Phase Goals

1.
    a.
    b.

2.
    a.
    b.

Vignette: Individual

Michael, age 7, has three younger siblings and is being seen individually with monthly family sessions. Michael was potty trained at age 3 and has been wetting the bed at night for 3 weeks, since his seventh birthday. His physician has ruled out biological causes. Michael states that his father is always at work and his mother is busy with the younger children. His academic and social functioning is normal, and the enuresis is only at home. Michael's mother states that they have tried "everything" and does not know what else to do.

Cognitive-Behavioral Treatment Plan for Individual

Early-Phase Goals

1. Maintain a sense of respect for Michael while establishing a therapeutic relationship.
   a. Model open communication.
   b. Positively reinforce times when Michael does not wet his bed.
   c. Begin process of shaping Michael not wetting his bed through positive reinforcement and highlighting times when he does not wet bed.

2. Identify and explore Michael wetting his bed and obtain a baseline of functioning.
   a. Ask parents and Michael to track baseline functioning by using a daily chart and a journal of when he wets his bed, including triggers, intensity, and frequency. Use a chart with different colors and stickers to assist in charting.
   b. Use functional analysis to assess context of problem by having Michael write a story about times when he wets his bed or have him draw pictures and verbally discuss.
   c. Observe Michael's behavior and interaction in the monthly family sessions to further assess family functioning and rule out abuse and other stressors.
   d. Explore family schema and listen for dysfunctional qualities present in parenting and/or interactional "rules" that may be contributing to Michael's wetting his bed.
   e. Develop and discuss a therapeutic contract that specifies goals and therapist/Michael roles and responsibilities.

Middle-Phase Goals

1. Decrease frequency of Michael wetting his bed, while increasing use of the restroom at home.
   a. Shape using the restroom by identifying specific positive and negative reinforcements for targeted behavior, such as adding/taking away privileges; educate parents about the importance of consistent reinforcement.
   b. Initiate a token system, rewarding and punishing when Michael wets/does not wet his bed.

c. Negotiate quid pro quo contingency contract between child and parents to increase privileges if Michael does not wet bed.
d. Have Michael chart the frequency of wetting his bed between sessions.
e. Consult with parents to identify a consistent, appropriate reinforcement schedule for targeted behavior.

Late-Phase Goals

1. Increase Michael's sense of being included in the family.
   a. Refer parents for psychoeducation to address parenting issues, including parent-skill and communication training, highlighting how to parent Michael with younger children in the family and how to communicate love and concern to each child.
   b. Identify ways family schema needs to change or has changed; identify irrational beliefs that reinforced bedwetting.
   c. Identify and renegotiate relational contract between parents and children, highlighting how they interact and communicate needs and feelings.

2. Extinguish Michael's bedwetting and develop prevention plan.
   a. Contract with Michael by stating that he must cease wetting the bed for 30 consecutive days before terminating therapy.
   b. Continue charting and tracking times Michael wets the bed to highlight improvement.
   c. Implement a contingency contract between Michael and his parents to sustain gains and improvement.
   d. Identify symptoms that would signal a return of Michael wetting his bed and devise a prevention plan.
   e. Consult with parents to identify which reinforcements are most likely to help maintain progress and improvements.

Vignette: Couple

Alexis and Chris have been married for 3 years and initiated counseling to address lack of sexual intimacy in the relationship. Chris and Alexis report that, in the beginning of their relationship, they had an active sex life, having intercourse at least five times a week. However, for the last 3 months, "things have changed." Chris and Alexis state that they have not been sexually intimate for 2 months and that they would like to increase frequency.

Cognitive-Behavioral Treatment Plan for Couple

Early-Phase Goals

1. Maintain a sense of respect for Chris and Alexis while establishing a therapeutic relationship.
   a. Model communication, such as reflecting what was heard and asking questions.
   b. Positively reinforce desired couple interaction and interest in sex and intimacy.

2. Identify problem and obtain a baseline of individual and couple functioning, highlighting baseline for sexual and relational functioning.
   a. Ask Chris and Alexis to behaviorally and measurably define sexual relationship and dysfunction.
   b. Use functional analysis to identify the antecedents, consequences, and contexts of the sexual dysfunction, exploring sexual history, levels of intimacy, and relationships.
   c. Observe individual and couple behavior and interaction in session to assess relational issues related to the dysfunctional sexual relationship.
   d. Identify the current family schema, listening for dysfunctional communication and interactional qualities contributing to dysfunctional sexual relationship.
   e. Develop a therapeutic contract to identify specific goals, roles, and responsibilities.

Middle-Phase Goals

1. Decrease sexual dysfunction in the relationship while increasing sexual intimacy.
   a. Use psychoeducation to provide couple with information on sexual physiology and techniques.
   b. Explore and dispute irrational beliefs Chris and Alexis hold related to sexuality that sustain their inability to be sexually intimate.
   c. Explore family schema, negative attributions, and related assumptions that support lack of intimacy.
   d. Negotiate good-faith contingency contract to increase the frequency of sexual intimacy.
   e. Use sex therapy techniques, such as sensate focus, to address sexual dysfunction.
   f. Have Alexis and Chris track and report changes in the sexual relationship.

Late-Phase Goals

1. Address remaining couple issues and improve communication patterns.
   a. Use psychoeducation to address relationship and communication issues, as well as the connection between irrational beliefs, dysfunctional rules/schema, and so on, that may be contributing to the sexual dysfunction.
   b. Identify ways schema needs to change or has changed; identify irrational beliefs that sustained problem behaviors.
   c. Renegotiate relational contract between intimate partners, including specific behaviors.

2. Extinguish sexual dysfunctions and maintain a satisfying level of sexual intimacy.
   a. Contract with Chris and Alexis by agreeing on a specific length of time that their sexual relationship is satisfying before terminating therapy.
   b. Chart the couple's sexual relationship to track improvements.
   c. Continue to use good-faith contingency contracting to help sustain gains.
   d. Identify symptoms that would signal a return of lack of intimacy and develop a plan of how to address.

Vignette: Family

Eddie initiated counseling for his 17-year-old daughter Roxanne, his 15-year-old son Robert, and his 12-year-old son Derek. Eddie states that, since his wife's death (6 months ago), Roxanne has been leaving without telling him and Robert has been talking back to him. Eddie states that the family received grief-counseling services immediately following the death; however, he terminated services after 3 months.

Cognitive-Behavioral Treatment Plan for Family

Early-Phase Goals

1. Maintain respect for family members and establish a therapeutic relationship.
   a. Model appropriate communication.
   b. Compliment effective communication between family members.
   c. Begin process of shaping desired behaviors in Roxanne and Robert by positively reinforcing times when they appropriately communicate with father.

2. Identify reported problems with Roxanne and Robert and obtain a baseline of individual and family functioning.
   a. Discuss the problem behavior and inappropriate communication to behaviorally and measurably define Roxanne's and Robert's problem behaviors.
   b. Ask Roxanne and Robert to track baseline functioning by using a daily chart to monitor their problem behaviors; involve Derek by gaining his perspective on siblings' behaviors.
   c. Observe Roxanne's and Robert's behavior and family interaction in session to assess communication difficulties; observe Derek's and Eddie's roles in the family and how they communicate.
   d. Identify the current family schema, listening for dysfunctional qualities and unresolved grief issues that may be contributing to Roxanne's and Robert's communication problems.
   e. Develop a therapeutic contract that specifies goals and therapist/family roles and responsibilities.

Middle-Phase Goals

1. Decrease Roxanne's leaving without informing father while increasing appropriate communication.
   a. Shape desired behavior by identifying specific positive and negative reinforcements for Roxanne communicating needs and whereabouts with father; educate Eddie about the importance of consistent reinforcement.
   b. Initiate token system, rewarding and punishing Roxanne's ability/inability to communicate with father.
   c. Dispute Eddie's and Roxanne's irrational beliefs associated with their roles and communication that sustain Roxanne's lack of communication with father.

   d. Explore negative attributions and related assumptions that support problem behavior, highlighting grief and loss issues.
   e. Negotiate good-faith contingency contract between Roxanne and father to increase the frequency of desired communication.
   f. Have Roxanne chart the frequency of appropriate/inappropriate communication between sessions.
   g. Involve Eddie and Roxanne in identifying a consistent, appropriate reinforcement schedule for appropriate communication.
   h. Use psychoeducation to provide Eddie and Roxanne with educational information about how unresolved grief and loss issues, death of mother, and changes in parenting influence disruption in the family.

2. Decrease Robert's "talking back" to father and increase appropriate communication.
   a. Shape Robert's not talking back to father by identifying specific positive and negative reinforcements for appropriate communication; educate father about the importance of consistent reinforcement.
   b. Initiate token system, rewarding and punishing talking back.
   c. Dispute Robert's and Eddie's irrational beliefs associated with parenting, changes in roles, and developmental changes that sustain Robert's talking back.
   d. Explore family schema, negative attributions, and related assumptions that support Robert's talking back to father.
   e. Negotiate quid pro quo contingency contract between father and Robert to increase the frequency of appropriate communication.
   f. Have Robert chart the frequency of inappropriate and appropriate communication between sessions.
   g. Consult with Eddie and Robert to identify an appropriate reinforcement schedule for appropriate communication.
   h. Identify times and strategies for using time outs when Robert talks back to father.
   i. Use psychoeducation to provide client with educational information about contributing factors and developmental issues that support inappropriate communication.

Late-Phase Goals

1. Reduce grief related to mother's death and facilitate adjustment to single-parent family.
   a. Use psychoeducation to address relationship, grief and loss, communication, and single-parenting issues.
   b. Encourage family to attend a grief/loss support group; encourage Eddie to attend a support group for loss of spouse and single-parent group.
   c. Identify ways family schema needs to change or has changed; identify children's irrational beliefs related to loss of mother that sustained Roxanne's and Robert's problem behaviors.
   d. Encourage father to model appropriate communication with children.

e. Renegotiate relational contract between father and children, addressing how they will communicate needs, feelings, grief, and thoughts.
f. Have family clarify rules for behaviors and the corresponding privileges and consequences for following and breaking rules.

2. Extinguish Roxanne's and Robert's problem behaviors and maintain a satisfying level of communication.
   a. Discuss extinction of problem behaviors with family and contract for a specific length of time that symptoms must be under control before terminating therapy.
   b. Have entire family use charting to track changes and improvements in communication.
   c. Refer Robert and Roxanne to psychoeducation or support groups to support appropriate communication.
   d. Use contingency contracting between family members to maintain appropriate communication patterns.
   e. Identify symptoms that would signal a return of inappropriate communication patterns and devise plan to address.
   f. Identify which reinforcements have been effective and which will maintain changes.

Suggested Readings

Bandura, A. (1969). *Principles of behavior modification.* New York: Holt, Rinehart, & Winston.

Baucom, D. H., & Epstein, N. (1990). *Cognitive-behavioral marital therapy.* New York: Brunner/Mazel.

Beck, A. T. (1976). *Cognitive therapy and the emotional disorders.* New York: International Universities Press.

Craighead, L. W., Craighead, W. E., Kazdin, A. E., & Mahoney, M. J. (1994). *Cognitive and behavioral intervention: An empirical approach to mental health problems.* Deedham, MA: Allyn and Bacon.

Ellis, A. (1962). *Reason and emotion in psychotherapy.* New York: Lyle Stuart.

Falloon, I. R. H. (Ed.). (1988). *Handbook of behavioral family therapy.* New York: Guilford Press.

Falloon, I. R. H. (1991). Behavioral family therapy. In A. S. Gurman and D. P. Kniskern (Eds.), *Handbook of family therapy,* volume 2 (pp. 65–95). Philadelphia, PA: Brunner/Mazel.

Holtzworth-Munroe, A., & Jacobson, N. S. (1991). Behavioral marital therapy. In A. S. Gurman and D. P. Kniskern (Eds.), *Handbook of family therapy,* volume 2 (pp. 96–133). Philadelphia, PA: Brunner/Mazel.

Lazarus, A. A. (1968). Behavior therapy and group marriage counseling. *Journal of the American Society of Medicine and Dentistry, 15,* 49–56.

Lazarus, A. A. (1971). *Behavior therapy and beyond.* New York: McGraw-Hill.

LoPiccolo, J., & LoPiccolo, L. (1978). *Handbook of sex therapy.* New York: Plenum.

Mason, M. J. (1991). Family therapy as the emerging context for sex therapy, in A. S. Gurman and D. P. Kniskern (Eds.), *Handbook of family therapy,* volume 2 (pp. 479–507). Philadelphia, PA: Brunner/Mazel.

Pavlov, I. P. (1932). Neuroses in man and animals. *Journal of the American Medical Association, 99,* 1012–1013.

Reincke, M., Dattilio, F. M., & Freeman, A. (1996). *Casebook of cognitive-behavior therapy with children and adolescents.* New York: Guilford Press.

Wolpe, J. (1969). *The practice of behavior therapy.* New York: Pergamon Press.

Solution-focused therapy "focuses on people's competence rather than their deficits, their strengths rather than their weaknesses, their possibilities rather than their limitations" (O'Hanlon & Weiner-Davis, 1989, p. 1).

10 CHAPTER SOLUTION-FOCUSED THERAPY

KEY THEORISTS

Kim Insoo Berg
Steve de Shazer
Patricia Hudson
Eve Lipchik
Scott Miller
William O'Hanlon
Jane Peller
Michelle Weiner-Davis
John Walter

HISTORICAL OVERVIEW

Steve de Shazer (1985, 1988, 1994) and his colleagues at the Brief Family Therapy Center in Milwaukee developed solution-focused therapy, which evolved from their initial work with the MRI problem-focused approach. They have applied these ideas to "numerous clinical issues, including" substance abuse (Berg & Miller, 1992), domestic violence (Lipchik & Kubicki, 1996), and divorce (Weiner-Davis, 1992). Bill O'Hanlon (O'Hanlon & Martin, 1992), who trained with Milton Erickson, has also been a prominent proponent of solution-oriented therapy and, more recently, possibility therapy. Walter and Peller (1992), located in Chicago, also have written and present on applications of solution-focused therapy. Solution-focused therapy grew out of the systemic therapy tradition but has evolved more postmodern approach to therapy.

KEY CONCEPTS

Solution and Future Focus

Unlike most other forms of therapy, solution-focused therapy posits that one does not need to understand the problem to resolve it and that the solution may not be directly related to the problem. In fact, de Shazer (1988) states, "the [idea of a] solution always comes before the problem" (p. 6). Therefore, the therapist does not need to explore and understand the past and only needs minimal information about the present to resolve client concerns. Instead, a solution-focused therapist's primary interests are existing and possible solutions and future possibilities.

Strengths and Resources

Solution-focused therapists highlight and focus on the client's existing strengths and resources. Strengths and resources are believed to be present in every individual. The therapist helps clients identify their strengths and adapts these to resolve the clients' current difficulties.

Beginner's Mind

Beginner's mind refers to a Zen saying: " 'In the beginner's mind there are many possibilities; in the expert's mind there are few' " (O'Hanlon & Weiner-Davis, 1989, p. 8). The concept refers to the therapists' stance, which ensures that they are able to conceptualize a client and a client's situation without interference from preconceived ideas and beliefs. This mindset allows the therapist to assist the client in reaching solutions consistent with the client's worldview rather than the therapist's preconceived theory or ideas. In addition, a beginner's mind assists in attaining an understanding of the clients' perceptions, while providing the therapist with the ability to learn and identify the most appropriate way "to work with them [clients] and how to help solve their dilemmas" (p. 8).

Change Is Constant

In the solution-focused approach, change is viewed as a process that is inevitable and constant (de Shazer, 1985). Solution-focused therapists assume that clients' situations are always in flux but that these changes often go unnoticed by clients and therapists (O'Hanlon & Weiner-Davis, 1989). Therefore, the solution-focused therapist is curious about times when changes occur and attempts to identify circumstances and behaviors that encourage the desired change.

Language and Meaning

Solution-focused therapists closely attend to language and meaning. The language people use shapes their reality and assists in establishing the meaning of situations, relationships, others, and self. The meanings people assign to a situation may limit the range of alternative solutions to a problem, which is of particular interest to solution-focused therapists. Every individual constructs his or her own meaning based on previous experiences, beliefs, family of origin, and worldview (de Shazer, 1988; O'Hanlon & Weiner-Davis, 1989). As such, when the therapist and client interact, there is a "co-creation of realities"; therefore, differing perspectives and meanings must be negotiated and defined. The therapeutic process is essentially the negotiation of meaning between therapist and client with the intent to increase possibilities and solutions to problems.

Hope

"Hope is the expectation of good" (Miller, Duncan, & Hubble, 1996, p. 218). In therapy, *hope* generally refers to the belief that the presenting difficulty will improve. In the solution-focused approach, therapists are sensitive to and aware of the importance of hope in the therapy process and continuously and collaboratively ensure that clients have a sense of hope. Furthermore, recent research indicates that hope may play a significant role in the successful attainment of desired outcomes (Miller et al., 1996).

GOALS OF THERAPY

Solution Focus

In the solution-focused approach, a shift occurs from the traditional problem focus on the individual's history and/or problem situation to a focus on solutions and future possibilities. This shift involves a focus on identifying and taking steps toward the individual's or family's preferred solutions to the current difficulties.

Goals and Goal Setting

Goals are central in a solution-focused approach. In this approach, the client defines goals and the therapist ensures that they are concrete and attainable. Initially, the goals are small to ensure that the client will gain a sense of confidence and accomplishment early in the therapy process.

Solution-focused therapy goals identify specific preferred behaviors and interactions, such as a couple increasing the number of times each partner demonstrates concern for the other. More than any other family approach, solution-focused therapy emphasizes "setting up ways to measure goals achievement" (de Shazer, 1988, p. 93). Solution-focused goals should be specific and attainable. In addition, goals should include concrete descriptions about *how* one will know when the problem is solved: what specifically will be different. Therapy may be terminated when clients feel that the goals have been reached or when clients believe that they are sufficiently "on track" and no longer need the assistance of the therapist (Walter & Peller, 1994).

STRUCTURE OF THERAPY

de Shazer (1988) describes the process of therapy as occurring within a "central map," which identifies "what we do rather than prescribe[s] what should be done" (p. 84).

First Session

During the first session, the therapist joins with the client/family with "nonjudgmental interest" (O'Hanlon & Weiner-Davis, 1989). This process assists in creating a sense of comfort and safety and in establishing rapport. The initial session continues by addressing the client's complaint, while giving compliments for present and/or past strengths and resources.

In the first session and initial phases of therapy, three processes are highlighted:

1. First, the problem is defined in the clients' or family's language and interpreted from their perspective. The therapist assesses for the possibility of unexplored solutions and meanings.
2. Second, exceptions are identified and highlighted, while clients and their situation is normalized (de Shazer, 1988; O'Hanlon & Weiner-Davis, 1989). If exceptions are apparent, therapy continues by exploring these exceptions and their deliberate or spontaneous nature (de Shazer, 1988).
3. From this point, exceptions are highlighted and goals are established. However, if exceptions are not apparent, a hypothetical solution is constructed and compared to the presenting problem (de Shazer, 1988). This leads to the next road on de Shazer's "central map": the goal-setting stage.

Setting Goals

In the goal-setting stage, the client and therapist attempt to identify *how* the problem will be solved and *how* they will know when the problem has been alleviated (de Shazer, 1988). This stage involves the exploration of exceptions and identifies small changes that will contribute to the elimination of the problem issue and the realization of the preferred solutions, which are defined in terms that are concrete and attainable (de Shazer, 1988).

Subsequent Sessions

de Shazer (1988) depicts the second and subsequent sessions as following the first session "map." The process continues with the therapist inquiring about positive patterns. If positive patterns have occurred, the client is encouraged to "do more of the same" (de Shazer, 1988, p. 86). If no apparent changes or positive patterns have occurred, the presenting problem is "redesigned" or "deconstructed" and the therapist explores the client's situation in great detail (p. 86). The solution-focused therapist *deconstructs* the problem by inquiring about and questioning the "logic of the behavior, thoughts, feelings, and perceptions within the client's frame" (p. 114). This process challenges the client's meaning and assists in identifying, creating, and negotiating solutions, as well as present strengths and resources. This line of inquiry is followed by monitoring exceptions, strengths, and positive alterations.

Throughout the process of therapy, the therapist is complimenting, inquiring about, and highlighting strengths and resources. Therapeutic techniques, such as the formula first session task, are applied in the first session, as are the miracle and crystal ball questions. Scaling questions and exception questions are applied throughout the therapeutic process to monitor and identify solutions, strengths, and progress.

ASSESSMENT

"The assessment process is influenced by the therapist's metaphors and assumptions with regard to people and the nature of problems and by the theory of resolution he or she holds" (O'Hanlon & Weiner-Davis, 1989, p. 54). The assessment process involves (a) identifying client motivation for therapy, (b) acknowledging the problematic issues as solvable, (c) identifying what has worked, (d) exploring exceptions, and (e) highlighting strengths and resources.

Motivation

While several levels and degrees of motivation exist, de Shazer (1988) identified three types of clients, including (a) the "visitor," (b) the "complainant," and (c) the "customer" (p. 87), that highlight his/her view toward the therapeutic process.

- " 'Visitors' must have somebody to visit with, 'complainants' somebody to complain to, and 'customers' somebody from which to buy" (p. 87). The "visitor" enters therapy without an identified complaint or problem issue. The visiting client may initiate counseling at the request of others and may be "resistant" or noncompliant.
- The "complainant" client identifies a complaint and/or problem issue. The therapeutic relationship with the "complainant" client is "one in which the client has developed some expectation of solution[s]" (p. 88).
- The "customer" is similar to the "complainant" in that each identifies a complaint; however, the "customer" will utilize behavioral tasks, while the "complainant" will utilize "observational or thinking tasks" (p. 89). The "customer" is highly cooperative and willing to change disruptive patterns.

Assessing for client motivation and perspective of therapy will assist the therapeutic process and knowing how to proceed.

Solvable Problems

Problems are discussed in terms of solutions. Detailed descriptions of behavioral patterns and exceptions to those patterns are used to assess the situation. Information gathered from this descriptive process is used to identify a solution.

As part of the therapeutic process, the client's perception of the problem is challenged and renegotiated in terms of a solution. The therapist's attempt to attain a "new outlook. . . . dissolves the idea that there is a 'problem' " (O'Hanlon & Weiner-Davis, 1989, p. 57). Through this process, the problem is increasingly perceived as manageable and solvable.

What Worked

The therapist uses information about attempted solutions that have worked in the recent and distant past to develop treatment goals and strategies. The process of gathering information about what has worked is associated with the assessment of exceptions to the problem. By identifying what has worked, the therapist identifies current solutions, addresses the client's strengths, and begins to establish goals.

Exceptions

Identifying exceptions involves answering the question, *When is the problem not a problem?* In the assessment process, the therapist focuses on past and present exceptions to identify the client's strengths and resources, which may be helpful in reaching solutions. The assessment process involves the identification of when the problem was not a problem or was less of a problem (de Shazer, 1988; O'Hanlon & Weiner-Davis, 1989). This process assists in identifying past solutions, strengths, and possible goals.

Strengths and Resources

The solution-focused therapist assesses for strengths in all aspects of the client's life to identify resources that may be helpful in the current situation. Often, clients do not make a connection between strengths and abilities they have in one area and the problem at hand (O'Hanlon & Weiner-Davis, 1989). Therefore, the therapist assists the client in identifying strengths and resources that may assist in addressing the presenting issue. Furthermore, the assessment of strengths and resources assists in identifying exceptions and goals while providing the opportunity for complimenting the client on what has worked.

TECHNIQUES

Formula First Session Task

During the first session, the therapist reorients the individual or family to notice the unacknowledged positive aspects of the situation, which is often accomplished through the *formula first session task.* It is a technique that provides the client with the opportunity to notice times when the problem was not a problem, as well as identify present strengths. de Shazer (1985) presented the task as follows: "Between now and next time we meet, we would like you to observe, so that you can describe to us next time, what happens in your family that you want to continue to have happen" (p. 137). This technique assists in goal setting while highlighting strengths, resources, and what has worked.

The Miracle Question and the Crystal Ball Technique

The *miracle question* and the *crystal ball technique* are used for assessment, goal setting, and intervention. Clients are asked to behaviorally describe what their lives would look like without the problem. This technique is an assessment tool used to specifically inquire about what the solution may "look like" while addressing the client's expectations and goals (de Shazer, 1985, 1988).

The miracle question, established by de Shazer (1988), is as follows: "Suppose that one night, while you were asleep, there was a miracle and this problem was solved. How would you know? How will your husband know without saying a word to him about it?" (p. 5).

The crystal ball technique was originated by Milton Erickson and creates a "pseudo-orientation to time" (de Shazer, 1985, 1988; O'Hanlon & Weiner-Davis, 1989). In this process, the client is oriented to a hypnotic state and asked to envision a scenario in the future that involves him or her telling the therapist how he or she "resolved" the problem. As in the miracle question technique, the crystal ball technique is used to inquire about the client's future without the problematic issue. In addition, these techniques can be extended to include the use of a magic wand or spell and applied with the appropriateness of the client. The techniques are often adapted for use with children by including the use of drawings, puppets, and other play media to represent the preferred future scenario.

Exception Questions

When clients describe a problem, they typically describe the problem as *always* happening, occurring, and being present. In applying exception questions, therapists alter totalizing language and intervene to assist clients in identifying exceptions. Exception questions are questions that allow the client to search for times in the past and present when the problem was/is not apparent (de Shazer, 1988; O'Hanlon & Weiner-Davis, 1989). Exceptions reveal past solutions that have worked and identify the client's strengths.

These questions include: "When is the problem not a problem or when was it not as much of a problem?" "What do you do that is different during these times?" Exception questions provide the client with the opportunity to identify solutions that have worked and are working, thus creating possibilities and solutions for change.

Compliments

Compliments are a technique that provides the therapist with the opportunity to highlight the clients' progress, strengths, and resources. Compliments "highlight positive trends" (O'Hanlon & Weiner-Davis, 1989, p. 104). The technique of using compliments allows the "therapist to reflect back to clients what they have already done to begin to solve the problem" (p. 105). Furthermore, de Shazer (1988) notes that the use of compliments assists in the process of establishing a therapeutic relationship.

Scaling Questions

Solution-focused therapists use a 10-point scale to measure incremental change. *Scaling questions* can be used to set goals from week to week and to measure progress. For example: "On a scale from 1 to 10 with 1 being the most depressed you've ever been, where are you today? What will it take to go from the 3 you are today to a 4 during this next week?" When presenting scaling questions, "clients are asked to rate, on a one-to-ten scale, their situations prior to coming for therapy" (O'Hanlon & Weiner-Davis, 1989, p. 150). The process continues by asking clients to rate their last week and where on the scale they would have to be to feel "satisfied." O'Hanlon and Weiner-Davis (1989) note that this process of questioning allows clients to realize that things do not have to be a ten for them to be okay or to feel satisfied. Furthermore, the use of scaling questions and ratings can be applied to the treatment and assessment process by inquiring if clients have ever experienced or reported a particular rating, and/or what will have to happen or what will be different if the rating is incrementally increased.

"On Track"

The notion of being "*on track*" is "a technique for opening new meaning where clients are stuck in thinking of their goal as an endpoint or in some either/or fashion" (Walter & Peller, 1994, p. 112). Remaining "on track" involves establishing goals (a) stated in positive terms, (b) reflecting process form, (c) framed in the present and in the "here and now," (d) that are specific, (e) within the client's ability to accomplish, and (f) in the client's language (p. 113). "On track" provides the therapist and client with the opportunity to terminate services with the client's perception that he/she has the ability to reach or maintain the solution without the assistance of the therapist.

Eliciting Strengths and Resources

"Everyone has some resources, such as skills, capabilities, talents, interests, admirable character traits, and so forth, that can be utilized in solving the problem" (Furman & Ahola, 1994, p. 49). Identifying individual strengths and resources can assist in providing exceptions, possibilities, and solutions to the problem issue.

Inspiring Solutions and Solution Building

Furman and Ahola (1994) identify one of the most difficult initial tasks as generating solutions to the problem issue(s). Some questions that can be asked follow:

- If you were to do something different the next time the problem presents itself, what might you do?
- If we could invent a solution to the problem, what would it be?
- How do you think people in other geographical areas, possibly with limited access to therapy, would solve the problem?
- One possible solution may be . . . . What would happen if you tried it?
- There was once someone who tried . . . .
- What additional possible solutions do you think may be helpful to you? (p. 54–55)

These and similar questions keep the therapeutic conversation solution-oriented and assist in the process of solution building (Berg & De Jong, 1996; Hoyt, 1996). "When a discussion is solution-oriented, the atmosphere tends to inspire the creation of solutions" (Hoyt, 1996, p. 53).

SOLUTION-FOCUSED TREATMENT PLANS

The following general treatment plan identifies possible goals and interventions for each stage of therapy that could be used in treating individuals, couples, and families. Not all goals and techniques are applicable to all clients.

General Solution-Focused Treatment Plan

Early-Phase Goals

1. Develop a supportive working relationship with client.

Possible Interventions

a. Maintain a beginner's mind to assist in providing information about problem issues and to ensure understanding of client meanings.
b. Allow clients to tell the problem story, while listening for and highlighting examples of strengths, resources, and exceptions spontaneously offered by client.

2. Begin process of identifying (a) exceptions, (b) possibilities, (c) previous solutions, and (d) strengths and resources.

Possible Interventions

a. Offer formula first session task to identify what is working.
b. Discuss problem issues in terms of solutions.
c. Identify strengths and resources from all areas of life.
d. Ask about previous solutions.
e. Ask about exceptions (times when the problem was not a problem) that have worked.
f. Ask about existing strengths and resources.

3. Identify and create concrete, attainable goals stated in positive terms.

Possible Interventions

a. Present miracle question or crystal ball technique to identify goals. Ask clients to provide specific details about preferred solutions.
b. Present scaling question to determine status of current situation and to identify small steps toward goals.
c. Ask about times already experiencing solution.

Middle-Phase Goals

1. Take steps toward specific goal(s) that addresses specific solution (one goal for each major issue).

Possible Interventions

a. Identify specific outcome in terms of what solutions would look like.
b. Use scaling questions to identify small steps to be taken between sessions that will move client closer to goal; often given as "homework" assignments.

c. Monitor exceptions to the problem issues and times when the problem was not a problem; identify ways to do more of those behaviors.
d. Compliment progress and solutions.
e. Scale changes from week to week.
f. Identify existing resources and mobilize to address concerns.

Late-Phase Goals

1. Highlight progress and attainment of goals.

Possible Interventions

a. Compliment achievements.
b. Readdress and identify strengths and resources.
c. Scale present functioning and compare to initial scaling process and identify what has worked and how to keep "on track" with changes.

2. Create a plan to prevent or address possible future problems using the resources and strengths clients have developed while in therapy.

Possible Interventions

a. Focus on future-oriented talk and highlight use of solutions in future.
b. Readdress strengths and resources.
c. Use scaling questions to highlight progress and changes.
d. Develop a plan to address possible setbacks and staying "on track."

Vignette: Individual

Pamona is a 24-year-old, Native American female. She is a post baccalaureate student living alone and states that she has felt very "sad" and "lonely" since her significant other ended their intimate, 2-year relationship. Pamona reports that several months ago she was unfaithful to her significant other and states that she does not understand why she was unfaithful and deceptive about the affair. Pamona reports feeling very confused, "lost," and uncertain about how to go on.

Practice Solution-Focused Treatment Plan for Individual

Early-Phase Goals

1.
   a.
   b.

2.
   a.
   b.

Middle-Phase Goals

1.
   a.
   b.

2.
   a.
   b.

Late-Phase Goals

1.
   a.
   b.

2.
   a.
   b.

Vignette: Couple

Reynaldo, a Cuban American male, and Sue, a European American woman, are a married couple in their mid-thirties. They have no children; however, they report that they would like to have children in the near future. Reynaldo and Sue initiated counseling due to their inability to resolve conflict in the relationship. Reynaldo and Sue report that when a conflict arises Sue withdraws because Reynaldo will "explode" and become loud and "verbally abusive." Reynaldo states that he has displayed this type of "irrational" behavior since childhood and that his parents would often ignore his outbursts. Sue reports that the yelling and verbal abuse have to stop before they have children.

Practice Solution-Focused Treatment Plan for Couple

Early-Phase Goals

1.
    a.
    b.

2.
    a.
    b.

Middle-Phase Goals

1.
    a.
    b.

2.
    a.
    b.

Late-Phase Goals

1.
    a.
    b.

2.
    a.
    b.

Vignette: Family

Matthew requested an appointment for therapy, and stated that the reason was that his "kids are upset that their mother has been arrested for drugs again." Matthew reported that his 12-year-old son Jesse has a problem with his anger and there is a lack of communication between them. Matthew reported that his 10-year-old daughter Lindsay is always getting into trouble and is doing poorly in school. Matthew reported that both children have been held back 1 year in school; he stated that he is worried that they will be held back again if things do not improve. Matthew reported that Lindsay was evaluated by a physician and was diagnosed with AD/HD and was prescribed medication. Matthew stated that the medication was helpful and that Lindsay improved academically. However, Matthew stated that mother, Kiara, took Lindsay off the medication because she did not like her daughter taking drugs.

Practice Solution-Focused Treatment Plan for Family

Early-Phase Goals

1.
    a.
    b.

2.
    a.
    b.

Middle-Phase Goals

1.
    a.
    b.

2.
    a.
    b.

Late-Phase Goals

1.
    a.
    b.

2.
    a.
    b.

Vignette: Individual

Pamona is a 24-year-old, Native American female. She is a post-baccalaureate student living alone and states that she has felt very "sad" and "lonely" since her significant other ended their intimate, 2-year relationship. Pamona reports that several months ago she was unfaithful to her significant other and states that she does not understand why she was unfaithful and deceptive about the affair. Pamona reports feelings very confused, "lost," and uncertain about how to go on.

Solution-Focused Treatment Plan for Individual

Early-Phase Goals

1. Establish and maintain a supportive relationship with Pamona.
   a. Maintain a beginner's mind to assist in gaining information about Pamona's symptoms and problem issue while striving to understand client's meaning, as well as exploring her Native American heritage.
   b. Allow Pamona to tell problem story while listening for and highlighting Pamona's examples of strength, resources, and exceptions to reported sadness and loneliness.

2. Begin process of identifying exceptions, possibilities, and previous solutions to current complaints and the termination of the relationship.
   a. Offer formula first session task to identify what is working in her life.
   b. Discuss termination of relationship and reported symptoms in terms of solutions.
   c. Identify Pamona's strengths and resources in every aspect of her life and connect to cultural strengths and resources.
   d. Ask about times Pamona is not feeling sad, alone, and guilty.

3. Identify and create concrete, attainable goals stated in positive terms.
   a. Present miracle question or crystal ball technique to determine Pamona's goals.
   b. Ask about times when Pamona is already experiencing the identified solution.
   c. Present scaling question to determine status of Pamona's current situation and to identify small steps toward goals.

Middle-Phase Goals

1. Increase times that Pamona feels contentment and happiness.
   a. Identify Pamona's specific outcome in terms of what a solution would look like.
   b. Use scaling questions to identify small steps to be taken between sessions that will move Pamona closer to diminishing symptoms. Ask Pamona to scale her sadness/loneliness symptoms daily, one being the saddest she's ever felt and ten representing no signs of sadness.

   c. Monitor exceptions to the problem issues and times when the sadness and loneliness are absent and/or not a problem. Direct Pamona to engage in behavior that reflects the times when the symptoms are not a problem.
   d. Compliment progress and solutions.
   e. Scale feelings weekly and identify tasks each week to incrementally enact preferred solution.
   f. Identify existing resources/strengths that have helped and encourage to do more.

2. Focus on existing, satisfying relationships and identify her strengths that allow her to maintain these relationships and past relationships.
   a. Identify what positive relationships look like/have looked like/will look like.
   b. Use scaling questions to identify small steps to be taken between sessions that will move Pamona closer to creating more satisfying relationships.
   c. Monitor and identify exceptions to Pamona not being able to move on and times when it was not a problem.
   d. Compliment Pamona's progress and establishment of solutions.
   e. Scale Pamona's progress and changes.

Late-Phase Goals

1. Increase positive emotions and rebuild future while identifying her strengths in relationships with others.
   a. Compliment Pamona on identifying and implementing solutions to assist in diminishing symptoms and moving past her stated loss issues.
   b. Readdress and identify Pamona's strengths and resources, including cultural resources.
   c. Scale present functioning and compare initial scaling progress, while identifying what has worked and how to keep "on track" with changes.

2. Create a plan identifying Pamona's strengths, resources, and solutions to apply with future problem issues.
   a. Focus on future-oriented talk and highlight use of solutions in future.
   b. Compliment while reidentifying strengths and resources.
   c. Identify possible warning signs of setbacks and ways to stay "on track."

Vignette: Couple

Reynaldo, a Cuban American male, and Sue, a European American woman, are a married couple in their mid-thirties. They have no children; however, they report that they would like to have children in the near future. Reynaldo and Sue initiated counseling due to their inability to resolve conflict in the relationship. Reynaldo and Sue report that when a conflict arises Sue withdraws because Reynaldo will "explode" and become loud and "verbally abusive." Reynaldo states that he has displayed this type of "irrational" behavior since childhood and that his parents would often ignore his outbursts. Sue reports that the yelling and verbal abuse have to stop before they have children.

Solution-Focused Treatment Plan for Couple

Early-Phase Goals

1. Develop and maintain a supportive relationship with Sue and Reynaldo.
   a. Maintain a beginner's mind to assist in understanding each client's perspective on Reynaldo's outbursts and other couple issues, while exploring and remaining sensitive to couple's perspective and cultural influences.
   b. Allow Sue and Reynaldo to share their versions of the problem story, while listening for and highlighting strengths, resources, and exceptions.

2. Begin process of identifying exceptions, possibilities, and possible solutions to Reynaldo's outbursts/Sue's withdrawal and the couple's ability to resolve conflict.
   a. Offer formula first session task to identify what is working in the relationship.
   b. Discuss the communication issue as something that is solvable and in terms of solutions.
   c. Identify Sue's and Reynaldo's strengths and resources as individuals and as a couple.
   d. Inquire about why couple wants to stay together, what attracted them initially to each other, and their hopes for the future.
   e. Ask about times when they do not have the problem.

3. Identify and create concrete, attainable goals stated in positive terms.
   a. Present miracle question or crystal ball technique to identify couple's goals. Ensure that desired behavior of each partner is addressed and described.
   b. Present scaling question to determine current status and identify small steps toward goals.

Middle-Phase Goals

1. Highlight cultural differences/similarities and increase number of respectful communication exchanges between Sue and Reynaldo that allow each to feel heard.

a. Identify specific outcome in terms of what the solutions to outbursts/withdrawal would look like, including new behaviors for Reynaldo and Sue.
b. Use scaling questions to identify small steps to be taken by Sue and Reynaldo between sessions that will move them closer to maintaining open, healthy communication by directing them to scale improvements in communication (one being no positive changes in communication and ten representing the desired communication interaction).
c. Monitor exceptions to Reynaldo's outbursts/Sue's withdrawal and times when the outbursts were not a problem.
d. Compliment couple on progress and identified solutions.
e. Scale changes experienced and observed by Sue and Reynaldo.

2. Help couple learn to resolve conflict without episodes of angry explosions or withdrawal.
   a. Identify specific outcomes in terms of what the solutions to improved conflict resolution would look like.
   b. Use scaling questions to identify small steps to be taken between sessions that will move Sue and Reynaldo closer to improvements in conflict resolution. Direct Sue and Reynaldo to individually scale communication and conflict resolution daily.
   c. Monitor exceptions when Reynaldo and Sue have been able to resolve conflict successfully and identify factors that led to the successful outcome.
   d. Compliment progress and solutions.
   e. Scale changes in conflict-resolution skills.

Late-Phase Goals

1. Increase couple's readiness for parenting and children.
   a. Allow Reynaldo and Sue to talk about readiness for parenting and children while listening for strengths and resources.
   b. Scale the couple's readiness to parent and take steps to get "on track."
   c. Compliment existing strengths and resources and identify additional strengths and resources.

2. Highlight progress and attainment of goals and develop a plan for anticipated challenges, identifying Sue's and Reynaldo's strengths, resources, and solutions.
   a. Compliment on progress, change, and achievement in communication and conflict-resolution skills and Reynaldo's diminished verbal outbursts.
   b. Scale present functioning and compare to initial scaling process; identify what would indicate that they are getting off track.
   c. Identify what has worked and how to keep "on track" with changes.
   d. Focus on future-oriented talk and highlight use of solutions in future.
   e. Identify best strategies for staying "on track."

Vignette: Family

Matthew requested an appointment for therapy, and he stated that the reason was that his "kids are upset that their mother has been arrested for drugs again." Matthew reported that his 12-year-old son Jesse has a problem with his anger and there is a lack of communication between them. Matthew reported that his 10-year-old daughter Lindsay is always getting into trouble and is doing poorly in school. Matthew reported that both children have been held back 1 year in school; he stated that he is worried that they will be held back again if things do not improve. Matthew reported that Lindsay was evaluated by a physician and was diagnosed with AD/HD and was prescribed medication. Matthew stated that the medication was helpful and that Lindsay improved academically. However, Matthew stated that the mother, Kiara, took Lindsay off the medication because she did not like her daughter taking drugs.

Solution-Focused Treatment Plan for Family

Early-Phase Goals

1. Create and maintain a supportive working relationship with family.
   a. Maintain a beginner's mind to assist in gaining information about problem issue to ensure that the family's meaning is heard and understood.
   b. Allow each member to tell the problem story while listening for and highlighting the family's examples of each member's strengths, resources, and exceptions.

2. Begin process of identifying exceptions, possibilities, and previous solutions to the children's adjusting to their mother being arrested for drugs again.
   a. Offer formula first session task to identify what Matthew, Jesse, and Lindsay would like to continue to have happen that is currently working.
   b. Discuss disruptive behaviors in terms of possibilities and solutions.
   c. Identify individual and family strengths and resources from all areas of each member's life.

3. Identify and create concrete, attainable goals stated in positive terms.
   a. Present miracle question or crystal ball technique to identify goals; use drawings to help children identify their miracle and goals.
   b. Present scaling question to determine status of current situation and to identify small steps toward goals; may use drawings to help children scale.

Middle-Phase Goals

1. Decrease Jesse's anger while increasing mutually satisfying exchanges between him and other family members.
   a. Identify specific outcomes in terms of what Jesse's improved ability to manage anger and communicate would look like; may use role play or drawing to facilitate.

   b. Use scaling questions to identify small steps to be taken between sessions that will move Jesse toward diminishing anger and improving communication by directing him to scale anger and communication daily (one being very angry and ten being no presence of anger).
   c. Monitor exceptions to Jesse's anger and times when the anger and poor communication were not a problem and direct family to do more of this.
   d. Compliment Jesse on his progress and identified solutions.
   e. Scale Jesse's changes and progress weekly.

2. Increase the number of positive relationships Lindsay has at school and improve her school performance.
   a. Identify specific outcome in terms of what the solutions to improvements in Lindsay's behavior would look like; may draw or role-play.
   b. Use scaling questions to identify small steps to be taken between sessions that will move Lindsay toward improving behavior by directing her to scale behavior daily (one being highly disruptive behavior and ten being improved behavior).
   c. Monitor exceptions to Lindsay's behavior and times when her behavior was not a problem.
   d. Compliment Lindsay on her progress and identified solutions.
   e. Scale changes week to week to monitor what works.
   f. Consider reevaluation for medication since this had worked before.

Late-Phase Goals

1. Increase cohesion between the family members while mother, Kiara, is not present in the home by improving communication and increasing frequency of positive interactions.
   a. Discuss each family member's reaction to mother's situation. Discuss their hopes for the future.
   b. Identify specific outcome in terms of what the solutions to increasing cohesion, communication, and positive interactions would look like.
   c. Use scaling questions to identify small steps to be taken between sessions that will move family toward a sense of cohesion by directing each member to scale changes in the family daily (one representing current level of distance and ten being close, cohesive family).
   d. Monitor exceptions to current lack of cohesion and communication and times when the lack of cohesion and inappropriate communication were not a problem.
   e. Compliment family on progress and identified solutions.
   f. Scale the family's changes and progress.

2. Facilitate adjustment to mother not being present and address their reactions to her substance abuse.
   a. Allow each member to discuss the problem story and his/her reactions to mother's substance abuse while listening for and highlighting strengths and resources.

   b. Ask about exception times when mother not being present is less of a problem, perhaps in terms of what they are learning without her there.
   c. Identify family strengths and resources.

3. Highlight progress and attainment of goals and discuss strategies for handling future challenges or setbacks.
   a. Compliment progress and each member's achievements.
   b. Identify individual and family strengths and resources.
   c. Scale present functioning and compare to initial scaling process; identify what would indicate a setback.
   d. Identify what has worked and how to keep "on track" with changes.
   e. Focus on future-oriented talk and highlight use of solutions in future.

Suggested Readings

Berg, I. K., & De Jong, P. (1996). Solution-building conversations: Co-constructing a sense of competence with clients. *Families in Society,* 77(6), 376–391.

Berg, I. K., & Miller, S. (1992). *Working with the problem drinker: A solution-focused approach.* New York: Norton.

De Jong, P., & Berg, I. K. (2000). *Interviewing for solutions* (2nd ed.). New York: Brooks/Cole.

de Shazer, S. (1985). *Keys to solution in brief therapy.* New York: Norton.

de Shazer, S. (1988). *Clues: Investigating solutions in brief therapy.* New York: Norton.

de Shazer, S. (1994). *Words were originally magic.* New York: Norton.

de Shazer, S., & Kral, R. (Eds.), (1986). *Indirect approaches in therapy.* Rockville, MD. Aspen Systems.

Furman, B., & Ahola, T. (1994). Solution talk: The solution-oriented way of talking about problems. In M. F. Hoyt (Ed.), *Constructive therapies 1.* New York: Guilford Press.

Hoyt, M. F. (1996). Solution building and language games: A conversation with Steve de Shazer. In M. F. Hoyt (Ed.), *Constructive therapies, Vol. 2.* New York: Guilford Press.

Lipchik, E., & Kubicki, A. (1996). Solution-focused domestic violence views: Bridges toward a new reality in couples therapy. In S. Miller, B. Duncan & M. Hubble, (Eds.), *Handbook of solution-focused brief therapy.* San Francisco: Jossey-Bass.

Miller, S. D., Duncan, B. L., & Hubble, M. A. (1997). *Escape from Babel: Towards a unifying language for psychotherapy practice.* New York: Norton

Miller, S. D., Duncan, B. L., & Hubble, M. (Eds.), (1996). *Handbook of solution-focused brief therapy.* San Francisco, CA: Jossey-Bass.

O'Hanlon, W. H., & Martin, M. (1992). *Solution-oriented hypnosis: An Ericksonian approach.* New York: Norton.

O'Hanlon, W. H., & Weiner-Davis, M. (1989). *In search of solutions: A new direction in psychotherapy.* New York: Norton.

Walter, J. L., & Peller, J. E. (1992). *Becoming solution-focused in brief therapy.* New York: Brunner/Mazel.

Walter, J. L., & Peller, J. E. (1994). "On track" in solution-focused brief therapy. In M. F. Hoyt (Ed.), *Constructive therapies I,* (pp 111–125). New York: Guilford Press.

Weiner-Davis, M. (1992). *Divorce busting.* New York: Summit Books.

"The narrative therapist draws from her own patient and thoughtful persistence to help the client rediscover the remnants of favored experience in his life" (Monk, 1997, pp. 3–4).

NARRATIVE THERAPY

CHAPTER 11

KEY THEORISTS

Gene Combs
Vicki Dickerson
Robert Doan
David Epston
Jill Freedman
Stephen Madigan
Gerald Monk
Alan Parry
Michael White
John Winslade
Jeff Zimmerman

HISTORICAL OVERVIEW

Michael White, an Australian, and David Epston, a New Zealander, first articulated narrative therapy theory in their book *Narrative Means to Therapeutic Ends* in 1990. Their unique approach introduced the work of philosopher Michel Foucault to psychotherapy and is one of the most prominent postmodern approaches to therapy. Over the past decade, narrative therapy has rapidly grown in popularity around the world, and numerous therapists have expanded on these ideas, including Freedman and Combs (1996) in Illinois, Parry and Doan (1994) in Canada, Winslade and Monk (1999, 2000) in New Zealand, and Zimmerman and Dickerson (1994) in California. Narrative therapists vary in the emphasis they place on Foucault's sociopolitical analysis versus other postmodern and social-constructionist theories, but they generally share a commitment to addressing sociopolitical issues in therapy and to employing the narrative metaphor in their work.

KEY CONCEPTS

The Textual and Narrative Metaphors

Narrative therapy is distinguished by its reliance on the *textual* (White & Epston, 1990) or *narrative* (Freedman & Combs, 1996) *metaphor.* Narrative therapists use the narrative metaphor to describe the primary tool people use to make sense of their lived experiences: stories. People make sense of life experiences by storying their experiences in sequences across time. These stories provide meaning, allowing a person to "make sense" of their experience. Furthermore, from a narrative perspective, events do not have inherent meaning outside these narratives. The characteristics of the narrative (i.e., tragic or heroic are determined by what is and is not included in a person's life narrative. "Persons are rich in lived experience . . . [but] only a fraction of this experience can be storied and expressed at any one time" (White & Epston, 1990, p. 15). Therefore, there are multiple ways to story one's life. Society provides dominant narratives that provide readily available "templates" for storying and interpreting a person's everyday lived experiences, such as what it means to be a "mother," a "construction worker," or "successful." However, when a person's lived experience differs from these social narratives, one experiences a "problem." Narrative therapists use the resources available in a person's unnoticed and unstoried events to address the problems brought to therapy.

Unique Outcomes

"Unique outcomes are experiences that would not be predicted by the plot of the problem-saturated narrative" (Freedman & Combs, 1996, p. 67). Therapists look for unique outcomes in problem-saturated narratives to create narratives that reflect local knowledges, alternative possibilities, and more hopeful accounts of the client's lived experience. Grounded in social-constructionist theory, the narrative therapist maintains that unique outcomes can always be found. For example, often parents will bring a "problem" child into therapy reporting that the child "never" listens, yet it is usually quite easy to find numerous events in the family life that do not fit with this problem-saturated description of the child's behavior, such as following rules in public, listening to grandparents, or cooperating to get some ice cream.

Dominant and Subjugated (Local) Knowledges

The distinction between dominant and subjugated knowledges is drawn from Michel Foucault's work on power/knowledge, which Foucault views as inseparable (White & Epston, 1990). Foucault asserts that society's "normalizing truths" and "unitary knowledges" have power in the sense that they are the norms around which people construct their lives. *Dominant knowledge* is shaped by those in power in a given culture and prescribes "the good" thereby implying how one should live. However, in any society, there are many accounts of the good; those that do not fit with the dominant accounts are generally denied voice and are therefore referred to as *subjugated knowledges.* Narrative therapy often serves to "resurrect" subjugated knowledges that fit more closely with an individual's lived experience when the dominant knowledges do not adequately account for the person's lived reality. For example, a client may come to therapy with the sense that she is a "failure" in intimate relationships based on the societal interpretation of divorce as "bad" and a sign of weakness. In this situation, the narrative therapist would explore local and subjugated knowledges that may view divorce as a healthy and logical decision in the face of a loveless or abusive relationship and will consider the implications of these alternative knowledges in her personal life narrative.

Language

Consistent with social-constructionist theory, narrative therapists maintain that reality is constructed and given meaning through language. "Our understandings of our lived experience, including those that we refer to as 'self-understandings,' are mediated through language" (White & Epston, 1990, pp. 27–28). Therefore, language is not viewed as a neutral activity; it shapes reality and has many political consequences.

Politics

More than any other approach, narrative therapists closely attend to sociopolitical issues in therapy and avoid practices that subjugate others or capitalize on the therapist's power. This attentiveness to politics includes awareness that the therapist's descriptions, including diagnoses, impact how clients and those around them construct their identities and experience problems. Therefore, narrative therapists attend closely to social issues such as culture, gender, race, disability, social class, social status, sexual orientation, religion, and other marginalizing practices.

The Problem Is the Problem

If narrative therapy were to have a motto, it would most likely be: "The person is not the problem. The problem is the problem." This statement reveals the therapist's basic assumption that people are separate from their problems and that no single description can fully capture a person's identity or life history.

Therapist Positioning

The positioning of the therapist has been described as both a co-editor (Parry & Doan, 1994) and co-author (Freedman & Combs, 1996; Monk, Winslade, Crocket, & Epston, 1997). These descriptions attempt to capture the importance of positioning oneself in such a way as to make room for the voices of clients and to remain mindful of sociopolitical issues that can subtly direct the process (Monk et al., 1997). Therefore, most narrative therapists emphasize that the success of the approach is not in the creative techniques but rather in the positioning of the therapist. Without proper positioning, which requires a sincere commitment to the philosophical underpinnings of the theory, the techniques can be viewed as manipulative or simply word games.

GOALS OF THERAPY

Enacting Preferred Narratives

In narrative therapy, the most common goal is to alter the problem-saturated story to reflect a preferred narrative (Freedman & Combs, 1996; White & Epston, 1990). The preferred or alternative narrative is defined by the client rather than the therapist. Often this goal involves helping clients to "thicken the plot" around alternative accounts of their identity and relational narratives.

STRUCTURE OF THERAPY

Freedman and Combs (1996) identify a format for story development as an "ideal shape for a therapy conversation" (p. 101). However, they note that therapy rarely goes as planned and that, often, unexpected changes arise that warrant new directions. Their prescribed format follows:

- Begin with a unique outcome. "It is only necessary that one unique outcome be identified in order to facilitate performance of new meaning" (White & Epston, 1990, p. 55).
- Make sure the unique outcome represents a preferred experience.
- Plot the story (of the unique outcome) in the landscape of action: "How did you do that?"
- Plot the story in the landscape of consciousness: "What does this act say about you as a person? What does this say about your life goals?"
- Ask about a past experience that has something in common with the unique outcome or its meaning. Plot this second story in the landscape of action and consciousness.
- Ask questions that link the past episode with the present.
- Ask questions to extend the story into the future.

ASSESSMENT

Knowing the Person Apart from the Problem

Narrative therapists take time to ask about who the person is when he or she is not having the problem. This questioning helps facilitate the externalization process, "a practice supported by the belief that a problem is something operating or impacting on or pervading a person's life, something separate and different from the person" (Freedman & Combs, 1996, p. 47). Knowing the person apart from the problem also helps identify strengths and resources that would otherwise not be explored. Finally, this process expands the client's sense of self to include a sense of competence: "As persons become separated from their stories, they are able to experience a sense of personal agency; as they break from their performance of their stories, they experience a capacity to intervene in their own lives and relationships" (White & Epston, 1990, p. 16).

Unique Outcomes

Therapists assess for unique outcomes to the problem-saturated narrative, which are times when the problem is not a problem. Unique outcomes can be from the past, present, future, or imagination. Historical unique outcomes are "identified through a historical review of the person's influence in relation to the problem" (White & Epston, 1990, p. 56). Current unique outcomes "present themselves in the course of the session" (p. 59). Future unique outcomes are anticipated to occur in the future. Imagination can be utilized in identifying possible unique outcomes by imagining "what sort of response might constitute a unique and unexpected outcome" (p. 61).

Mapping Effects

When learning more about a client's situation, narrative therapists generally inquire about the effects of problems and persons. As described later in more detail in the section on relative-influence questioning, narrative therapists are curious about the effects problems have had on clients and about how clients have affected the life of the problem.

TECHNIQUES

Deconstructive Listening

Deconstructive listening refers to a type of listening that opens up space for new meaning and understandings. "The meaning a listener makes is, more often than not, different from the meaning that the speaker has intended. We seek to capitalize on this by looking for gaps in our understanding and asking people to fill in the details. . . . Many of the gaps we notice haven't yet been filled in; people must search their experience to find the details" (Freedman & Combs, 1996, p. 47).

Deconstructive Questions

"Deconstructive questions help people unpack their stories or see them from different perspectives, so that how they have been constructive becomes apparent" (Freedman & Combs, 1996, p. 120). These questions often encourage clients to situate their narratives in broader contexts, such as personal background, social history, or family traditions, and then allow them to identify the influence of these on their current life narrative.

Externalization of the Problem

Externalization involves linguistically separating the problem from the person and often entails personifying the problem, for example "The Temper" or "Anorexia" (White & Epston, 1990). Externalizing the problem involves (a) defining the problem to be externalized and (b) utilizing externalizing questions (White & Epston, 1990).

Defining the Problem to Be Externalized Problems are externalized in the client's language and develop from conversation. The problem definition is "fluid and evolves through time" (White & Epston, 1990, p. 49). This occurs through "deconstructive listening," where the therapist does not go along with taken-for-granted realities and practices but is open to new meanings.

Externalizing Questions These questions turn the adjectives people typically use to describe themselves into nouns; this linguistic shift leads to problems being viewed as objects external to the person (Freedman & Combs, 1996). As exemplified in Table 11.1, externalizing questions that refer to the problem as a noun imply greater agency on the part of the person than traditionally informed questions that refer to the problem as an adjective, implying that the problem is descriptive of the person.

Relative-Influence Questioning

Relative-influence questioning assists the person in externalizing the problem (White & Epston, 1990). This process involves (a) mapping the influence of the problem and (b) mapping the influence of the person.

Mapping the Influence of the Problem This questioning involves broadening the description of the problem, including identifying the problem's influence on "behavioral, emotional, physical, interactional, and attitudinal domains" (White & Epston, 1990, p. 42). "Once details of the effects of the problem have been established, it becomes easier for persons to specify their own influence in relation to the problem" (p. 56). For example, a family may be asked not about the child and the reported tantrums but also about how the tantrums have affected each person's emotional life, social life, professional life, spirituality, health, external relationships, identities, and overall attitude. In many ways, the effects of the problem are expanded.

Mapping the Influence of Persons This questioning facilitates the discovery of "unique outcomes" and new information that contradicts the problem-saturated

TABLE 11.1 | COMPARING EXTERNALIZING QUESTIONS TO TRADITIONALLY INFORMED QUESTIONS

Externalizing Questions: Problem as Noun (e.g., Depression)	Traditionally Informed Questions: Problem as Adjective (e.g., Depressed)
What made you vulnerable to Depression so that it was able to dominate your life?	How did you become depressed?
In what contexts is Depression most likely to take over?	What are you most depressed about?
What types of things happen that typically lead to Depression taking over?	What kinds of things happen that typically lead to your being depressed?
What has Depression gotten you to do that is against your better judgment?	When you are depressed, what do you do that you wouldn't do if you weren't depressed?
Does Depression blind you from noticing your resources or can you see them through it?	How is your self-image different when you are depressed?
Have there been times when you have been able to get the best of Depression? Times when Depression could have taken over but you kept it out of the picture?	If by some miracle you woke up some morning and you were not depressed anymore, how, specifically, would your life be different?

Note: Information for this table is adapted from *Narrative Therapy: The Social Construction of Preferred Realities* (p. 49) by J. Freedman and G. Combs, 1996, New York: Norton.

narrative. To identify unique outcomes, the therapist inquires about times when involved persons were able to have an effect on the "life" of the problem or were able to change the typical problematic outcome. These unique outcomes can be historical, contextual, current, and/or imagined in the future. These are the "sparkling moments" that therapists can use to develop an alternative narrative (Freedman & Combs, 1996). In the previous example, the family would be asked about times they did not give in to the tantrum, perhaps for the son not having a tantrum when he could have, and for the parents not allowing the tantrums to affect their attitude, social life, or identity as "good" parents.

Plotting Narratives in the Landscapes of Action and Consciousness

Based on the work of Jerome Bruner, Freedman and Combs (1996) propose mapping preferred and alternative narratives in the dual landscapes of "action" and "consciousness." These narratives are usually built around an identified unique outcome that the client would like to have continued.

Landscape of Action The therapist inquires about the specific actions that constitute the preferred narrative: Who was involved? What did each person do? In what sequence? These questions also highlight the agency of persons involved.

Landscape of Consciousness After obtaining a rich description of the preferred narrative's events, the therapist inquires about the *meaning* the person attributes to these events, which can include the implications, motivations, values, desires, and intentions. These questions often provide the foundation for alternative accounts of personhood and relationships. For example, if a client identifies a time when he or she did not give into depression by choosing to accept an invitation to go to dinner, the therapist can explore what this says about the client as person, what this might mean for the potential for a social life, and so on.

Preference and Permission Questions

To ensure that they are not pushing their ideas on the client, narrative therapists periodically ask questions to ensure that a unique outcome or line of discussion is consistent with the client's preferred reality: "Is this something you would like to have happen more often?" (Freedman & Combs, 1996; Monk et al., 1997). In addition, therapists may also ask for permission to pursue a line of questioning or discussion of a certain topic: "Would it be okay if I ask a little more about the events that lead up to the Trouble your mother reported?"

Exploring Specifications for Personhood

To a greater or lesser extent, each culture specifies and outlines certain forms of personhood, which can be based on gender, ethnicity, social class, profession, family relations, social role, age, religion, political affiliation, sexual orientation, values, or beliefs. People tend to use these specifications to define their "selfdom" (Parry & Doan, 1994). Although these may be helpful at times, these specifications are often experienced as narrow and limiting. In this situation, narrative therapists inquire about the outside influences that have shaped the client's identity, detailing the various sources, their history, and their effects in the client's life. For example, many clients find that the specifications for being a "real" man or woman limit the behaviors they see available in their relationships. Exploring their ideas about what a real man or woman should do or not do unveils assumptions and attitudes that may be creating unnecessary challenges in a person's life.

Situating Comments

Narrative therapists "situate" themselves as a way to publicly identify their own experiences and intentions that guide and affect their work, acknowledging shortcomings and inherent limitations as human beings (Freedman & Combs, 1996). Situating comments can help clients understand where the therapist is coming from and help to deconstruct the "expertise" of the therapist, inviting the client to attend to his or her own voice. For example, when working with a couple, the therapist could "situate" herself as a heterosexual woman who may be more likely to understand the woman's perspective and misunderstand that of the husband. Such practices make public the political undercurrents of heterosexual relationships and open a space for such issues to be freely discussed in therapy.

Letters and Certificates

Letters and certificates are used to document new narratives. "In storied therapy, the letters are used primarily for the purpose of rendering lived experience into a narrative or 'story,' one that makes sense according to the criteria of coherence and lifelikeness" (White & Epston, 1990, p. 125); certificates are "documents that celebrate the new story" (p. 192). Letters can be mailed weekly to clients and used as case notes to document the emerging narrative or can be used periodically to highlight significant shifts. Certificates are typically used to acknowledge accomplishments toward the end of therapy.

Audience/Witnesses

"If people constitute their preferred selves by performing their preferred stories, then it is important that there be audiences for those stories" (Freedman & Combs, 1996, p. 237). Therefore, therapists may have clients invite significant people in their lives to witness their new narrative by writing a letter, inviting them to a session, or involving them in outside rituals or conversations. "As preferred stories are circulated and shared in a subculture, *all* the participants in that subculture construct each other according to the values, beliefs, and ideas carried in that subculture's preferred stories" (p. 237). An audience can also be created with a reflecting team that shares its observations in front of the client.

NARRATIVE TREATMENT PLANS

The following general treatment plan identifies possible goals and interventions for each stage of therapy that could be used in treating individuals, couples, and families. Not all goals and techniques are applicable to all clients.

General Narrative Treatment Plan

Early-Phase Goals

1. Create openings and space for client/family stories to be told/heard.

Possible Interventions

a. Provide an open, inviting space for the story to be told and verbalized.
b. Maintain the sense that the client is the "privileged author" of his/her story, while ensuring therapist's role as a "co-author."
c. Ask questions to learn about the person(s) apart from the problem.
d. Ask permission to pursue particular lines of questioning, particularly those that address sensitive issues.
e. Situate therapist in relation to client and/or client issue.

2. Facilitate telling of problem narrative while listening for unique outcomes.

Possible Interventions

a. Listen from a deconstructive stance to better understand how the client makes sense of his or her story, while opening up space for new accounts and descriptions.
b. Reflect back content of story to ensure understanding and clarify meanings: inquire about client interpretations and meanings.
c. Begin listening for openings and unique outcomes to problem-saturated story.
d. "Situate" therapist comments and perspective to avoid dominating or directing session.

3. Identify preferred and/or alternative narratives, which may or may not involve externalization.

Possible Interventions

a. Use externalization questions to separate the person from the Problem. Examples: What made you vulnerable to the Problem and allowed the Problem to dominate your life? In what contexts is the Problem most likely to take over? What types of things typically happen that lead to the Problem taking over?
b. Use relative influence questioning to (1) map the influence of the problem by identifying its effects on those involved and (2) map the influence of persons to identify times when they are able to avoid or outsmart the Problem, thereby opening space for externalization.

c. Begin to identify unique outcomes and times when the Problem was not a problem; inquire to ensure this is a preferred experience.
d. Begin plotting preferred narrative in the landscapes of action and consciousness.
e. Use narrative letters to document emerging alternative accounts.
f. Identify the effects of sociopolitical issues or beliefs that may have strengthened the problem-saturated narrative (e.g., "assertive women are rude").

Middle-Phase Goals

1. Help clients develop a new relationship with the externalized Problem in which the person has a sense of agency and does not feel dominated by the Problem.

Possible Interventions

a. Use externalizing language, referring to the Problem as a noun rather than adjective, to identify how the person interacts and responds to the Problem.
b. Employ relative-influence questioning to assist in identifying times when the person is not dominated by the Problem but is able to "take a stand" against it.
c. Have clients identify what type of relationship they would prefer to have with the Problem; specify how this would look and what the clients would be doing differently.
d. Use unique outcomes and mapping of dual landscapes to develop descriptions of what actions clients can take to enact their preferred narratives.
e. Assess from week to week the client's progress in relating to the Problem and moving toward preferred outcomes.

2. Thicken the plots of alternative accounts around identified Problem.

Possible Interventions

a. Use deconstructive listening and questioning to continue to identify unique outcomes and ensure these are preferred experiences.
b. Plot the story, including the unique outcome, in the landscape of action and inquire how client(s) is able to function without the Problem; plot the story in the landscape of consciousness by inquiring about how client(s) can reflect on self and the future. Inquire about additional times when the unique outcome was apparent, and plot in landscape of action and consciousness.
c. Based on mapping of preferred narrative, identify specific actions that the client can take to move toward this reality. Inquire about progress from week to week.
d. Explore the effects of society's dominant discourse on the client's life and problem narratives.

e. Identify sources of specifications for personhood and explore their effects.
f. Invite reflecting teams to the session to generate alternative perspectives.
g. Use narrative letters to document newly emerging narrative or reflect on a particular session or event.
h. Explore possibilities for creating an audience to witness alternative narrative via letter writing, therapy sessions, or outside rituals.

Late-Phase Goals

1. Address any remaining issues, such as broader identity development and family narratives.

Possible Interventions

a. Explore new sources and/or interpretations of specified forms of personhood and how these will affect client (and Problem) in the future.
b. Identify the effects of these specifications of personhood on relationships.
c. Explore the effects of sociopolitical issues that may have strengthened the problem or may impinge on the preferred narrative in the future.
d. Specifically identify actions and corresponding meanings of the preferred narrative.
e. Identify what has been most helpful and least helpful in enacting the preferred narrative.

2. Solidify and explore potential of preferred narrative.

Possible Interventions

a. Ask questions that link the past story and unique outcome with the present.
b. Ask questions to extend the story into the future, including potential obstacles.
c. Invite reflecting team to reflect on clients' accomplishments and potential of new narrative.
d. Invite witnessing communities to experience, acknowledge, and become aware of newly enacted narrative.
e. Identify rituals and traditions that are relevant to the client and support preferred self-narrative.
f. Send client(s) a letter or certificate to document the new narrative.
g. Help client to create supportive input from chosen audience and other witnesses.

Vignette: Individual

Helen is a 72-year-old female who has been residing with her daughter and her son-in-law since an accident that left her with limited use of her legs. Helen reports being very active in the community before the accident; however, since the accident she reports being "stuck at home." Furthermore, she reports feeling "depressed" and "lonely."

Practice Narrative Treatment Plan for Individual

Early-Phase Goals

1.
   a.
   b.

2.
   a.
   b.

Middle-Phase Goals

1.
   a.
   b.

2.
   a.
   b.

Late-Phase Goals

1.
   a.
   b.

2.
   a.
   b.

Vignette: Couple

Corina, a 35-year-old female, and Veronica, a 37-year-old female, are a lesbian couple that has been in a committed relationship for 5 years. Corina is a recovering drug user and has not informed her family of her sexual orientation and current relationship. Veronica is a working professional who is open about her relationships. The couple initiated counseling to address the stress and tension in the relationship, reportedly resulting from Corina's inability to be open about their relationship. Furthermore, Veronica reports high levels of anxiety and Corina reports feeling very "depressed" and on the verge of relapsing.

Practice Narrative Treatment Plan for Couple

Early-Phase Goals

1.
    a.
    b.

2.
    a.
    b.

Middle-Phase Goals

1.
    a.
    b.

2.
    a.
    b.

Late-Phase Goals

1.
    a.
    b.

2.
    a.
    b.

Vignette: Family

A 6-year-old male, Peter, was referred to counseling by his teacher because he has recently been to the principal's office and suspended a number of times. The teacher complains that Peter is very disruptive in class, uses obscene language, fights with other students, and consistently talks out of turn. The parents, Scott and Norma, corroborate that their child shows similar behaviors at home and that he does not respond to punishment. The parents also report that their son seems unresolved in his grief over his baby sister's recent death.

Practice Narrative Treatment Plan for Family

Early-Phase Goals

1.
    a.
    b.

2.
    a.
    b.

Middle-Phase Goals

1.
    a.
    b.

2.
    a.
    b.

Late-Phase Goals

1.
    a.
    b.

2.
    a.
    b.

Vignette: Individual

Helen is a 72-year-old female who has been residing with her daughter and her son-in-law since an accident that left her with limited use of her legs. Helen reports being very active in the community before the accident; however, since the accident she reports being "stuck at home." Furthermore, she reports feeling "depressed" and "lonely."

Narrative Treatment Plan for Individual

Early-Phase Goals

1. Create openings and space for Helen's story to be told/heard.
   a. Provide an open, inviting space for Helen's story to be told and verbalized.
   b. Maintain a sense that Helen is the "privileged author" of her story, while ensuring therapist's role as a "co-author."
   c. Ask about Helen's life before the accident, listening for strengths, interests, and a sense of identity apart from the accident.
   d. Ask questions to clarify meaning and ensure understanding of Helen's perspectives.
   e. Situate therapist in relation to client age, disability, culture, and so on.
   f. Begin listening for openings and unique outcomes in Helen's problem-saturated story.

2. Obtain a rich description of Helen's life and identity since the accident, after which Depression and Loneliness have been dominant; then identify possible alternative and preferred accounts of her life and identity.
   a. Begin the externalization process by inquiring about when Helen is not taken over by the Depression and Loneliness.
   b. Inquire about who she was before the accident. Obtain rich account of what she did and how she viewed herself.
   c. Use relative-influence questioning to map the influence of the Depression and Loneliness in her life and relationships. Then map the influence of Helen to identify times when she resisted the Depression and Loneliness, thereby further opening space for externalization.
   d. Begin externalizing Depression by presenting externalizing questions such as, What made you vulnerable to the Depression and Loneliness and allowed them to dominate your life? In what contexts are the Depression and Loneliness most likely to take over? And what types of things typically happen that lead to the Depression and Loneliness taking over?
   e. Begin to identify unique outcomes—times when the Depression and Loneliness were not a problem, while ensuring these are preferred experiences.

Middle-Phase Goals

1. Reduce the effects/influence of Depression and Loneliness in Helen's life by encouraging a proactive stance.
   a. Use externalization language and questions to separate Helen from Depression and Loneliness and help her to see how she interacts with each of them.
   b. Map the effects of Depression and Loneliness on the client and have her map how she has affected the lives of Depression and Loneliness. Identify specific strategies that have helped her to be in charge of them.
   c. Check in weekly about her progress in "taking a stand against" or "outsmarting" Depression and Loneliness.
   d. Use letter writing to document her progress and respond to setbacks regarding Depression and Loneliness.

2. Thicken plot of Helen's "active" identity (or other preferred account of her life), focusing on new possibilities she may not have considered since the accident. Work with Helen to identify ways to move toward enacting her preferred account of herself and her life.
   a. Identify a time since the accident (or before) when she felt she was living an "active" life. Plot this unique outcome in the landscape of action and inquire how Helen was able to do this; plot the story in the landscape of consciousness by inquiring about the meaning this incident holds for her and her future.
   b. Each week identify small steps Helen has taken to enact her active or preferred life narrative.
   c. Inquire about how the accident may have changed her view of herself, especially in relation to specifications for people who are "elderly," "crippled," or "disabled." Has she interpreted the accident to mean she is now "elderly" or "closer to death"?
   d. Introduce and invite reflecting teams to expand Helen's view of her situation.
   e. Use narrative letters to document emerging narrative in session.
   f. Invite audience to witness the emerging alternative narrative, possibly Helen's daughter and son-in-law.

Late-Phase Goals

1. Restory personal identity to make sense of age and loss of motion in a way that creates a greater sense of autonomy & "living."
   a. Invite family members and/or friends in to witness new account and discuss implications for the family and her social life.
   b. Have Helen link prior life history and the accident with present and future accounts.
   c. Ask Helen questions to extend her new narrative into the future.
   d. Explore new interpretations of specifications of "elderly" or "disabled" personhood, perhaps with the help of her family.

  e. Invite a reflecting team to generate new perspectives on her situation.
  f. Identify significant rituals, activities, and traditions that support Helen's preferred self-narrative, such as involvement in community services.

2. Identify strategies for sustaining an "active life" or otherwise defined preferred narrative.
   a. Send Helen a letter or "Certificate of Youthfulness" to document changes she has made.
   b. Help her to identify how to create and maintain support from family and friends.
   c. Have her list out the most successful strategies for fighting off Depression and Loneliness.
   d. Have her identify the actions that are most closely associated with living an "active life" and specify how she can continue with these.

Vignette: Couple

Corina, a 35-year-old female, and Veronica, a 37-year-old female, are a lesbian couple that has been in a committed relationship for 5 years. Corina is a recovering drug user and has not informed her family of her sexual orientation and current relationship. Veronica is a working professional who is open about her relationships. The couple initiated counseling to address the stress and tension in the relationship, reportedly resulting from Corina's inability to be open about their relationship. Furthermore, Veronica reports high levels of anxiety and Corina reports feeling very "depressed" and on the verge of relapsing.

Narrative Treatment Plan for Couple

Early-Phase Goals

1. Create openings and space for couple's stories to be told/heard.
   a. Provide an open, inviting space for Veronica and Corina's stories to be told and verbalized, allowing each space to be heard.
   b. Maintain a sense that Veronica and Corina are the "privileged authors" of their stories, while ensuring therapist's role as a "co-author."
   c. Ask permission to ask questions about the relationship.
   d. Situate therapist self in relation to sexual orientation, gender, substance abuse, and other relevant issues.
   e. Ask about Corina and Veronica's life without the Stress, Tension, and/or Depression, while listening for their strengths and sense of identity apart from the symptoms.
   f. Clarify meaning and ensure understanding.
   g. Begin listening for openings and unique outcomes to Veronica and Corina's problem-saturated stories.

2. Obtain a description of Corina and Veronica's problem narratives while listening for unique outcomes.
   a. Listen from a deconstructive stance to better understand how Corina and Veronica make sense of their stories, while opening up space for new accounts and descriptions.
   b. Explore the dominant discourse associated with their relationship and how it may play a role in the problem narrative. Explore sense of being marginalized as individuals and couple due to sexual orientation.
   c. Reflect content of their stories to ensure understanding and clarify meaning.
   d. Begin listening for openings and unique outcomes to problem-saturated stories. How have you kept self from relapsing or becoming more depressed?

3. Identify preferred and/or alternative narratives, while beginning to externalize the Stress and Tension in the relationship.
   a. Use externalization questions to separate Corina and Veronica from the Stress and Tension.
   b. Use relative influence questioning to (1) map the influence of the Stress and Tension by identifying its effects on those involved and (2) map the influence of persons to identify times when they are able to avoid or outsmart the Stress and Tension, thereby opening space for externalization.
   c. Begin to identify unique outcomes and times when the Stress and Tension were not problems; inquire to ensure this is a preferred experience.
   d. Begin plotting preferred narrative in the landscapes of action and consciousness.
   e. Use narrative letters to document emerging alternative accounts.
   f. Identify the effects of sociopolitical issues or beliefs associated with same-sex couples that have strengthened the problem-saturated narratives.

Middle-Phase Goals

1. Develop new relationships with Stress and Tension in which the couple has a sense of agency and does not feel dominated by Stress and Tension.
   a. Use externalizing language, referring to the Stress and Tension as nouns rather than adjectives.
   b. Continue to employ relative-influence and externalization questioning to assist in identifying times when the couple is not dominated by the Stress and Tension but is able to "take a stand" against Stress and Tension.
   c. Have the couple identify what type of relationship they would prefer to have with the Stress and Tension; specify how this would look and what Corina and Veronica would be doing differently.
   d. Use unique outcomes and mapping of dual landscapes to develop descriptions of what actions the couple can take to enact preferred narratives.
   e. Assess from week to week the couple progress in relating to the Stress and Tension and moving toward preferred outcomes.

2. Take steps toward increasing "openness" and communication in relationship and with families, including deciding on what type of action to take regarding "openness" with their families and others.
   a. Use deconstructive listening and questioning to continue to identify unique outcomes and ensure these are preferred experiences.
   b. Plot the emerging relational story, including the unique outcome, in the landscape of action plot the story in the landscape of consciousness by inquiring about how Corina and Veronica view themselves and the future of the relationship.

c. Based on mapping of preferred narrative, identify specific actions that the couple can take to move toward being more open/communicating better.
d. Explore subjugated knowledges that counter dominant discourses regarding same-sex relationships.
e. Invite reflecting teams to the session to generate alternative perspectives.
f. Explore possibilities for creating an audience to witness alternative narrative; may involve family and friends.

Late-Phase Goals

1. Enrich individual identity narratives by specifying new stance in relation to Depression and Anxiety and clarifying how they prefer to interact with society regarding their sexual orientation.
   a. Explore new sources and/or interpretations of specified forms of personhood and how these will affect Corina and Veronica.
   b. Identify the effects of these specifications of personhood on relationships.
   c. Identify effects of sociopolitical issues that may have strengthened the Depression and Anxiety or may impinge on the preferred narrative in the future.
   d. Identify what has been most helpful and least helpful in enacting preferred narrative on the alleviation of Depression and Anxiety.
   e. Monitor presence of Depression and Anxiety from week to week.

2. Explore ways to sustain "stress-free" identity and relationship narratives.
   a. Ask questions that link the past story and unique outcome with the present.
   b. Ask questions to extend the story into the future, including potential obstacles.
   c. Invite reflecting team to reflect on the couple's accomplishments and potential of new narrative.
   d. Identify rituals and traditions that are relevant to the couple and support preferred self-narrative.
   e. Send the couple a letter or certificate to document the new narrative.
   f. Help couple to create supportive input from chosen audience and other witnesses.

Vignette: Family

A 6-year-old male, Peter, was referred to counseling by his teacher because he has recently been to the principal's office and suspended a number of times. The teacher complains that he is very disruptive in class, uses obscene language, fights with other students, and consistently talks out of turn. The parents, Scott and Norma, corroborate that their child shows similar behaviors at home and that he does not respond to punishment. The parents also report that their son seems unresolved in his grief over his baby sister's recent death.

Narrative Treatment Plan for Family

Early-Phase Goals

1. Create openings and space for family's stories to be told/heard.
    a. Provide an open, inviting space for the story to be told and verbalized.
    b. Maintain a sense that the family is the "privileged author" of their story, while ensuring therapist's role as a "co-author."
    c. Ask questions to learn about Peter and the family apart from Peter's "disruptive behavior."
    d. Ask permission to ask questions about daughter/sister's death.
    e. Situate therapist self in relation to family.
    f. Begin listening for openings and unique outcomes to problem-saturated story.

2. Obtain a description of the disruptive behavior and problem narrative while listening for unique outcomes, including family life before the death of the sister.
    a. Listen from a deconstructive stance to better understand how family members make sense of their story.
    b. Reflect back content of story to ensure understanding and clarify meaning.
    c. Begin listening for openings and unique outcomes to problem-saturated story.
    d. Ensure that therapist comments and perspective avoid dominating or directing session.

3. Identify the family's preferred and/or alternative narratives, focusing on Peter's Bad Behavior and Loss.
    a. Use externalization questions to separate Peter from Bad Behavior. Examples: What made you vulnerable to Bad Behavior and allowed Bad Behavior to dominate your life? In what contexts is Bad Behavior most likely to take over? What types of things typically happen that lead to Bad Behavior taking over?

b. Use relative influence questioning to (1) map the influence of Bad Behavior by identifying its effects on those involved and (2) map the influence of persons to identify times when Peter is able to avoid or outsmart Bad Behavior.
c. Explore the effects of Bad Behavior at home and at school.
d. Begin to identify unique outcomes and times when Bad Behavior is not a problem; inquire to ensure that this is a preferred experience.
e. Begin plotting preferred narrative in the landscapes of action and consciousness.
f. Use narrative letters to document emerging alternative accounts.

Middle-Phase Goals

1. Help Peter and family develop a new relationship with Bad Behavior in which Peter has a sense of agency and does not feel dominated by Bad Behavior.
   a. Use externalizing language, referring to Bad Behavior as a noun rather than an adjective, to identify how Peter, Norma, and Scott interact and respond to Bad Behavior.
   b. Employ externalization questions to assist in identifying times when Peter and the family are not dominated by Bad Behavior and Peter is able to "take a stand" against Bad Behavior.
   c. Have Peter and family identify what type of relationship they would prefer to have with Bad Behavior; specify how this would look and what Peter would be doing differently.
   d. Use unique outcomes and mapping of dual landscapes to develop descriptions of what actions family can take to enact their preferred narratives.
   e. Assess from week to week Peter's progress in relating to Bad Behavior and moving toward preferred outcomes.

2. Thicken the plots of Cooperation and Friendliness at school and home.
   a. Use deconstructive listening and questioning to continue to identify unique outcomes and to ensure that these are preferred experiences.
   b. Plot preferred behaviors, in the landscape of action and consciousness.
   c. Based on mapping of preferred narrative, identify specific actions that Peter and family can take to move toward this reality. Inquire about progress from week to week.
   d. Explore the effects of society's dominant discourse on the family's life and problem narratives.
   e. Invite reflecting teams to the session to generate alternative perspectives.
   f. Use narrative letters to document newly emerging narrative or reflect on a particular session or event.

Late-Phase Goals

1. Renegotiate understanding/experience of sister/daughters's death so that her memory becomes a resource for Peter and family.
   a. Help Peter and family find preferred ways to interact with Grief using preferred outcomes.
   b. Explore new ways to define and describe their relationship with deceased sister, perhaps accessing spirituality and cultural traditions (e.g., as an angel, still part of family, etc.); explore possibility of wanting aspects of Grief around as a reminder of sister.
   c. Explore new sources and/or interpretations of specified forms of personhood and how these will affect Peter and family in the future. What does it mean to be parents who have lost a child? Identify the effects of these specifications of personhood on relationships.
   d. Identify actions and meanings of the preferred narrative.
   e. Identify what has been most helpful and least helpful in enacting preferred narrative.

2. Help couple "make sense" of loss and regain sense of hope.
   a. Share their individual and couple stories around the death, exploring themes of guilt, shame, and blame.
   b. Explore new sources and/or interpretations of specified forms of personhood (parents who lost child) and how these will affect the couple in the future.
   c. Explore the effects of sociopolitical issues that may have strengthened the couple issues or may impinge on the preferred narrative in the future.
   d. Specifically identify actions and corresponding meanings of the preferred narrative.
   e. Identify what has been most helpful and least helpful in enacting preferred narrative.

3. Solidify and explore new identity and family narratives and identify ways to meet future challenges.
   a. Ask questions that link the past story and unique outcome with the present.
   b. Ask questions to extend the story into the future, including potential obstacles.
   c. Invite reflecting team to reflect on the family's accomplishments and potential of new narrative.
   d. Identify rituals and traditions that are relevant to the family and support preferred narratives.
   e. Send the family a letter or certificate to document the new narrative.
   f. Help family to create supportive input from chosen audience and other witnesses.

Suggested Readings

Epston, D. (1994). Extending the conversation. *Family Therapy Networker, 18*(6), 30–37, 62–63.

Freedman, J., & Combs, G. (1996). *Narrative therapy: The social construction of preferred realities.* New York: Norton.

Freedman, J., & Combs, G. (1996). Gender stories. *Journal of Systemic Therapies,* 15(1), 31–44.

Gilligan, S., & Price, R. (Eds.). (1993). *Therapeutic conversations.* New York: Norton.

Monk, G. (1997). How narrative therapy works. In G. Monk, J. Winslade, K. Crocket, & D. Epston (Eds.), *Narrative therapy in practice: The archaeology of hope* (pp. 3–31). San Francisco, CA: Jossey-Bass.

Monk, G., Winslade, J., Crocket, K., & Epston, D. (Eds.). (1997). *Narrative therapy in practice: The archaeology of hope.* San Francisco, CA: Jossey-Bass.

Parry, A., & Doan, R. E. (1994). *Story re-visions: Narrative therapy in the postmodern world.* New York: Guilford Press.

White, M. (1988/9, Summer). The externalizing of the problem and the re-authoring of lives and relationships. *Dulwich Centre Newsletter,* 3–20.

White, M. (1991). Deconstruction and therapy. *Dulwich Centre Newsletter, 3,* 21–40.

White, M., & Epston, D. (1990). *Narrative means to therapeutic ends.* New York: Norton.

Winslade, J., & Monk, G. (1999). *Narrative counseling in schools: Powerful and brief.* Thousand Oaks, CA: Corwin/Sage.

Winslade, J., & Monk, G. (2000). *Narrative mediation: A new approach to conflict resolution.* San Francisco, CA: Jossey-Bass.

Zimmerman, J. L., & Dickerson, V. C. (1994). Using a narrative metaphor: Implications for theory and clinical practice. *Family Process, 33,* 233–246.

Zimmerman, J., & Dickerson, V. (1996). *If problems talked: Adventures in narrative therapy.* New York: Guilford Press.

"One of the most important features of life is conversation. We are in continuous conversation with each other and with ourselves. Through conversation we form and reform our life experiences; we create and recreate our meanings and understandings; and we construct and reconstruct our realities and ourselves" (Anderson, 1997, p. xvii).

12 CHAPTER COLLABORATIVE THERAPIES

KEY THEORISTS

Harlene Anderson
Tom Andersen
Harry Goolishian
Lynn Hoffman
Peggy Penn

HISTORICAL OVERVIEW

Several therapists have contributed to what is loosely referred to as the "collaborative therapies." The late Harry Goolishian, Harlene Anderson, and their colleagues at the Houston Galveston Institute have explored the implications of social-constructionist and postmodern ideas in therapy; their approach is most frequently known as *collaborative language systems.* In Norway, Tom Andersen, who trained with the Milan team early in his career, has explored the possibilities of postmodern reflecting practices, most notably the reflecting team. Lynn Hoffman, who has been closely associated with many family therapy theorists, has been a strong proponent of a collaborative approach to therapy in the past decade. Peggy Penn has explored the implications of these ideas using various forms of writing at the Ackerman Institute. Although each theorist maintains a distinct voice, these theorists share similar social-constructionist premises and practices, creating more points of connection than distinction.

KEY CONCEPTS

Human Systems as Language Systems

Human systems are *language-generating* and, simultaneously, *meaning-generating systems* (Anderson, 1997; Anderson & Goolishian, 1992). Through language, people give meaning to their experiences and thereby determine what is "good," "right," or otherwise in each social situation. Determinations of meaning occur between people in relationship, both at personal and societal levels. This shared meaning—rather than some external factor—forms the core of any social system.

Problem-Organizing, Problem-Dissolving Systems

A therapy system is a special form of language-generating system that organizes itself around the identification of a "problem." "Problems live and breathe in language" (Anderson, 1997, p. 82). Therefore, therapy systems can be viewed as problem-organizing, problem-dissolving systems (Anderson & Goolishian, 1992). This description of therapy systems implies the following:

"Problems" Problems are not experienced unless someone interprets a situation as "problematic." What one person sees as a problem, another person may view as "normal," "a phase," or something other than a problem that requires therapeutic intervention.

Problem Organizing Therapy systems are created (i.e., a person seeks a therapist) because a "problem" has been identified. Therapeutic systems therefore dialogically coalesce around an identified "problem." This type of system differs from predefined social structures, such as the family, and is therefore more fluid in its membership and life span.

Problem Dissolving Through dialogical conversation, clients and therapists co-create new meanings regarding the problem. Each new interpretation or description of the problem informs different actions and attitudes toward the problem. This ongoing process of reinterpretation leads to the problem no longer being experienced as a problem but rather as something that the client has learned to "manage," "handle," or "deal with." Rather than describing this as problem *solving* in a traditional sense, the problems are described as *dissolving* through this unique dialogical process. Problem dissolving also refers to the fact that the therapy system "dissolves" once talk about a "problem" ends.

Who Is Involved? Anyone who is talking about the "problem" should be invited into the conversation in some form. This may include family, friends, school personnel, medical doctors, and probation officers.

Shifting Membership "The therapy system is defined by those participating in it" (Anderson, 1997, p. 84). As the definition of the problem changes, so do the people who need to be in conversation.

Philosophical Stance: Postmodernism and Social Constructionism in Action

The therapist's primary "tool" is his or her philosophical stance. This stance is really a "way of being in relationship" (Anderson, 1997, p. 94). This stance reflects *postmodern* and *social-constructionist* assumptions about knowledge, language, people, and problems. These assumptions include:

- Rather than being "out there" waiting to be discovered, knowledge is created, negotiated, and transformed through language in human relationships.
- Language is not a mirror of reality but a medium for constructing our reality.
- "Reality" and "truth" are constructed through language in everyday human relationships and therefore are continually open to renegotiation.

Role of the Therapist

The role of the collaborative language systems therapist is that of a conversational artist whose expertise is in the area of creating space for and facilitating a dialogical conversation. The therapist is an expert on the therapeutic process rather than on the content of the client's life. The therapist's role has been described as a "conversational partner," which requires valuing what the client brings to the process (Anderson, 1997). As a facilitator of two-way dialogue, the therapist must be open to hear what the client is saying, strive to understand from the client's unique perspective, and avoid assuming that the client's interpretations are similar to his/her own. This openness requires openness at a personal level and a willing to question one's own beliefs. In therapeutic conversation, *both conversational partners are changed.*

Dialogical Conversation

Therapeutic conversation is described as *dialogical conversation,* conversation in which a mutual exchange of ideas and understandings takes place. This exchange of ideas allows for the generation of new meanings and ideas, which opens new possibilities for action and relating. This two-way exchange of ideas occurs between the therapist and the client, between two or more clients, and/or between clients and persons outside the session. The therapist's primary task in this approach is to facilitate meaning-generating, dialogical conversations.

Relational Identity

"A linguistic and dialogic view emphasizes this social nature of the self—as emerging in and embodied in relationships—and it emphasizes our capacity to create meaning through conversation" (Anderson, 1997, p. 224). The basic tenant here is that we cannot know ourselves without being in relation to another. Our identities are intimately bound to our understanding of ourselves in relationship to others. For example, taken-for-granted identities and descriptions are relationally bound either to a specific person or to others more generally. Identities, such as mother, son, therapist, manager, friendly, and beautiful, all imply a relationship of some form, if even a general comparison, with another. When in dialogue or two-way conversation, we are able to renegotiate our identities and these relationships.

Outer Talk and Inner Talk

Outer talk and *inner talk* are used to distinguish those conversations we have with others and those that we have with ourselves while in conversation with others (Andersen, 1991). Therefore, one can say that, really, three conversations are going on between two people in the therapy room: one outer conversation and an inner conversation in each person. Therapists must attend to and allow space for all three dialogues. It is precisely in the interplay between these inner and outer talks that new ideas and meanings are constructed and reconstructed.

Appropriately Unusual

Tom Andersen (1991) recommends that a therapist's comments be *appropriately unusual*. If a therapist's comments are too usual, there is no difference from which one can construct new meaning. If a therapist's comments are too "unusual," the client will not be able to engage the ideas in a way that promotes new perspectives. Therefore, therapists should strive to offer comments that are appropriately unusual, reflecting the familiar and the unfamiliar. Such comments are most likely to promote alternative perspectives and new meanings.

GOALS OF THERAPY

Transformation

Rather than attempting to "change" clients or family structure, collaborative therapists view themselves as promoting dialogues that are transformative. The transformational quality of therapeutic dialogue lies in its capacity to relate the events of our lives in the context of new and different meanings. Transformation is a shift in meaning that is usually characterized by "self-agency" or "sense of freedom" (Anderson, 1997, p. 109).

Client-Determined Goals

Goals for therapy are jointly determined with the client and are continually open to renegotiation and change over the course of therapy. As the problem is redefined, the goals may also change. If a treatment plan is required, the plan is jointly created and negotiated with the client's active involvement.

No Theory- or Therapist-Defined Goals

The collaborative approach does not propose or advocate any theory-defined or therapist-defined goals for clients. The therapist's role is one of facilitating a dialogic process. Therefore, it could be said that the *therapist's* goal is to create and sustain two-way dialogic conversations that promote the generation of new meanings and possibilities.

STRUCTURE OF THERAPY

"The structure of the therapy conversation is spontaneous, determined by moment-to-moment exchanges that zigzag and crisscross" (Anderson, 1997, p. 126). This spontaneous dialogical process involves six components:

1. The therapist initiates an internal dialogical space.
2. The therapist engages in an external dialogue with the client.
3. The client engages in an internal dialogue.
4. The clients engage in external dialogue with each other.
5. The client engages in internal and external dialogue outside therapy.
6. The therapist engages in internal and external dialogue outside therapy. (p. 128)

The therapy process then involves accessing all of these conversations in determining what needs to be discussed, with whom, and how. The therapy process is fluid and evolving based on the inner and outer dialogues of all involved.

ASSESSMENT

Problem-Organizing System

This approach does not support a standardized or formal assessment procedure. However, therapists are generally curious about how all persons in the language systems view the problem and therefore seek to involve all persons talking about the problem in the therapy system. Therefore, friends, "unofficial" family members, school personnel, probation officers, and others discussing the problem are contacted and, if possible, invited to participate in discussions about the problem.

Client's Worldview

Rather than assessing clients using the therapist's predefined categories and theories, collaborative therapists "assess" the situation by trying to obtain a rich and detailed description of how all people talking about the problem understand the problem situation. How do the different people involved believe the problem began? How does each person describe or name the problem? How does each person describe his or her role and the roles of others in the situation? What does each think the best course of action may be? Questions such as these, which should follow from the therapist's curiosity about a particular client's story rather than from a predefined assessment "script," are the therapist's primary means of making sense of (or assessing) where the client is. This "assessment" process is simultaneously a transformative process in which the client and therapist both begin to explore new understandings of the problem situation.

TECHNIQUES

The therapist's primary concern is the creation and maintenance of a "*dialogical space*" (Anderson, 1997). This approach does not support the use of predetermined techniques or interventions. Instead, the therapist's primary focus is to maintain dialogical conversations that allow for the generation of new meanings and possibilities.

Not Knowing and Curiosity

Not knowing frees therapists "from needing to be experts on how clients ought to live their lives" (Anderson, 1997, p. 64). Not knowing implies that the therapist recognizes that clients are the experts in the understanding and interpretation of their experiences. The therapist maintains a stance of not knowing and genuine *curiosity* to explore how clients are making sense of their situation. This curiosity, uncertainty, and openness to "seeing anew" promote a dialogue in which new meanings and possibilities can be explored. Not knowing and curiosity require that the therapist sincerely believe and trust clients as the "expert" of their stories.

Specifics of Not Knowing

Humility "Not knowing means humility about what one knows" (Anderson, 1997, p. 136). It is important to be humble when offering opinions or questions. "Humble does not mean meek, unsure, or timid; I want to have an unassuming manner" (p. 136).

Uncertainty "To be uncertain requires that we leave our dominant professional and personal discourses—what we know or think we know—suspended, hanging in front of us; that we be continually aware of, reflect on, and be open to examination by ourselves and others" (Anderson, 1997, p. 134). When a therapist is "certain" about what is happening or should happen, therapy is no longer a dialogue but a monologue in which only a small range of possibilities can be considered.

Mutual Puzzling "A therapist genuinely wants to learn how a client makes sense of things" (Anderson, 1997, p. 137). As the therapist curiously attends to the client's story, the client often becomes curious and more open to other ways of looking at the situation. This joint exploration of meaning is often a "wondering together" or "mutual puzzling" in which the client and therapist are working together to make sense of the problem situation.

Multiple and Contradictory Ideas The therapist entertains multiple ideas simultaneously, allowing all voices and perspectives about the problem to be heard and explored.

Not Understanding Too Quickly The therapist does not try to understand too quickly, if ever, and therefore is careful not to assume he or she knows exactly what is meant by commonly used terms, especially those that often have many shades of meaning, such as "upset," "angry," "unfair," or "hurtful." The therapist also avoids making assumptions in meaning about common life situations—marriage, death, loss, births—and, instead, invites clients to share their meanings for these events.

Conversational Questions

"Questions are the core of any interview or therapy conversation" (Anderson, 1997, p. 144). Conversational questions are used to maximize new meanings and prompt further questions:

- Conversational questions are based on what the client is saying rather than theory; therefore, conversational questions come from *within* the conversation rather than being predefined by the theory or therapist.
- Therapists avoid asking any questions to which they think they know the correct answer.
- Any suggestions or ideas that the therapist proposes must "emerge" from within the conversation.

Maintaining Coherence with the Client's Story

"Clients say that they want a chance to tell their stories" (Anderson, 1997, p. 156). Therefore, the therapist must create a space for clients to tell their stories in their own way:

- When a therapist assumes a curious stance, the therapist is open to the client's meaning and strives to maintain coherence and follow the flow and logic of the client's story.

- *"Staying in sync"* and *"keeping pace"* help the therapist to maintain coherence with the client's story. "We sometimes make the mistake of going along at our own pace and ignoring the client's, and in doing so, we do not stay in sync with or match his or her rhythm" (Anderson, 1997, p. 160).

Accessing the "Not Yet Said"

The resource for change is in the yet-to-be-said private conversations that clients have never spoken or thought about. Dialogical conversations access unspoken "assumptions" or meanings; once these are voiced, they become open to question and change.

Being Public

Being public requires that therapists share their private inner dialogues (Anderson, 1997). This "inner dialogue" includes "thoughts, prejudices, wonderings, speculations, questions, opinions, and fears" (Anderson, 1997, pp. 102–103). Being public also refers to being open about the "business" of therapy, such as diagnoses and conversations with outside systems.

Addressing the Therapeutic Impasse

The *therapeutic impasse* is the point when the dialogue breaks down and becomes a monologue (Anderson, 1997). Dialogue or a "dialogical process" is a two-way conversation or exchange of ideas. This process requires that therapist and client "take in" the other person's ideas and that there is a "cross-fertilization" of ideas. When this process breaks down, the conversation becomes "monologic" in that each person keeps telling the same story without really listening to the other. When a dialogic conversation breaks down, the therapist should ask either internally or externally, "What am I not hearing?" If a client seems to be telling the story over and over, what is the therapist not hearing?

Reflecting Teams

Tom Andersen developed the idea of *reflecting teams* in an attempt to make public the dialogues about clients that therapists previously held behind closed doors and one-way mirrors. Reflecting teams are used to promote new ideas by offering multiple perspectives about a problem. Teams can be used in a variety of ways. Generally, the team is invited to observe the first half of a session and then offers its reflections while the family and therapist observe. Team members offer multiple perspectives and appropriately unusual comments to provide opportunities for clients to construct new meanings about their situation. This process can be adapted by individual therapists who may share their inner conversations and/or have conversations with imagined others.

Guidelines for reflecting teams follow (Andersen, 1995):

- Use reflecting teams only with the permission of the family.
- Have the team and family in the same room, but they should not talk to each other directly.
- The therapist should give the family permission to listen or not to listen.
- Team members should speak from something they see or hear in the family's talk with the therapist. The team can comment on an event and then "wonder" about it. For example, "When the father said 'x', I wonder if he meant 'y' or 'z'."
- Team members should talk from a questioning perspective, which may include present, future, or hypothetical questions (i.e., "If 'x' were to happen, I wonder . . ."). Statements, opinions, and meanings should be avoided because they tend to close down possibilities.
- Team members should comment on what they hear but not on all that they see. If the family tries to cover something up, they should be allowed privacy and the right to not talk about all that they think and feel.

Accessing Multiple Voices in Writing

Peggy Penn and her associates (Penn & Frankfurt, 1994; Penn & Sheinberg, 1991; Penn, 2001) access multiple voices using letter writing and multiple hypothetical descriptions to generate alternative perspectives and make room for silenced inner voices or the voices of significant persons not currently in the therapeutic dialogue. Penn's letter writing has a different intent than letters that are meant to express repressed emotions, bring resolution to a past situation, or achieve a similar clinical aim. Instead, Penn's letter writing invites different voices into the conversation with the expectation that each new voice offers new possibilities for understanding rather than achieving a predetermined therapeutic effect.

COLLABORATIVE LANGUAGE SYSTEMS TREATMENT PLANS

The following general treatment plan identifies possible goals and interventions for each stage of therapy that could be used in treating individuals, couples, and families. Not all goals and techniques are applicable to all clients.

General Collaborative Language Systems Treatment Plan

Early-Phase Goals

1. Create a collaborative relationship with the client(s) by creating and maintaining a dialogical conversation.

Possible Interventions

a. Allow each person talking about the problem to share his or her thoughts about the problem, its history, and possible/preferred ways to address it.
b. Use client's language when referring to the problem issue.
c. Maintain a curious, not-knowing stance by using conversational questions to inquire about the meanings clients attribute to situations and terms.
d. Be public about therapist biases, diagnoses (if any), communications with outside systems, and any other "business" matters.
e. Invite clients to join in mutual puzzling about the problem; avoid certainties and singular descriptions.
f. Encourage clients to ask questions and be active participants in the therapeutic conversations.
g. Take a humble position and avoid making assumptions.

2. Obtain a description of the "problem" from all persons in dialogue about the problem (i.e., identify who is in the "language system").

Possible Interventions

a. Inquire about each person's thoughts about whether he/she sees a problem, what the problem is, how it developed, and where to go from here.
b. Maintain coherence with each client's story by inquiring about how all of the various themes and pieces fit together.
c. Listen for special meanings and descriptions of the problem issue that may be unique to a person or to the family.
d. Make room for inner and outer dialogues by allowing for silence, curious inquiry, and/or sharing one's own inner dialogue.

3. Jointly discuss goals, hopes, expectations, and possibilities of therapy.

Possible Interventions

a. Inquire about how clients see therapy as being helpful to their situation.
b. Discuss and agree upon where to start and who needs to be involved in the conversation(s).

Middle-Phase Goals

1. Based on goals and agendas set in the early phase, the therapist and client will identify specific goals for the middle phase of therapy that address the client's issues. Each middle-phase goal is unique and is open to modification as new ideas emerge in conversation.

Possible Interventions

a. Inquire about the client's view and meaning of problem issue through conversational questions; try not to understand too quickly and, instead, obtain rich descriptions.
b. As jointly agreed upon, include significantly involved others to participate in conversation around the problem issue.
c. Access the not yet said and make room for inner dialogues by allowing for silence, curious inquiry, and/or sharing one's own inner dialogue.
d. Respectfully encourage multiple, contradictory accounts of problem situations and avoid establishing certainties.
e. Offer reflections that are appropriately unusual to encourage curiosity and alternative perspectives.
f. Invite reflecting teams or visiting therapists to provide alternative perspectives.
g. Stay in sync and keep pace with clients' communication styles and with their willingness to make changes.
h. Explore implications of the problem situation on each person's identity, attending to points of jointly constructed meanings and interdependence.
i. Use letter writing to invite the silenced inner voices or voices of others into the therapeutic dialogue.
j. Maintain a two-way exchange of ideas and address any breakdowns or therapeutic impasses.

Late-Phase Goals

1. Address any new issues that have emerged that clients want to address; invite anyone else who may need to be in conversation.

Possible Interventions

a. Inquire about client's view and meaning of problem issue through conversational questions; try not to understand too quickly and, instead, obtain rich descriptions.

b. As jointly agreed upon, include significantly involved others to participate in conversation around the problem issue.
c. Access the not yet said and make room for inner dialogues by allowing for silence, curious inquiry, and/or sharing one's own inner dialogue.
d. Respectfully encourage multiple, contradictory accounts of problem situations and avoid establishing certainties.
e. Offer reflections that are appropriately unusual to encourage curiosity and alternative perspectives.
f. Invite reflecting teams or visiting therapists to provide alternative perspectives.
g. Stay in sync and keep pace with clients' communication styles and with their willingness to make changes.
h. Explore implications of the problem situation on each person's identity, attending to points of jointly constructed meanings and interdependence.
i. Maintain a two-way exchange of ideas and address any breakdowns or therapeutic impasses.

2. Jointly decide when to terminate meetings, and discuss progress that was made and any concerns about the future.

Possible Interventions

a. Reflecting teams can be used to encourage a comprehensive and/or outsider's view of changes and accomplishments.
b. Curiosity and conversational questions can be used to explore client's motivation to end, fears about ending, feelings about therapy, and hopes for the future.
c. In cases where client may anticipate future difficulties, the therapist and client can discuss how to address these concerns given what has been helpful thus far.
d. The therapist can be public about ending by reflecting on client's process or progress and/or sharing the therapist's thoughts about ending.

Vignette: Individual

Rachel is a Caucasian American female in her mid-thirties. She initiated counseling services to address past molestation issues and current abuse issues. She states that her uncle molested her when she was 10. Rachel reports that the memories of the sexual abuse were repressed until she began experiencing flashbacks and memories following involvement with her second husband. Rachel reports that she "kicked" him out of the house last week due to 3 years of verbal and physical abuse. She reported that, prior to kicking him out of the house, he beat her and threatened her life. Presently, Rachel reports trouble sleeping, flashbacks of the childhood molestation, and feelings of fear and depression.

Practice Collaborative Language Systems Treatment Plan for Individual

Early-Phase Goals

1\.
   a.
   b.

2\.
   a.
   b.

Middle-Phase Goals

1\.
   a.
   b.

2\.
   a.
   b.

Late-Phase Goals

1\.
   a.
   b.

2\.
   a.
   b.

Vignette: Couple

Amelia and Miguel have been cohabitating on and off for 7 years. The couple has four children, ages 8, 6, 3, and 1. The couple states that they are unable to communicate effectively due to frequent use of the "silent treatment" that can last up to 3 days. Amelia states that she is "tired" of staying home with the children while Miguel works and returns home late. Amelia reports that when Miguel gets home, he retreats to the bedroom, watches TV, then goes to bed. Amelia states that she cannot care for the kids without his help and will move in with her mother if things do not change. Miguel reports no noteworthy complaints and comments that "everything is great."

Practice Collaborative Language Systems Treatment Plan for Couple

Early-Phase Goals

1.
   a.
   b.

2.
   a.
   b.

Middle-Phase Goals

1.
   a.
   b.

2.
   a.
   b.

Late-Phase Goals

1.
   a.
   b.

2.
   a.
   b.

Vignette: Family

Margaret initiated counseling services for herself, her husband, and their two children. Margaret states that her 12-year-old daughter Carrie was diagnosed with general anxiety disorder by the family's general medical physician and that her 17-year-old son Alan was diagnosed with depression. Margaret reports that she and her husband have been diagnosed with anxiety disorders in the past; however, Margaret and Joe are no longer on medication. Margaret states that the children are not functioning well and have been on and off medications for the last 2 years.

Practice Collaborative Language Systems Treatment Plan for Family

Early-Phase Goals

1.
   a.
   b.

2.
   a.
   b.

Middle-Phase Goals

1.
   a.
   b.

2.
   a.
   b.

Late-Phase Goals

1.
   a.
   b.

2.
   a.
   b.

Vignette: Individual

Rachel is a Caucasian American female in her mid-thirties. She initiated counseling services to address past molestation issues and current abuse issues. She states that her uncle molested her when she was 10. Rachel reports that the memories of the sexual abuse were repressed until she began experiencing flashbacks and memories following involvement with her second husband. Rachel reports that she "kicked" him out of the house last week due to 3 years of verbal and physical abuse. She reported that, prior to kicking him out of the house, he beat her and threatened her life. Presently, Rachel reports trouble sleeping, flashbacks of the childhood molestation, and feelings of fear and depression.

Collaborative Language Systems Treatment Plan for Individual

Early-Phase Goals

1. Create a collaborative relationship with Rachel and maintain a dialogical conversation.
   a. Create a space for Rachel to talk about thoughts, feelings, and history of the sexual and physical abuse, as well as her thoughts about ways to deal with her pain and fears; allow her to share at her own pace.
   b. Attend to the unique words and meanings Rachel uses to describe her situation; avoid filling in the blanks with professional knowledge and assumptions.
   c. Maintain a not-knowing stance by utilizing conversational questions: "What does the abuse mean to you? How do you make sense of it?"
   d. Encourage mutual puzzling about the sexual and physical abuse, flashbacks, and life events.
   e. Give Rachel permission to ask questions and not share until ready.
   f. Maintain a humble presence.

2. Gain a rich description of Rachel's disrupted sleeping patterns, flashbacks, fears, depression, and abuse and the meanings each has for her.
   a. Inquire about Rachel's thoughts about the abuse, how the symptoms are a problem, how the symptoms developed, and how Rachel wants to proceed.
   b. Maintain coherence with Rachel's story by exploring the sexual, verbal, and physical abuse and how they are or are not related, as well as how each is defined.
   c. Allow Rachel time to be with her inner dialogue by allowing silence; share relevant aspects of therapist's inner dialogue.
   d. Identify and explore Rachel's perception of the family and societal and cultural beliefs about abuse and depression.

3. Collaboratively identify hopes, expectations, and possibilities for therapy and its outcome.
   a. Explore the possibilities of therapy and how Rachel hopes it will impact her life and situation.
   b. Identify a place to start and encourage Rachel to consider inviting significant others into the conversation as it makes sense to her.

Middle-Phase Goals

1. Collaboratively develop goal with client to address concerns, such as alleviate the disrupted sleeping patterns, flashbacks, fear, and depression; explore new understandings related to these symptoms.
   a. Inquire about Rachel's view and meaning of the symptoms through conversational questions.
   b. Access the not yet said and make room for Rachel's inner dialogues by allowing for silence, curious inquiry, and/or sharing one's own inner dialogue.
   c. Respectfully encourage multiple, contradictory accounts of the symptoms and situations.
   d. Offer reflections that are appropriately unusual to encourage curiosity and alternative perspectives.
   e. Invite reflecting teams or visiting therapists to provide alternative perspectives.
   f. Stay in sync and keep pace with Rachel's openness to making changes.
   g. Maintain a two-way exchange of ideas and address any breakdowns or therapeutic impasses.
   h. If Rachel is interested, invite her to write letters to the parts of herself that are fearful from the parts that are stronger (use her language to define these parts); when she is ready, also consider writing letters to the person who molested her and/or other significant persons during that time.

2. Collaboratively develop goal with Rachel to address abuse, possibly, reduce emotional pain associated with sexual abuse and begin to "take back" her sexual identity/body/self.
   a. Explore Rachel's view and meaning of the abuse and family betrayal through conversational questions.
   b. Make room for Rachel's inner dialogues to avoid certainty by allowing for silence.
   c. Present reflections that are appropriately unusual to invite fresh perspectives.
   d. Invite reflecting teams or visiting therapists to provide alternative perspectives.
   e. Invite relevant and available family members with whom Rachel would like to discuss the abuse.

   f. If interested, use letters or writing to dialogue with aspects of herself and/or others.
   g. Stay in sync and keep pace with Rachel.

3. Collaboratively develop goal with Rachel to address spousal abuse and "kicking out" spouse, such as eliminate guilt and fears related to second marriage and strengthen inner voice and sense of self.
   a. Inquire about Rachel's view and meaning of abusive spouse and obtain a rich description through conversational questions.
   b. Encourage Rachel's multiple and contradictory accounts of the abuse, giving voice to the parts of her that were afraid to leave and parts that wanted change.
   c. Offer reflections that are appropriately unusual to encourage curiosity and alternative perspectives.
   d. Invite reflecting teams and/or use writing to generate alternative voices and perspectives.
   e. Stay in sync and keep pace with Rachel's willingness to make changes.
   f. Maintain a two-way exchange of ideas and address any breakdowns or therapeutic impasses.

Late-Phase Goals

1. Address new issues that have emerged, such as how to go on with a single life, dating, and interacting with family.
   a. Inquire about Rachel's new perspective on life after surviving abuses through conversational questions; "What does it mean that you have survived abuse, confronted, and so on?"
   b. Inquire about how she would like to see her life move forward and take steps to enact desired changes.
   c. Offer reflections that are appropriately unusual.
   d. Explore implications of the abuse on her identity.

2. Jointly decide when to terminate, highlight progress, and explore Rachel's future.
   a. Invite a reflecting team or visiting therapist to provide a review of Rachel's accomplishments in alleviating symptoms and obtaining new meaning of abuse and abusive relationships.
   b. Explore Rachel's feelings about terminating and hopes for the future.
   c. Identify possible obstacles and explore utilization of newly gained ideas, perspectives, meanings, and so on.
   d. Be public and reveal inner dialogue by discussing Rachel's progress and other thoughts and feelings.

Vignette: Couple

Amelia and Miguel have been cohabitating on and off for 7 years. The couple has four children, ages 8, 6, 3, and 1. The couple states that they are unable to communicate effectively due to frequent use of the "silent treatment" that can last up to 3 days. Amelia states that she is "tired" of staying home with the children while Miguel works and returns home late. Amelia reports that when Miguel gets home, he retreats to the bedroom, watches TV, then goes to bed. Amelia states that she cannot care for the kids without his help and will move in with her mother if things do not change. Miguel reports no noteworthy complaints and comments that "everything is great."

Collaborative Language Systems Treatment Plan for Couple

Early-Phase Goals

1. Create a collaborative relationship with Amelia and Miguel by supporting a dialogical conversation.
   a. Allow Amelia and Miguel to share their thoughts, perspective, and history of the relational interaction, contradictory perspectives, and ideas and possibilities for addressing healthier relational interaction.
   b. Attend to Amelia's and Miguel's language and the specific meaning of words, concepts, and so on.
   c. Maintain a curious, not-knowing stance without taking sides with either.
   d. Be public about process and concerns about Miguel possibly not wanting to be there.
   e. Maintain a humble position.
   f. Encourage Amelia and Miguel to ask questions about therapy, therapist, and so on.

2. Obtain a rich description of the relational problems from Miguel and Amelia.
   a. Inquire about Amelia's and Miguel's perspectives of the relationship, as well as how they became so disconnected from one another.
   b. Discuss with each their ideas about how to proceed.
   c. Maintain coherence by inquiring about both perspectives and their similarities and differences.
   d. Listen for special meanings of relational issues from Amelia and Miguel.
   e. Provide space for Amelia's and Miguel's inner dialogues and cultural beliefs about relationships and conflict.

3. Discuss goals and expectations and possibilities of therapy.
   a. Explore how Amelia and Miguel perceive therapy and how it can be helpful.
   b. Decide on where to start and explore possibility of occasionally bringing children into conversation.
   c. Develop an initial agenda for therapy that both are willing to work on.

Middle-Phase Goals

1. Start with the couple's primary concern, which may be breaking pattern of "silent treatment" and, instead, communicating in a more loving way.
   a. Inquire about Miguel's and Amelia's views and meanings of the "silent treatment" through conversational questions to obtain Amelia's and Miguel's descriptions of how they resolve conflict.
   b. Access Amelia's and Miguel's inner dialogues by allowing for silence, curious inquiry, and/or sharing one's own inner dialogue.
   c. Encourage Amelia's and Miguel's accounts of the relational communication and conflict-resolution skills while avoiding certainties and "prepackaged" advice.
   d. Offer reflections that are appropriately unusual to encourage curiosity and alternative perspectives, such as, "I wonder how the children experience the silent treatment and/or other conflict between the two of you."
   e. Invite reflecting teams or visiting therapists to provide alternative perspectives on the couple's conflict.
   f. Stay in sync and keep pace with Amelia's and Miguel's communication styles, focusing on willingness to make changes.
   g. Explore implications of the problem situation on Amelia's and Miguel's identities, attending to the couple's meanings of the marriage and interdependence.
   h. Maintain a two-way exchange of ideas and address any breakdowns or therapeutic impasses.

Late-Phase Goals

1. Address any newly emerging issues, such as balancing marriage, family, and individual needs.
   a. Obtain a rich description of how the couple has created moments of balance and/or wants to create balance.
   b. Explore Amelia's and Miguel's inner dialogues about how they prefer to balance the competing needs.
   c. Invite a reflecting team and/or utilize writing to explore alternative perspectives and reflections.
   d. At couple's pace, identify small steps to pursuing this goal.

2. If child and parenting issues are important to the couple, discuss how they want to parent together and their vision for the family.
   a. Invite children into the session to share their perspectives on the family.
   b. Inquire about each family member's view and meaning of family through conversational questions; try not to understand too quickly and, instead, obtain rich descriptions.
   c. Explore each family member's inner dialogue and explore how the family can work together.
   d. Invite reflecting teams to introduce alternative, outside perspectives.

3. Jointly decide when to terminate, discuss progress, and address concerns for the future.
    a. Invite reflecting team to highlight an outsider's view of the family and couple's progress.
    b. Utilize conversational questions to explore Amelia's and Miguel's thoughts about therapy and hopes for their future as a couple and as a family.
    c. Highlight what has been helpful and discuss applying in future.
    d. Reflect on Amelia and Miguel's progress and remain public about terminating therapeutic relationship.

Vignette: Family

Margaret initiated counseling services for herself, her husband, and their two children. Margaret states that her 12-year-old daughter Carrie was diagnosed with general anxiety disorder by the family's general medical physician and that her 17-year-old son Alan was diagnosed with depression. Margaret reports that she and her husband have been diagnosed with anxiety disorders in the past; however, Margaret and Joe are no longer on medication. Margaret states that the children are not functioning well and have been on and off medications for the last 2 years.

Collaborative Language Systems Treatment Plan for Family

Early-Phase Goals

1. Create a collaborative relationship with family by maintaining dialogical conversation.
   a. Encourage each member to share his/her thoughts, history, and preferred solutions regarding the problems.
   b. Invite all people talking about the problem to be part of the therapy dialogue; contact doctors, other significant family members, teachers, and so on.
   c. Maintain a curious and not-knowing position, focusing on how the family characterizes their unique experiences of "anxiety," "depression," and so on.
   d. Be public about thoughts and biases associated with the children's diagnoses and communication with the family's general medical physician.
   e. Invite family to wonder about the diagnoses and other family problems.
   f. Encourage family members to ask questions, especially the children.
   g. Use humor and playful communication to engage children and assist in opening up dialogue and sharing of each member's perspective.

2. Obtain a rich description about the problems from each family member.
   a. Identify how each member describes the problem, how it developed, and how to proceed.
   b. Maintain coherence by closely attending to each member's story.
   c. Identify unique meanings and descriptions of the diagnoses and other relational problems; allow understanding of diagnoses to evolve in ways that more accurately fit with their experience than "expert" knowledge.
   d. Allow each member to experience and/or share inner dialogues by sitting with silence, maintaining curiosity, and sharing own inner dialogue.

3. Discuss goals, hopes, expectations, and possibilities of therapy.
   a. Explore each member's perception of therapy and how each believes therapy could be helpful or unhelpful.
   b. Discuss how to start and who they believe should be involved in the conversations.
   c. Set an initial agenda that addresses their concerns and that they are willing to work on.

Middle-Phase Goals

1. Begin with family's stated goals, such as reduce Carrie's anxiety and Alan's depression; allow the name of the problems to shift and evolve based on the family's actual experiences and ideas.
   a. Inquire about each family member's view and description of the depression and anxiety through conversational questions.
   b. Include significantly involved others to participate in conversation around the problem issue, including Carrie's and Alan's teachers, physicians, and so on.
   c. Discuss if family feels the need to "do" something besides what it is already doing; if so, jointly identify possible new ways to approach problem situation.
   d. Invite the family's multiple accounts of the anxiety and depression.
   e. Invite visiting therapist or reflecting team to provide alternative perspectives.
   f. Stay in sync and keep pace with the family's communication styles and with their willingness to make changes.
   g. Explore implications of the problem situation on each person's identity and how each member experiences the symptoms.
   h. Inquire about Margaret's and Joe's views and meanings of children's symptoms as related to the couple's prior medical history using conversational questions.

Late-Phase Goals

1. Based on family input, identify how to adjust family life so that everyone can remain "medication-free."
   a. Explore the not yet said by inquiring about family life in the past and present and their perspective of what, if anything, needs to change.
   b. Based on each person's ideas for what needs to change, work with family to identify and take steps to make the desired changes.
   c. Provide reflections that are appropriately unusual to encourage curiosity and alternative perspectives on how to create the family life they want.
   d. Stay in sync and keep pace with family's communication styles and with their willingness to make changes.
   e. Explore implications of Carrie and Alan's symptoms on their identity and family identity, attending to interdependence of identities.
   f. Invite a reflecting team and/or use writing to highlight alternative views.

2. Jointly decide when to terminate, discuss progress, and address family concerns about the future.
   a. Invite a reflecting team to highlight individual and family accomplishments.
   b. Explore feelings associated with terminating therapy.
   c. Address any identified future obstacles by considering how family can adapt what was learned and was helpful.
   d. Remain public about individual and family progress and share thoughts about ending therapy.

Suggested Readings

Andersen, T. (1991). *The reflecting team: Dialogues and dialogues about the dialogues.* New York: Norton.

Andersen, T. (1992). Relationship, language and pre-understanding in the reflecting process. *Australian and New Zealand Journal of Family Therapy, 13*(2), 87–91.

Andersen, T. (1995). Reflecting processes: Acts of informing and forming. In S. Friedman (Ed.), *The reflecting team in action: Collaborative practice in family therapy* (pp. 11–37). New York: Guilford Press.

Anderson, H. (1995). Collaborative language systems: Toward a postmodern therapy. In R. Mikesell, D. D. Lusterman, & S. McDaniel (Eds.), *Family psychology and systems therapy* (pp. 27–44). Washington, DC: American Psychological Association Press.

Anderson, H. (1997). *Conversations, language, and possibilities: A postmodern approach to therapy.* New York: Basic Books.

Anderson, H., & Goolishian, H. (1988). Human systems as linguistic systems: Preliminary and evolving ideas about the implications for clinical theory. *Family Process, 27,* 157–163.

Anderson, H., & Goolishian, H. (1992). The client is the expert: A not-knowing approach to therapy. In S. McNamee & K. J. Gergen (Eds.), *Therapy as social construction* (pp. 25–39). Newbury Park, CA: Sage.

Gergen, K. (1999). *An invitation to social construction.* Newbury Park, CA: Sage.

Gergen, K. (2001). *Social construction in context.* Newbury Park, CA: Sage.

Hoffman, L. (1990). Constructing realities: An art of lenses. *Family Process, 29,* 1–12.

Hoffman, L. (1993). *Exchanging voices: A collaborative approach to family therapy.* London: Karnac Books.

Hoffman, L. (2001). *Family therapy: An intimate history.* New York: Norton.

Penn, P. (2001). Chronic illness: Trauma, language, and writing: Breaking the silence. *Family Process, 40,* 33–52.

Penn, P., & Frankfurt, M. (1994). Creating a participant text: Writing, multiple voices, narrative multiplicity. *Family Process, 33,* 217–231.

Penn, P., & Sheinberg, M. (1991). Stories and conversations. *Journal of Systemic Therapies, 10*(3–4), 30–37.

A APPENDIX VIDEO AND INTERNET RESOURCES

VIDEO RESOURCES

Aponte, H. *A house divided: Structural therapy with a black family.* Pittsburgh, PA: Western Psychiatric Institute and Clinic Library.

Berg, I., & de Shazer, S. *Success story.* Washington, DC: AAMFT.

Boscolo, L., & Cecchin, G. *Luigi Boscolo and Gianfranco Cecchin: What to call it?* Washington, DC: AAFMT.

Bozermenyi-Nagy, I. *I would like to call you Mother: Ivan Boszemenyi-Nagy.* Washington, DC: AAMFT.

Bowen, M. *Family interview.* Pittsburg, PA: Western Psychiatric Institute and Clinic Library.

Bowen, M. *Family reaction to death.* Pittsburg, PA: Western Psychiatric Institute and Clinic Library.

Bowen, M. *Founders series: Murray Bowen.* Washington, DC: AAMFT.

Bowen, M., & Kerr, M. *The best of family therapy.* Pittsburgh, PA: Western Psychiatric Institute and Clinic Library.

Carlson, J., Kjos, D., & Aponte, H. *Family therapy with the experts: Structural therapy with Dr. Harry J. Aponte.*

Carter, B. *On not becoming a wicked stepmother.* Washington, DC: AAMFT.

Carter, B., Papp, P., Silverstein, O., & Walters, M. *The women's project: new clinical issues in family therapy, Betty Canter, Peggy Papp, Olga Silverstein, and Marianne Walters.* Washington, DC: AAMFT.

de Shazer, S. *Brief therapy: Constructing solutions.* Washington, DC: AAMFT.

Framo, J., Friedmann, Paul, N., Wynne, L., Kerr, K., & Kerr, M. *Conversations about Murray Bowen.* Washington, DC: AAMFT.

Hardy, K. *Race, class, and culture.* Washington, DC: AAMFT.

LoPiccolo, J. *Joseph LoPiccolo: Echoes from the past.* Washington, DC: AAMFT.

LoPiccolo, J. *Joseph LoPiccolo: Treatment of sexual deviation.* Washington, DC: AAMFT.

Minuchin, S. *Anorexia is a Greek word.* Pittsburgh, PA: Western Psychiatric Institute and Clinic Library.

Minuchin, S. *The case of the dumb deliquent.* Philadelphia, PA: Philadelphia Child Guidance Center.

Minuchin, S. *I think it's me.* Philadelphia, PA: Philadelphia Child Guidance Center.

Minuchin, S. *Salvador Minuchin: Unfolding the laundry.* Washington, DC: AAMFT.

Montalvo, B. *A family with a little fire.* Philadelphia, PA: Philadelphia Child Guidance Center.

Satir, V. *Satir family series: Teaching family therapy/family interview, intro to family reconstruction/making of maps, father's reconstruction, mother's reconstruction, son's parts party & question period, couple's parts party, mother's parts party, father's parts party.*

Satir, V. *The teachings of Virginia Satir: Temperature reading, the process of change, the origins & transformation of survival copings, the dynamics of a parts party, communication stances, the seed model.*

Satir, V. *Virginia Satir: The lost boy.* Washington, DC: AAMFT.

Satir, V. *Virginia Satir: Of rocks and flowers.* Kansas City, MO: Golden Triad Films.

Satir, V. *Virginia Satir: The use of self in therapy.* Evanston, IL: Menninger Video Productions.

Silverstein, O. *Putting the brakes on mother: Olga Silverstein.* Washington, DC: AAMFT.

Watzlawick, P. *Paul Watzlawick: Mad or bad?* Washington, DC: AAMFT.

Whitaker, C. *Carl Whitaker: Usefulness of non-presented symptoms.* Washington, DC: AAMFT.

Whitaker, C., & Connell, G. *Carl Whitaker and Gary Connell: Creating a symbolic experience through family therapy.* Washington, DC: AAMFT.

White, M. *Escape from bickering.* Washington, DC: AAMFT.

White, M. *Recent developments in the narrative approach.* Washington, DC: AAMFT.

INTERNET RESOURCES

Ackerman Institute
www.ackerman.org

American Association for Marriage and Family Therapy
www.aamft.org

AVANTA The Virginia Satir Network
www.avanta.net

Bay Area Family Therapy Training Associates (narrative therapy)
www.baftta.com

Bill O'Hanlon's Possibility Land
www.brieftherapy.com

Brief Family Therapy Center (solution-focused therapy)
www.brief-therapy.org

Dulwich Centre Website (narrative therapy)
www.dulwichcentre.com.au/homepage.html

Houston Galveston Institute (collaborative language systems)
www.neosoft.com/~hgi

Kenneth J. Gergen
www.swarthmore.edu/SocSci/kgergen1

Master's Work Video Productions
www.masterswork.com

Narrative Approaches
www.narrativeapproaches.com

Narrative Psychology Internet and Resource Guide
maple.lemoyne.edu/~hevern/narpsych.html

Narrative Training Associates
www.narrativetherapy.org

Philadelphia Child and Family Therapy Training Center, Inc.
www.philafamily.com

Postmodern Therapies News
www.california.com/~ rathbone/pmth.htm

Satir Systems Development Programs
www.satir.org

Solutions Focused Therapy
thesolutionfocus.com

Taos Institute (postmodern therapy)
www.taosinstitute.org

NAME AND SUBJECT INDEX

TO THE OWNER OF THIS BOOK:

I hope that you have found *Theory-Based Treatment Planning for Marriage and Family Therapists* useful. So that this book can be improved in a future edition, would you take the time to complete this sheet and return it? Thank you.

School and address: ____

Department: ____

Instructor's name: ____

1. What I like most about this book is: ____

____

____

2. What I like least about this book is: ____

____

____

3. My general reaction to this book is: ____

____

____

4. The name of the course in which I used this book is:

____

5. Were all of the chapters of the book assigned for you to read? ______________________

   If not, which ones weren't? ____

6. In the space below, or on a separate sheet of paper, please write specific suggestions for improving this book and anything else you'd care to share about your experience in using this book.

____

____

____

DO NOT STAPLE. PLEASE SEAL WITH TAPE.

FOLD HERE

NO POSTAGE
NECESSARY
IF MAILED
IN THE
UNITED STATES

BUSINESS REPLY MAIL
FIRST-CLASS MAIL PERMIT NO. 34 BELMONT CA

POSTAGE WILL BE PAID BY ADDRESSEE

Counseling Editor

Brooks/Cole
20 Davis Drive
Belmont, CA 94002-3098

FOLD HERE

OPTIONAL:

Your name: ______________________________ Date: ______________

May we quote you, either in promotion for *Theory-Based Treatment Planning for Marriage and Family Therapists*, or in future publishing ventures?

Yes: __________ No: __________

Sincerely yours,

Diane R. Gehart and Amy R. Tuttle

CPSIA information can be obtained
at www.ICGtesting.com
Printed in the USA
FFOW01n0642231215
19880FF